THE BIBLE IN AMERICAN LAW,
POLITICS, AND POLITICAL RHETORIC

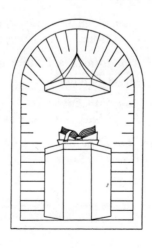

SOCIETY OF BIBLICAL LITERATURE

The Bible in American Culture

General Editors:

Edwin S. Gaustad
Professor of History
University of California, Riverside

Walter Harrelson
Distinguished Professor of Old Testament
Vanderbilt University

THE BIBLE IN AMERICAN LAW, POLITICS, AND POLITICAL RHETORIC

edited by

JAMES TURNER JOHNSON

FORTRESS PRESS
Philadelphia, Pennsylvania

SCHOLARS PRESS
Chico, California

SOCIETY OF BIBLICAL LITERATURE

CENTENNIAL PUBLICATIONS

Editorial Board

© 1985
Society of Biblical Literature

9826152

Library of Congress Cataloging in Publication Data
Main entry under title:

The Bible in American law, politics, and political rhetoric.

(The Bible in American culture ; 4) (Centennial publi-
cations / Society of Biblical Literature)
    1.   Bible—Influence—Addresses,   essays,   lectures.
2. United States—Politics and government—Addresses,
essays, lectures. 3. Religion and politics—United States—
Addresses, essays, lectures. I. Johnson, James Turner.
II. Series. III. Series: Centennial publications (Society of
Biblical Literature)
BS538.7.B55 1984   261.7   83-16327
ISBN 0-89130-625-0 (Scholars Press)
ISBN 0-8006-0614-0 (Fortress Press)

K965K84   Printed in the United States of America   1–614

CONTENTS

Editor and Contributors

EDWARD McGLYNN GAFFNEY, JR., Director of the Center for Constitutional Studies at the University of Notre Dame, is the editor of *Private Schools and the Public Good: Policy Alternatives for the Eighties* (1981).

JAMES TURNER JOHNSON, the editor of this volume, is the author of *Ideology, Reason, and the Limitation of War* (1975) and *Just War Tradition and the Restraint of War* (1981); he is a professor in the Department of Religion at Rutgers–The State University of New Jersey.

DENNIS P. McCANN, the author of *Christian Realism and Liberation Theology: Practical Theologies in Creative Conflict*, teaches in the Department of Religious Studies at DePaul University.

MARK A. NOLL, of the History Department at Wheaton College (Illinois), is joint editor (with Nathan O. Hatch) of *The Bible in America: Essays in Cultural History* (1982).

JAMES E. SELLERS, David Rice Professor of Religious Studies at Rice University, is the author of *Theological Ethics* (1966), *Public Ethics: American Morals and Manners* (1970), and *Warming Fires: The Quest for Community in America* (1975).

MAX L. STACKHOUSE, the author of *Ethics and the Urban Ethos* (1974), is Professor of Christian Social Ethics at Andover Newton Theological School.

MARK VALERI is currently writing a dissertation on the thought of Joseph Bellamy, in completion of his work for the doctorate at Princeton University; he is a member of the faculty at Whitworth College.

LOUIS WEEKS, of Louisville Presbyterian Theological Seminary, is the author of *A New Christian Nation*, volume 5 in the Faith of Our Fathers series.

JOHN F. WILSON, Collord Professor of Religion at Princeton University, is the author of *Public Religion in American Culture* (1979) and *Pulpit in Parliament: Puritanism during the English Civil Wars, 1640–1648* (1969).

Preface to the Series

To what extent are Americans a "people of the book"? To what degree is the history of their nation intermixt with the theology and story and imagery of the Bible? These and other questions are addressed in the several volumes of our series, The Bible in American Culture.

Initially conceived as part of the 1980 centennial celebration of the Society of Biblical Literature, this series explores the biblical influence—for good or ill—in the arts, music, literature, politics, law, education, ethnicity and many other facets of American civilization in general. It is the task of other series to examine biblical scholarship per se; these books, in contrast, search out the way in which the Bible permeates, subtly or powerfully, the very fabric of life within the United States.

The undersigned heartily commend the individual editors of each volume. They have persisted and pursued until all authors finally entered the fold. We also gladly acknowledge the wise counsel of Samuel Sandmel in an earlier stage of our planning, regretting only that he is not with us at the end.

Finally, we express our deep appreciation to the Lilly Endowment for its generous assistance in bringing this entire series to publication and wider dissemination.

EDWIN S. GAUSTAD
WALTER HARRELSON

Introduction

James Turner Johnson

As one in a series of books focusing on the Bible in American culture, the present collection of essays has for its subject the relation between the Bible and politics and political rhetoric in American life. "Politics" is almost as difficult a term to define—and as difficult a reality to circumscribe—as is "religion," and it is equally pervasive. Yet just as there are institutional forms of religion (however diverse) in America, so there is institutional politics, and the figures, ideas, and movements of this somewhat more easily recognizable reality have oriented the discussions of the contributors to this volume. At the same time, though, we have also had to attend to the broader context within which this particular aspect of American cultural life has taken shape. Numerous observers of the American religious scene have pointed out that there is a particular "style" to being religiously American or Americanly religious—a style expressed in the denominational character of religious bodies, in historic links between religious moral values and public values, in symbolic and linguistic connections between the self-consciously religious and secular spheres. A cross-flow has existed between religion and American culture from the early colonial settlements onward to the present, and through much of American history that flow has involved reference to symbols, rhetoric, moral guidance, and an understanding of history derived from the Bible.

Even if we take at full face value the religious sincerity of such biblicism, however, there remains the question whether the impact of the Bible on the language and practice of politics has gone equally deep. How much were those who referred to the Bible in attempting to shape the political life of this culture in fact drawing wisdom from it and not simply laying a familiar biblical veneer over ideas they received from elsewhere? How profound has biblical reliance been—even in the presence of biblical imagery—at different stages in American history, in different historical social movements or crises? How important is the Bible for American politics today? The task of the present volume is to attempt to answer such questions as these regarding the use of the Bible in American political life.

What We Do Not Attempt to Cover

Every book, whatever its subject, must leave some matters aside in order to give the proper attention to others. With a subject like the use of the Bible in American politics, a great deal obviously has to be left untreated in order to manage the flow of the main currents. Where possible, the essays in this volume have paused to explore some of the tributary streams and to sample the eddies along the banks, but our principal purpose has been to chart the mainstream. At the same time, some political figures, ideas, and movements have already been singled out for close scrutiny in other volumes in the SBL Centennial Publications; the slavery debate is one such, the women's rights movement another, and the role of the Bible in public education still another (see Sandeen; Barr and Piediscalzi). These are all clearly political issues, but they are so large that in our present framework they would have been difficult to treat adequately without danger of their overwhelming the rest of the volume. Since this is a book on the broad sweep of the Bible in American politics and not one on the use of the Bible in movements seeking social change or the proper place of the Bible in public moral education, we gratefully acknowledge that, with topics like these in other hands, our task in the present volume has been made easier.

Another task our topic has required but that we avoid is attempting to survey the entire realm of the interaction between religion and politics in America. Religiously based attempts to shape the formation of public policy or law have not been universally characterized by use of the Bible. American Jews, for example, however religiously motivated they may have been, have tended to enter the political sphere as pragmatic secularists, and at least until recently Roman Catholics have done the same, likely for the same reason—a perceived Protestant hegemony. But beyond this, as the entry of religiously motivated people of both these faiths into the political controversy over abortion has revealed, both look first for religious guidance on politics to specific interpretive traditions—to the Talmud and collected rabbinical wisdom in the case of Judaism and to the idea of natural law and the composite social teaching of the church in the case of Catholicism. Both these are biblically based religious faiths; yet neither ordinarily applies the Bible directly to social and political issues. Doing so has typically been a Protestant pattern, derived from the Reformation principles of "scripture alone" and individual, direct interpretations of the Bible. Even so, this pattern has not been universal among American Protestants, which restricts our focus still further. The various American religious descendants of John Calvin have been the more likely to bring the Bible into political debate, and among the Calvinists the reformist tradition begun by the Puritan movement has been the most prolific in producing efforts to use the Bible in politics. Additionally, from the colonial through the early national periods at least, there were many more Calvinists around in America than Lutherans, pietists, Catholics, or Jews. So an effort to chart the mainstream of the presence of the Bible in American politics and political rhetoric is not the same as one to explore the impact of religion generally on this nation's political life. Not only must we look more closely at one branch of Judeo-Christian tradition at the expense of others, but American religious movements outside this broad tradition are omitted entirely from this volume. Such a definition of our field is not without costs, but it produces benefits. The ability to narrow our concerns in this way means that in this study it is the more possible for our essayists to question the quality and depth of the political use of the Bible based in religious sensibility and to offer some judgments on the degree to which biblical religion has benefited American political life.

Finally, this is not a book on the Bible in American *culture* as a whole, but rather it is a collection of essays on one significant aspect of this entire culture, which together with the other volumes in this series aims to form a picture of the whole. Nor is it a study of the relation between religion in American political life and that in other societies, though we have not avoided reference to such relations where useful.

So far I have discussed what we have not, or in some cases could not, examine in this volume. It is time now to turn to what we have in fact set out to do in our efforts to chart the mainstream of the presence of the Bible in American politics and political rhetoric. Broadly, we begin at the beginning, with the transition from the Old World to the New, and end in the present with some reflections on the nature and future of political community in America. Let us look more closely at what is included in this broad sweep.

The Shape of This Volume

The essays in this volume are divided into two groups, reflecting differences in their approach and specific subject matter. Those in Part One focus on various stages in American historical development, treating specific themes as they arose in these contexts; in Part Two the procedure is reversed, with the principal object of attention being certain major themes in American political life, while the essays range over those portions of American history relevant to the development of the theme in question. The overall aim, however, has been to achieve complementarity among the essays taken as a whole, and this means that the distinctions implied by this division should not be taken as absolute. Themes raised in the essays of Part One have, in many instances, continued at or near the center of American religious and political life through much later historical periods, and thus the raw material of the "historical" essays might easily be transformed into "thematic" treatments. Similarly, there is a historical overlapping and a progression evident in the essays of Part Two, which reach back into the periods discussed in Part One and carry forward to the contemporary period the historical investigation artificially halted there at about the turn of the century.

Another way of thinking about the two parts of this volume, their differences and their interrelationship, is to reflect upon the idea that something of a sea change has occurred over American history in the use of the Bible in political rhetoric and the shaping of policy decisions. Early in the history of this society, up through much of the nineteenth century, when the cultural roots of Americans were still relatively homogeneous and the nation could meaningfully be described in terms of its dominant Protestant Christian faith, the outstanding pattern was of the use of the Bible by public figures as individuals working in the political realm. Whether sincere or opportunistic, whether they had a clear grasp of the biblical meaning or only a superficial understanding, these individuals spoke for what they identified as a common religious heritage rather than for institutional religious bodies. But beginning with the religiously motivated efforts of the nineteenth century at social reforms, this earlier pattern has been gradually replaced by another one that has become virtually universal by our own time: the use of the Bible within particular religious groups in society to inform the consciences of their members, to influence their political behavior, and in some cases to attempt to impose policies rooted in such sectarian religious belief upon the public at large. The flavor of this shift can be tasted quickly in this collection by comparing the political use of the Bible described in such essays as those by Mark Noll (representing the first pattern) and Max Stackhouse (representing the second). The first way of using the Bible politically presupposes a Christian cultural homogeneity within which it is possible, across the breadth of the society, to appeal to common (and biblically based) values and to measure moral and political behavior by a commonly recognized standard. The second approach recognizes the fact of sectarian divisions and political pluralism, making the Bible into a symbol of an ideology that defines a social group and may seek the heteronomous domination of other groups within the pluralistic whole. Within the context of this book, the essays of Part One have more to do with the first pattern of political use of the Bible, while those of Part Two correlate more closely with the second pattern.

Once more, though, these categories overlap, as can be seen by considering a figure like Reinhold Niebuhr (see Dennis McCann's essay). Viewed from the latter perspective I have described, Niebuhr appears as an anachronism, for he consciously sought to appeal to a national consensus about moral value, though this was for him a Judeo-Christian, and not merely a Christian, consciousness. His use of the Bible in political criticism accordingly relied heavily on themes from the Hebrew prophets, in some contrast to an earlier generation that had sought to guide the body politic by "the ethic of Jesus." While a preacher, Niebuhr was a spokesman for a general rather than a sectarian point of view. By the standards of the two patterns of political use of the Bible sketched above, he was less a modern man than is Jerry Falwell or the members of the Catholic right-to-life movement. Yet the enormous influence Niebuhr exerted shows that even if he was an exception to the general rule, something may be learned from considering his case. If the first general way of using the Bible in the political sphere assumes cultural homogeneity while the second assumes pluralism, what the example of Niebuhr may suggest is that in spite of its multifaceted diversity in the twentieth century, American culture nevertheless maintains an important level of cohesiveness, and one element helping to sustain that cohesion remains a common set of symbols, imagery, values, assumptions, and expectations rooted in the Bible. A sea change may have taken place, but it is not yet clear that the implications of the new wave have washed over all of American society.

If this is in fact so, as I suggest it is, then to reflect on the political use of the Bible in American history may be a helpful step toward understanding possible political roles for the Bible in the present time. For what this history tells us, as the essays in this volume reveal, is that there has never been a "golden age" in the application of biblical wisdom to the political guidance of American culture. As disputatious as Americans have been over the correct interpretation of the Bible for religious life, no one should expect more consensus over the possible implications of the Bible for political life. Moreover, where clear evidence of the use of the Bible is found in historical political movements and biblical rhetoric or example is employed to justify policy decisions, this is always one element of influence alongside many, so that it is difficult or impossible to know just how much weight was borne by reference to the Bible. These observations are no less true, as these essays demonstrate, of American political life a century and a half ago than of contemporary politics. Today's Americans are no better or worse—indeed, not much different—from their predecessors in this regard.

It is clear that the Bible represented a closer presence, a nearer object of attention, the focus of a different kind of honor when the country was yet small in population, when the dominant form of religion was Protestant Christian, when the Bible was often employed as a textbook in elementary education, and when few other books existed to serve as alternative sources of moral, social, or political wisdom. What is much less obvious is that all these factors worked together to produce a positive effect of the Bible on American politics. American political life has always been complicated and multidimensional, and even in the colonial period and the early years of the republic this many-sidedness shaped the impact of the Bible on public attitudes and decisions. The subject of this volume is, then, a curious though often profound and passionate ambivalence over the political aspect of the presence of the Bible in and for American culture.

The Scope of the Essays

In Mark Valeri and John Wilson's essay the problem is how the Reformation ideas of the proper place of the Bible in religious life and its implications for politics were transplanted to American soil. Their specific focus is on the way in which this background ultimately found expression in the religious and social changes brought about in the context of the Great Awakening. Thus the story told in their essay begins in sixteenth-century continental Europe and moves on to identify certain critical developments in the English Reformation a century later before tracing them finally into the establishment of a new culture in America. Puritan scholar Perry Miller once described the reactions of the first native-born generation of New Englanders to their cultural situation with the words "Having failed to rivet the eyes of the world upon their city on the hill, they were left alone with America" (Miller: 15). The social and the political, as well as the religious, fruits of the Great Awakening a long generation later were among the first results of this realization of being "left alone with America."

But Americans did not in fact cease trying to "rivet the eyes of the world upon their city on the hill," as subsequent history was to show, though this might ultimately take the secular form, in H. Richard Niebuhr's phrase, of giving "light to the gentiles by means of lamps manufactured in America" (Niebuhr: 179). As the remaining essays in the present volume show, the religious-secular dynamic, and particularly the use of the Bible in politics, remained a vital one, though many-sided and often ambiguous in its implications.

We find this vitality, along with the multiplicity and ambiguity, well described in the historical essays by Mark Noll and Louis Weeks, who carry the development of American political life through the Revolution, the early national period and the remainder of the nineteenth century. Noll's principal focus is on certain of the nation's founders, showing that while they regularly referred their thinking to biblical ideas and language, it is much less possible to say that this habitual manner of giving depth to their thinking reveals the Bible as their principal inspiration. These men used the Bible because it formed a consort with what they were thinking, Noll argues, and not because—beginning with a Lockean *tabula rasa* for their political conceptions—they found the Bible the most useful source of wisdom for writing on that blank table. Louis Weeks, examining less well-known figures and the political issues that activated them, finds essentially the same pattern. The Bible was so deeply buried in American culture during the period Weeks treats that it was naturally employed by all sorts of political figures; yet the evidence of this use does not go far enough to prove that these men's positions were, in the first place, biblically based or inspired.

Edward Gaffney, in questioning the place of the Bible in the formation of the American legal tradition, reaches a similar conclusion but also implicitly shifts the balance back the other way toward allowing that biblical influence has been more of a factor than the hard historical evidence employed by Noll and Weeks suggests. Writing on the impact of biblical tradition on American constitutional law, Gaffney finds the undercurrents of interaction to be more significant than particular legal language. By arguing that the Bible has had a genuine, if limited, influence on American public life Gaffney's essay reminds us again of the need to exercise caution in giving a general answer to the question of the political use of the Bible.

Clear and unequivocal examples of biblical influence on the formation of political consciousness and political goals form the meat of the essays by Max Stackhouse and Dennis McCann. Both these authors are dealing with self-consciously Christian actors whose ethical reflections led them into the political arena; this differentiates the subjects of these essays from those treated by Noll, Weeks, and Gaffney. For Stackhouse the orienting issue is the gradual development of a Christian social consciousness regarding economic inequality and injustice and the associated definition of political goals and programs aimed at ending such evils. The protagonists on his stage are all prominent figures in the history of American Protestant social and political thought; they are, in addition, all representatives of the Calvinist heritage identified earlier as producing most of the political usage of the Bible in American culture. It is abundantly clear in the writings that Stackhouse examines that their authors were engaged directly in a social critique inspired by biblical examples and were seeking sociopolitical goals patterned on the biblical ideal of the kingdom of God. Stackhouse's achievement in this essay goes beyond demonstrating the Bible-rootedness of this Christian approach to economics; he also establishes that this approach defines a tradition of how to deal with social and political issues that remains at the core of the contemporary ecumenical movement. Beyond this, his discussion exemplifies the transformation, mentioned above, from the use of the Bible by individuals engaged in politics to the employment of the Bible by self-consciously Christian groups, first to educate themselves and inform their own consciences and then to seek change in the broader society.

Dennis McCann's focus is the origins of political realism, the major theoretical concept in twentieth-century American politics. McCann compares two of the foremost secular authors of this approach to politics, George F. Kennan and Hans Morgenthau, with the foremost exponent of political realism from a theological point of view, Reinhold Niebuhr, and attempts to make out the differences that the latter's conspicuous use of biblical ideas, examples, imagery, and rhetoric make in separating his position from Kennan's and Morgenthau's. Is there a difference at all? The problem is made more difficult by the fact that Morgenthau as well as Niebuhr from time to time brought biblical rhetoric into his argumentation. McCann's conclusion is that there is a difference and that the difference does in fact matter for the way in which one tries "realistically" to think about policy. The implications of his analysis reflect back on the earlier essays in the volume, for Morgenthau, as McCann analyzes him, employs the Bible in decidedly unbiblical ways. Thus we are confronted with the reminder that, whether it is always obvious or not, references to the Bible or the employment of biblical-sounding rhetoric may point in directions at odds with those of the Bible itself. Thus acceptance of the use of the Bible in American political life requires a hermeneutical as well as an ethical decision.

Finally, James Sellers in the concluding essay picks up the threads of his earlier investigations into the religious aspects of American political community, arguing that the shape of the contemporary usage of the Bible in political affairs is such as to undermine community rather than to enhance it. The European neo-orthodox efforts to capture again the Reformation sense of the Bible left no lasting impression on America, Sellers argues. Yet the contemporary American alternatives offer no real hope for a future renewal of the political community, either. Caught between secularity and "born-again" Christianity, there is no use of the Bible in contemporary political life that Americans can readily accept without suspicion. Revitalization of the idea of community will require,

Sellers believes, escaping the secular versus born-again dilemma, and the suggestions he offers are reminiscent of the best positive indication of Miller's phrase. "Left alone with America," Americans must discover a commonalty that is simultaneously true to our diverse heritages as a people and reflective of the conditions of contemporary social and political life together.

WORKS CONSULTED

Miller, Perry
    1956   *Errand into the Wilderness*. New York: Harper & Row.

Niebuhr, H. Richard
    1959   *The Kingdom of God in America*. New York: Harper & Row.

Sandeen, Ernest R., ed.
    1982   *The Bible and Social Reform*. Philadelphia: Fortress; Chico, CA: Scholars Press.

Barr, David, and Nicholas Piediscalzi, eds.
    1982   *The Bible in American Education*. Philadelphia: Fortress; Chico, CA: Scholars Press.

Part One
HISTORICAL PERSPECTIVES

I

Scripture and Society: From Reform in the Old World to Revival in the New

Mark Valeri and John F. Wilson

This essay attempts to sketch the stages through which the Bible came to exercise formative influence in the political culture of late colonial America. It reaches back to note the commitment made by the first generation of Protestant reformers, following Luther, to recover the authoritative role of the scriptures for the renovated Christian community. Thus, it was the source for and the standard of correct teaching and practice. As English reformers received this heritage and made it their own in the course of prolonged struggles in that kingdom, it took on a special coloration. In this English setting an identification of the national community with the scriptural narrative was further specified by concentration on the apocalyptic sections of the Bible. This was the special legacy brought to the New World by the Puritans, and it set the fundamental terms for political appropriation of the Bible within American culture. Further development of these ideas about the relationship between scripture and society traces their expression in the Great Awakening of the eighteenth century, a decisive episode that stands at the foundation of the American political community./1/

The Reformers' Recovery of the Bible

Seventeenth-century Puritan culture owed to the first and classical generation of Protestant reformers, among many debts, the confidence that the Bible could and should be the authoritative source for its religious thought and communal identity. Two central innovations—or renovations—made in the use of the Bible by the magisterial reformers dominated early Protestant theology on the Continent and worked their way into positions of immense political and social influence in Lutheran and Calvinist territories: first, the claim that the scriptures principally contained the objective history of the covenant fidelity and saving acts of God; and second, the precept that the Bible should be the primary authoritative source for church doctrine and ethics.

When Martin Luther (1483-1546) discovered the passive nature of righteousness, he concomitantly found "a totally other face of the entire Scripture" (Spitz: 337). All the classical Protestant divines shared this new view: that biblical revelation was plain and literal—or historical. This historical reading sustained the doctrines of *sola fide* and *sola Christi*. For Luther, the Bible narrated the promises made by God to the Old Testament saints and the gracious fulfillment of those promises in the life of Jesus. For John Calvin (1509-1564), the Bible contained the history of the covenant of grace as it was committed to ancient Israel, broken by that people, and finally—and most evidently—secured for the elect in the Mediator. The historical events of redemption could be grasped through the exegetical methods dependent on grammatical and syntactical studies; texts were interpreted by their original presentation and intention, and key passages were set within the context provided by the whole biblical narrative. This new hermeneutical impulse obviously involved a rejection of the traditional fourfold exegesis of medieval Catholicism. The reformers denied not only the validity of the use of extrascriptural traditions as aids in interpretation but also any appeal to hidden meanings in the text. Tropological interpretation had moralized the historical accounts and had thrown the church back on its own efforts to secure salvation. Allegorical interpretation had led to a false justification of ecclesiastical traditions by substituting for the account of the work of Jesus the story of the church as the subject of scripture. According to the reformers, Roman exegesis had obscured the clear picture of Jesus in the Bible. Their literal reading recovered it and with it the operative means of justifying and sanctifying faith./2/

In this way the reformers at once distanced the Bible from contemporary traditions and communities (by arguing that it described the work of Jesus and not of the church) and centralized the Bible's position in their communities (by demanding that it exercise authority over the common life). These uses of the Bible influenced popular culture in two important ways: first, by providing a source of social cohesion and communal involvement for most members of Protestant societies; and second, by justifying active criticism of ecclesiastical, social, and political precedents. The social role thus taken by the Bible rested on both wide dispersion of the book and nurture of the means to use it. Protestantizers lost no time in producing widely printed vernacular translations; by 1535 editions were available in High and Low German, Swiss German, French, and English (see Greenslade: 94-153; Eisenstein). In order to foster the ability to read these scriptures the reformers founded and administered schools, academies (both public and private), and colleges; the curriculum of each centered on languages and Bible study. Schools took in both men and women from youths to adults; education was frequently compulsory and often free for the poor (see, for Lutheran Germany, Greenslade: 104; Spitz; Strauss; for Zwingli, see Potter: 216–24; for Calvin, see Graham: 145–51; Parker: 128–29).

Certainly the Reformation, which put into the hands of its common followers a means of religious and social criticism, resulted in the displacement of many political regimes, as the course of the Protestant movement in Geneva shows. But the political implications of the new use of the Bible went beyond a de facto challenge to established political powers. Ideal standards for government and for the character of political rule were derived from biblical doctrine and frequently stood in judgment over the practices of sixteenth-century politics. The ideal political rule maintained social order, administered justice equally under divine and civil law, and supported biblical religion (Skinner I)./3/

The reformers' use of the Bible mandated constant appraisal of political policies by the standards of biblical law, but thereby it also repudiated the presumption of any contemporary political entity to identify itself as the unique locus of God's reign on earth. The magisterial reformers had attacked the Catholic practice of identifying developments in the Church of Rome with a continuation of biblical history; consequently, they refused to say that any one nation, prince, or governmental policy particularly manifested the continuation of political orders instituted in biblical history. None of the early reformers wrote political manifestoes or extended prescriptions for a system of government. This reluctance to give the status of divine ordination to any specific body politic or form of political action derived from the reformers' commitment to literal interpretation of the Bible. The Bible decreed that every sovereign rule was instituted by God, that the kingdom of Christ existed within a variety of secular orders, and that the covenant status of Israel was transferred by the work of Jesus to the invisible number of those who had faith, not to any postbiblical political institution./4/

At the same time, however, the literal and historical reading of the Bible presented two challenges to the classical Protestant divines— challenges which they failed to meet and which were thus bequeathed to the reforming parties of the next century, especially in England. First, a consistent literalism made difficult the task of articulating the supposed cohesion between the Old and the New Testament. Luther posited a tension within the Hebrew writings between the law that condemned and the gospel that spoke of grace (Althaus: 72–81), while Calvin and Ulrich Zwingli (1484–1531) argued that God had accommodated his revelation to ancient Israel through indirect, carnal, and mysterious means (Coolidge: 82; Potter: 113. Both of these answers proved inadequate for the Puritans, who sought to identify more thoroughly the continuity between the ancient and the new Israel. The Puritan attempt to make this identification eventually fostered the development of typology, which became prominent in eighteenth-century New England, especially in the thought of Jonathan Edwards. Second, the conviction that scriptural accounts were historical brought the reformers face to face with biblical apocalyptic—without the "distance" afforded by the anagogical and allegorical methods. The mysterious events described in Ezekiel, Daniel, and Revelation had to be taken literally, even if they referred to events, people, and places under names different from the ones given in the original visions of the future. The early reformers hesitated to designate the literal referents of these prophecies. Luther referred to the pope and to the Turks as the Antichrist—but in a general and rhetorical way only. He refrained from locating the fulfillment of prophecies in any detailed manner in his own lifetime. He questioned the canonical status and usefulness of Revelation, as did Zwingli, partly because of the central place the radicals gave it. No doubt the eschatologically-minded zeal of the Anabaptists also contributed to Calvin's thorough avoidance of apocalyptic. He did not write a commentary on Revelation. He argued that the prophecies in Daniel referred to events in ancient history and that those in 2 Thessalonians referred to events at the end of history (see Althaus: 418–22; Potter: 113, 258 n. 1; Calvin, 1852 [on Daniel 7], 1851 [on 2 Thessalonians 2]). The Puritans did not share this reticence about biblical apocalyptic. It seemed clear to them that prophecy was being fulfilled in their midst. They sought to uncover the contemporary referents of the veiled images of scripture, and they found themselves and their antagonists to be the subjects.

The transformation of the principles of the doctrinal authority and historic literalism of the scriptures facilitated profound changes in the use of the Bible in Puritan political culture. First in England and then in the New World, the idea of a sacred nation came to seem plausible. Through their use of the Bible the reformers had given to Protestant political culture a framework for envisioning corporate life and an ethos for participation in it. When the English reforming party had the chance to control a truly national church, fleetingly in England and more permanently in America, they could transform their critique into national policy and identify their religious loyalties with the nation-as-community. In the process, they would locate their nation in terms of biblical history—as the "New Israel"—and thus the fulfillment of biblical prophecy. The stages of this remarkable development can be traced in Old and New England.

England's Appropriation of the Bible

The Protestant Reformation in England did not conform to the patterns that characterized continental societies. Here there was no dominant and dominating figure with a distinctive theological program comparable to Luther or Calvin—or even Zwingli. Here the break with Rome was initiated by the monarch (who had been a faithful son of the church) for reasons of personal concern and state need—namely, providing for succession to the throne—not religious allegiance. Here the period of attempted reformation lasted for well over a century, culminating in civil war and then compromise rather than being resolved for particular territories on the basis of the sovereign's religious allegiance (as was the case on the Continent). In these among many other ways the Reformation in England was anomalous, so that in its appropriation decisive transformations were worked upon Reformed teaching and practice./5/ One means of illustrating this point is the penchant for "Englishing the Bible," which culminated in the majestic King James or Authorized Version of 1611. A second is the increasingly common pattern of interpreting the trials and tribulations of English Protestants in terms of biblical precedents. Finally, a strong apocalyptic strand of biblical interpretation developed that identified the transformation of the world in the "last days" as possibly near at hand, which in later versions had England slated to play a decisive role. These separate commitments distinguished English approaches to the scriptures and influenced the distinctive New World culture as it began to form.

The commitment to translate the Bible into English was, by legend at least, made by John Wycliffe (ca. 1329–1384) in the latter half of the fourteenth century. Two partial versions often identified with him and his movement circulated at the end of the fourteenth and the beginning of the fifteenth century and closely followed the Latin Vulgate. The subsequent development of printing and circulation of Hebrew and Greek texts, along with increasing familiarity with vernacular European renditions, made possible the flowering of English translations in the sixteenth century. William Tyndale (1494?–1536) translated first the New Testament and then related sections of the Old while he was expatriate on the Continent. In 1535 Miles Coverdale (1488–1568) issued a complete translation of the Bible into English, making use of Tyndale's version as well as other European ones. Two years later the so-called Matthew's Bible, probably edited by John Rogers (1500?–1555), was printed. The Great Bible followed in 1539 and was ordered set up in churches; Miles Coverdale appears to have been the active agent behind both of these versions.

With the succession of the Catholic Mary, Protestants undertook to issue a new version, including verse divisions and substantial notes embodying a strong Protestant bias. This Geneva Bible remained a favorite among Puritans for some decades while a revision of the Great Bible known as the Bishop's Bible was used in the succeeding Elizabethan church. This version adopted the verse divisions begun with the Geneva Bible but eschewed marginal notations. An indication of the strength of this impulse to translate the scriptures into English is the Roman Catholic translation of the New Testament done at Rheims (1582), followed by the Old Testament at Douai (1609–10). Since Catholic piety did not provide the pressure for vernacular translations as directly as did Protestantism, the production of this translation suggests how persistently the English sought to make the Bible a national possession. The culmination of this remarkable impulse to "English the Scriptures" came with the Authorized or King James Version (1611). Its success in superseding the other versions, including even the Geneva Bible among many Puritans, is undoubtedly due to the care with which it was done and the marked excellence of its language (see further Greenslade: 141–74). Though religious turmoil, including outright civil war, troubled the society for the rest of the century, the Authorized Version remained unsupplanted. The achievement of an English version of the scriptures for the whole nation may be the most significant feature of the Reformation in English society—as important to it as Martin Luther was to the German lands or as Calvin was to the Reformation in Swiss cantons and France. In no other nation was a translation of the scriptures supported by the sovereign and generally accepted by the populace. This is remarkable, for it suggests that the struggle for religious reform of England was collective in a special way and that it centered in attempts to possess the scriptures and shape the common life around them./6/

The owning of the scriptures among English folk also fed an increasing tendency to identify England with Israel. Martyrs stocked the imagination of Europe for a millennium and more before this tradition was turned to special account by John Foxe (1516–1587). Along with the production of the Geneva Bible, English expatriates in the Rhineland cities in the 1550s worked at English legend-making (Haller, 1963; Olsen). The prolonged internal divisions experienced by England fed the impulse to construe the frustrations of the Protestants (and also the Roman Catholics, for that matter) in terms of ancient patterns of martyrology, reaching to that of Jesus himself. In the sixteenth century this sense of a suffering community fostered a conviction that the nation was a peculiar subject of divine will. Resemblances and analogies to events and figures in the scriptures gave way to the assumption of their very identity. In the extreme formulation, England became thought of as Israel, or better, the new Israel in and through which Christ would come again into the world. This line of thought effectively extended sacred history down into the sixteenth and seventeenth centuries. This was of immense consequence, for it made a national community, not just the ecclesiastical supranational body of Christ, the unique bearer of divine purposes. The essential steps of this development exist in the *Book of Martyrs*, for in the Elizabethan parish churches it was set up alongside the Bible. The penumbra of this development lay in the attention given to legendary matters—like the mission of Joseph of Arimathea to England or the English origins of Constantine, who subjected the mighty Roman Empire to Christ. Even shadowy materials that pertained to the Lollards and other lay groups of the High Middle Ages were converted into evidence for the precedence of England in the Christian dispensation.

These legendlike and mythic perspectives on England and its special role as seen by English Puritans in the Bible were developed in specific ways in the late sixteenth and the early seventeenth century. They came to focus in the civil war period as they informed and also legitimated the Puritan program to reform the social and political, as well as the religious, life of the kingdom according to the principles manifest in the Bible. Although the Puritans argued about the specifics of their program, they commonly assumed that such a program could be identified and delineated. For example, in his first speech to the Barebones Parliament as Lord Protector, Oliver Cromwell (1599–1658) declared:

> It is our duties to *endeavor* this way; not merely to *look* at the Prophecy in Daniel, "And the Kingdom shall not be delivered to another people [than the saints of the most High]".... Truely God hath brought this to your hands; by the owning of your call; blessing the Military Power.... Truely seeing things are thus, that you are at the edge of the Promises and Prophecies.... Surely it is our duty to choose men that fear the Lord.... [This] puts me in mind of ... [the] Sixty-eighth Psalm; which indeed is a glorious Prophecy ... of the Gospel Churches .... "He will bring His People again from the depths of the Sea, as once He led Israel through the Red Sea." (*Old South Leaflets*, 1891:17–18)

Here the English development of the biblicism of the continental reformers is clear: attention shifted from the Bible as a means of recovering the true church to the ideal of Israel as a national people holy to the God of the Bible.

To this fundamental scripturalism was added the conviction that England was in some way the special subject of scriptural narrative, past and future (see further Wilson, 1969). This is seen in the increasing English fascination with apocalyptic portions of the Bible. The apocalyptic sections of the Old and New Testaments were written at periods in the history of ancient Israel, or in the early Christian church, when all seemed lost—the forces of enemies to the God of Israel seemed so overwhelming that only direct and massive intervention by God would save the faithful. Under these circumstances, the apocalyptic message was cast as an analysis of the times in symbols that would encourage the faithful and that held out promise that deliverance was possible—all signs to the contrary. Daniel served as encouragement to Israel in its dark days of persecution by pagans and the Revelation to John of Patmos held out hope to the early Christians threatened by the Roman Empire. These highly symbolic deliverances seemed to chart the mysteries of succeeding postbiblical history.

It was not surprising that in the context of prolonged English struggles of the sixteenth century some English exegetes began to turn attention to the apocalyptic books. Among the more important authors were Thomas Brightman (1562–1607) and Hugh Broughton (1549–1612), both writing at the end of the sixteenth and early in the seventeenth century. The great Joseph Mede (1586–1638), who worked in the second and third decades of the seventeenth century, also devoted extraordinary energies to analyzing the book of Revelation. He made significant advances in literary analysis of the synchronic structure of the book. The writings of continentals like Henry Alsted (1588–1638) were as well introduced in this setting. Of course, numerous lesser lights—some well trained and others scarcely literate—appropriated and applied this bizarre and troublesome literature to England (see further Ball; Christianson).

This apocalyptic strand closed the circle with respect to the question of England and its place in divine providence. The apocalyptic preoccupations suggested just how momentous and imminent its role was thought to be./7/ Not a little of the legitimation for the killing of a Stuart king was the conviction that the fourth monarchy in Daniel—a plausible identification of the Stuart line—was to be succeeded by the true monarch, the returning Jesus as Christ the King. So too the bizarre events surrounding the Rump Parliament or movements among the populace like the followers of James Naylor (1618–1660) and George Fox (1624–1691)—not to mention the Fifth Monarchists—have their significance in terms of this logic held to be disclosed to the faithful in these, the "last days." These extreme manifestations of how apocalypticism fused with nationalism and scripturalism are chiefly important for what they signal about the premises concerning the relationship between scripture and society that stand behind and inform the experiment of transposing a culture to the New World across the Atlantic.

The Bible and Early New England Society

In the failure of their program to make of England a new Israel, the Puritans turned toward realizing these high ideals in New England (Miller, 1933, 1956). These colonists were not adventurers on the model of Sir Francis Drake or Sir Walter Raleigh. Nor were they merchants who saw an opportunity to develop profitable trade, or even manufacturers. The generation that laid claim to Massachusetts Bay in the 1620s and 1630s was profoundly disappointed over failure to achieve a thoroughly reformed England—politically and religiously. Thus they stood ready to dedicate their lives and fortunes to realizing that social program in the New World. They had not the opportunity to see that in the 1640s another chance to achieve their ends would come at home. As they faced William Laud's repressive actions, they could only conclude that their New Israel would languish unless built up in another place. This intimate connection between despair over prospects for achieving a properly reformed society in England and hopes for its realization in the New World is most clearly visible in certain documents of the "great migration." John Cotton (1585–1652) and Thomas Hooker (1586–1647) were the great clerical lights of this venture, and a close look at the sermons associated with their departures from England will amply illustrate the scriptural pattern and prospect that framed their undertaking. Of these texts, which stand for a much larger set, the one by Thomas Hooker has a logical priority if not a temporal one.

In his "The Danger of Desertion," Hooker explored the reasons for departure from old England (Williams: Doc. VII). The sermon forthrightly exhibits the reduction of scripture to social warrant, the larger theme of this essay. Hooker's text was Jer 14:5, "And we are called by thy name; leave us not." The context is Israel's entreaty that God not "take away his presence." Hooker distinguished between the "outward calling" of God and an "effectual one." The example of the destruction of Jerusalem enabled him to propose that "God will never forsake such as are in outward covenant with him." He explained the ways in which God can "unchurch or discharge a people and cast a nation off." He concluded that England was ripe for destruction: "England's sins are very great, and the greater because the means are great, and our warnings are and have been great; but yet our mercies are far greater. England had been a mirror of mercies. Yet God may now leave it and make it the mirror of his justice." Hooker's central doctrine in this sermon was "that it is the importunate desire of the saints of God still to keep God present with them." He then detailed how the presence of the "ordinances" of religion, especially preaching, is the key to continued divine presence with the nation. If that is lacking, God cannot be present to a people. "I will deal plainly with you. As sure as God is God, God is going from England."

The remainder of this great sermon explored the appropriate responses of the saints, modeled on the repentance called for in ancient Israel. Hooker's own withdrawal to the Low Countries and subsequent migration to the New World, however, suggest that he saw little efficacy in such measures. Hooker's sermon voices the underlying assumption and incorporates a sense of the national communal covenant with God. Thus the scriptures were the pattern for England's life, and the apocalyptic visions of the future were an overwhelming reality.

These same themes were no less present in a sermon preached by John Cotton as the Winthrop fleet was preparing to depart for the Atlantic crossing. Here the destruction of old England, explored so graphically by Hooker, is premised, and the preacher addressed his remarks to the obverse: "God's Promise to his Plantation" (*Old South Leaflets*, 1894). Cotton's text was 2 Sam 7:10, "I will appoint a place for my people Israel, and I will plant them, that they may dwell in a place of their own, and move no more." His doctrine was a formal statement of this point: "The placing of a people in this or that country is from the appointment of the Lord" (*Old South Leaflets*, 1894:5). Cotton explored the circumstances and conditions under which this occurs, dwelling at some length on the conditions appropriate for a colony "to remove out of their own country, and settle a City or commonwealth else where" (*Old South Leaflets*, 1894:8). In elaboration of this point he touched on the particular circumstances, such as those under which the Bay venture was proceeding (*Old South Leaflets*, 1894:9–10). Cotton's second observation was that when planted correctly, "a people of God's plantation should enjoy their own place with safety and peace" (*Old South Leaflets*, 1894:11). Central to this enjoyment is the securing of ordinances among the people—a direct reference to the necessity for New England to reform correctly church institutions and practices. But he emphasized much more broadly the achievement by a people of a good society that should be the Lord's—dare we say a new Israel?

These two sermons indicate how the hopes for a popular reformed English society were focused by and condensed into the project to develop a "New England" across the Atlantic. The magisterial sermon by John Winthrop (1588–1649) in the course of the voyage takes on added meaning when set in this context. "A Modell of Christian Charity" (1630) reviewed the premises through which a people create a society (Miller and Johnson: 195–99). The cardinal point is differentiation of the population in all sorts of ways: rulers and ruled, rich and poor; many more frameworks are implied as well. But Winthrop stressed not how the many must be subject to the few for their own good—the classical development of this point—but rather the interdependence of each on every other, whatever their individual stations. Here the two great biblical principles of justice and mercy guide the development of the society. Thus Winthrop emphasized that the society is a collectivity in relationship to God. Indeed, he resorted to covenantal language to discuss the degree of interdependence required. That was the means to assure "that the God of Israel is among us," so that New England would be a "Citty upon a Hill" (Miller and Johnson: 198–99). So at Winthrop's hand the end or purpose of the venture was to create a new Israel, a scripture-based society.

In this perspective the founders of New England understood themselves to be creating or inaugurating a new stage in human history, that is, a society conformed to the scriptures. The particulars of this program ramify throughout most aspects of the early life of the colony, from the attempts to develop and secure a body of laws synthesizing biblical precedents and English practices with their experience to virtually utopian ventures in town planning and management. In the last decades numerous monographs and studies have chronicled aspects of this experiment (Breen; Haskins; Morgan, 1963; Rutman, 1965; Solberg). But throughout this rich and valuable literature the fundamental premise has not always been clear that this society was to realize and manifest patterns disclosed in the Bible.

The Bible and the Maturation
of Colonial Society

The growth of colonial society between the establishment of New England towns and the coalescence of American political aspirations in the 1760s involved significant changes in the ways colonists identified their destiny through biblical images. New Englanders continued to use the rhetoric of the new Israel to understand their status vis-à-vis God and the "outside world" of England, French Canada, and the native Americans. Puritans still thought that their society could be conformed to biblical patterns, and they still expected that New England would play a crucial role in the consummation of the end-times. But the second generation of Puritans saw their parents' dreams clouded by apostasy, worldliness, contention, greed, and assorted heresies and schisms. They also witnessed their society evolve so that many of its sectors were no longer under the control of the churches, but colonial culture began to fall increasingly under the shadow of English political and social life. It

remained for the third generation of leaders to reconcile the vision of the
"Citty upon a Hill" with the failure of Puritanism to dominate life in the
New World. This synthesis depended upon the application of biblical
motifs to a society no longer encompassed by the pure church but conceived of as a "nation."

The attempts to realize a holy and peaceful commonwealth suffered
setbacks during the last third of the seventeenth century. In terms of
external forces, king and Parliament increased their authority over
colonial affairs. In 1660 the Navigation Acts were initiated; in 1679
Charles II warned the General Court in Boston against anti-Anglican
discrimination; in 1686 all of the northern colonies became a royal
dominion under an Anglican governor; and in 1697 Massachusetts lost its
restored charter and with it any prerogative to deny toleration to Quakers and Baptists. With respect to internal developments, native Americans under King Philip destroyed nearly a third of the Connecticut and
Massachusetts settlements in the 1675–76 war. Accusations of witchcraft
made in Salem in 1692 signaled more widespread social divisions./8/

These crises, among others, spawned the jeremiads of the 1670s, 1680s,
and 1690s. Puritan lay and clerical leaders fell over each other in lament-
ing that native peoples, royal agents, epidemics, harsh weather, and social
schism manifested divine judgments against the new Israel./9/ But
throughout this literature of declension the covenant status of New England was presupposed. Biblical images provided the means for both social
criticism of the present and optimism about the future./10/ Because, as
God's people and his Israel, New England was about "an errand for God,"
it was chastised for its sins./11/ But because New England's role was special, its sins could never extinguish the confidence that it stood at the center
of redemptive history.

Preachers such as James Allin (1692–1747), William Hubbard (1621–
1704), and Samuel Torrey (1632–1707) argued that New England was
founded with a federal status. It rested on ecclesiastical and civil consti-
tutions, which, by promoting Reformed religion, the rule of law, and
participatory politics, imbued it with an indelible character. In 1701
Torrey prefaced the published election sermon of Joseph Belcher (1669–
1723) with such claims:

> *When the Lord our God planted these Heavens, and laid the founda-*
> *tions of this Earth, and said to* New England, *Thou art my People*:
> I mean when he first founded and Erected, both an Ecclesiastical
> and Civil Constitution here . . . and thereby made us not only a
> People, but *His People*; he put it into hearts of his Servants in both
> Orders to endeavour a Coalition of both those fundamental Interests,
> (*viz.*) that of Heaven, and that of Earth; which is to say, that of
> Religion, and that of Civil Government, that the latter might be

> sanctified by the former, and our Churches and People be confirmed
> and flourish. . . . (Belcher: 3–4)

In confirming the belief that New England's status was divinely grounded, Puritans adopted a distinctive reading of biblical types and prophecies. Divine election, typically expressed in the image of the New Israel, was no longer linked to English destiny; neither did it pertain simply to individual or ecclesiastical salvation. Thus, in *The Fountain Opened* (1700), Samuel Willard (1640–1707) argued for a national, as opposed to a spiritual, reading of Old Testament types. The 1668 election sermon of William Stoughton (1632–1701), *New England's True Interest*, both treated the references of biblical prophecy as contemporary and singled out America as their subject (Stoughton). He improvised upon the Authorized Version of his text, "so he was their Saviour" (Isa 63:8), giving it a more immediate reading, "so hath he been our Saviour":

> And here I shall consider the words of the text are spoken concerning
> *a People, even the Body of a Nation.* For many a day and year,
> even from our first beginnings hath this word of the Lord been veri-
> fied concerning us in this wilderness: *The Lord hath said of* New-
> England, *Surely they are my People, Children that will not lie, so
> hath he been our Saviour.* Upon this Basis have all the *Saviourly
> Undertakings* of the Lord been founded in the midst of us, and upon
> this bottom do we unto this day abide. This we must know, that the
> Lord's promises have singled out *New England*, above all sorts of
> and ranks of men amongst us, above any Nation or people of the
> world. . . .

Sermons such as Stoughton's reveal an accommodation of biblical imagery to a New World no longer conceived in terms of Puritan villages but as a whole colonial society. The writings of Cotton Mather (1663–1728) illustrate this transformation and new synthesis of the role of the Bible in colonial political culture. He emphasized his confidence in America's destiny in his 1690 election sermon, *The Serviceable Man*. Here he warned the royal governor that America may have been in the wrong regarding ordinary sentiments of justice, but as chosen of God it received special protection. "If they be Davids, or a Beloved and Repenting people, which we are prejudic'd against; God will make it a dangerous thing to meddle with them" (quoted in Morgan, 1965:248). This teleological confidence was reflected in Mather's enthusiasm for worldly activity as an expression of piety. His organization of religious societies devoted to upholding the moral law within a colony no longer committed to enforcing narrowly Puritan ecclesiastical polity revealed Mather's recognition that America's raison d'être as a community had replaced the specific objectives of orthodoxy (see Middlekauff: 229–78).

Mather coupled his confidence in the divine ordination of the New World and continuing favor toward it with an identification of America as an elect nation. He and his contemporaries juxtaposed much more clearly than their Puritan forebears the image of the new Jerusalem, a society covenanted in the New World, and America conceived as a chosen nation. Mather's use of biblical images to portray a sacred future for America can be illustrated through two chief developments in his work.

First, Mather accepted with increasing equanimity the growing religious pluralism within colonial society. He disassociated the idea of a pure Congregationalism from the idea of the true church. His quasi-ecumenism, which embraced most Protestant churches although it excluded the Quakers, was evident in his 1712 plans for a transatlantic Christian Union. In the 1690s he had endorsed the policy of toleration as a basis for Christian unity; by 1718 he was participating in the ordination of a Baptist (Middlekauff: 215–29). Thus, the transformation of New England church life did not threaten the identification of America with the new Jerusalem. The separation of the individual churches from the national identity, through minimalizing concern over ecclesiastical differences, identified the locus of God's activity as the society rather than isolated communities within it.

Second, throughout Mather's generation Puritan preachers divorced the American eschatological future from that of England. Puritan failures in England and the burdensome domination of the crown and court over the colonies led New World Puritans to distinguish their identity and aspirations from those of England. Mather's chiliastic speculations no longer yoked America's future with the fate of brethren across the Atlantic. Although late in life he gravitated toward universalistic chiliasm (Middlekauff: 335–49), Mather consistently associated the momentous events in the New World with the imminent fulfillment of biblical prophecy: "AMERICA is legible in these Promises [of Christ's return]" (Mather, 1710:43; quoted in Berkovitch, 1975:107). "Awake, Awake, put on thy strength, O New English Zion . . . O American Jerusalem. . . . Put on thy beautiful Garments, O America, the holy City!" (Mather, 1692; quoted in Berkovitch, 1975:107; see further Miller, 1953:173–90). Cotton Mather's *Magnalia Christi Americana* (1702) monumentalized the history of New England in epic proportions. To that extent it must be seen as both the summation of the early Puritan vision of New England and the transformation of New England's hopes into the vision of the American nation as central to providentially guided history. The *Magnalia* ransacked the hagiography and legends of New England to compile evidence for the unquestioned nature of the covenant status of America. To the critics of New England, Mather responded that "there are golden Candlesticks [more than twice seven times seven!] in the midst of this 'outer darkness': unto the upright children of Abraham, here hath arisen *light in darkness*" (1853, I:27).

The formation of an American identity separate from the English, buttressed by a renewed confidence in the elect status of and apocalyptic hope for America, foreshadowed the more explicit rejection of English cultural and political dominance later in the eighteenth century. This development of the New World culture depended partly on the particular exegetical tradition of Puritan biblicism. This tradition was internally complex. First, it justified a typological reading of the scripture. Second, it incorporated a communal and national reading of the types. Third, it located the eschatological fulfillment of those types in the New World.

This tradition stands forth in the 1698 election sermon by Nicholas Noyes (1647–1717). In *New-England's Duty and Interest* Noyes spoke of the appropriateness of expecting that in the near future, "a Nation shall be born." He based such hopes on the exegetical propriety of applying Old Testament prophecy to postbiblical institutions, particularly New England: "To teach us, that by how much more similitude there is between the State . . . of the Jews, and the State . . . of any *Christian People* or Plantation. . . . And if so, I conclude such accommodations will be easy to *New England*" (Noyes: 44–45). This likening of New England to Israel has followed, according to Noyes, a three-fold pattern (46–59). Like Israel, New England went into the wilderness to worship God. Second, both Israel and New England suffered through sin, divine warning, and aimless wandering. Third, God restored Israel to the status of a great nation—after which its religion was reformed. Would New England follow this pattern? Noyes, like Mather, argued against the pessimistic declension rhetoric that prophesied America would lose its promised glory. According to Noyes's sermon, restoration preceded reformation in the scheme of Providence (66–68). Without making explicit the promise of national status, Noyes did foresee great things for America, not just her pure saints or her holy churches:

> Restauration and Reformation will struggle like twins in the Womb, which shall be born first; *a Nation shall be born at once, and the earth shall bring forth in one day*. Isa. 66.8. . . . So we know that some notable Restaurations and Reformations are nigh. . . . And notwithstanding the present bad circumstances of *America*, I know no reason to conclude this Continent shall not partake of *the Goodness of the Lord* . . . the Son of God . . . took possession [from Satan's control through the French and Indians] of *America* for *Himself*. (64–65, 75–78)

When America experienced this great spirit of restoration and reforma-tion—renewal and repentance—there would be even more cause to expect God's special favor toward the nation.

The Bible and the Great Awakening

The development of "American" assumptions about the relationship between scripture and society has been sketched in the preceding sec-tion. The Great Awakening, that summary and transforming event of colonial life in the 1740s, produced a condensed and forceful expression of them./12/ While Cotton Mather had discoursed in a learned way on "the great acts of Christ in America," the Awakening was taken by its proponents to be the culmination of those acts. Drawing as it did on different cultural sources in the separate regions, it was thought to be—by those who were positively disposed toward it—the drawing near of the end-times, the prelude to (or even the first act in) the conclusion of God's great work of redeeming humanity and creation through events initiated in America. What the revivals professed to manifest was the agency of the Spirit working among God's people to clarify the meaning of the current dispensation and to complete it. No doubt the sources of the awakening phenomena can be effectively analyzed in numerous ways. Surely the occasions for and the outcomes of the revival of religion were many and varied, especially in disparate locations. But, for those caught up in the conviction that the times of refreshing for the church had come, these discriminations were insignificant and their importance finally nil. From this perspective, the Great Awakening might be seen as the completion of the Reformation—the achievement of what had been so elusive. With the Awakening, God was believed at last to be moving decisively among his people. Numerous congregations finally "separated" from established bodies, prepared to continue in pure churches as long as necessary; numerous preachers adopted the role of itineration—against all their instincts and traditions./13/ In sum, precedent and convention gave way before the force of the gospel to the contrary. In this respect the Awakening was viewed as God's coming to his people and in turn their decisive response to him.

These are precisely the terms in which the proponents of the Great Awakening understood the remarkable events of the era. For example, Jonathan Dickinson (1688–1747), preaching in Newark in May 1740, argued: "It's your Business to consider, whether you have had this *wit-ness of the Spirit with your Spirit*, or not. If you have been thus awak-ened out of your carnal Security, you have the testimony of *the Spirit himself*, that he has begun a good work in you" (Heimert and Miller: 102). Again, an assembly of pre-Awakening New England pastors, meeting in

Boston in July 1743, published a statement that centers in the following observation:

> When Christ is pleased to come into his Church in a plentiful Effusion of the Holy Spirit, by whose powerful Influence the Ministration of the Word is attended with uncommon Success, Salvation-Work carried on in an eminent Manner, and his Kingdom . . . is notably advanced. *This* is an event which above all others invites notice; and bespeaks the Praises of the Lord's People and should be declared abroad for the Memorial of the divine Grace. . . . (Bushman, 1970: 129)

These assessments of the event could be paralleled repeatedly, for the central conviction behind the Awakening was that in so coming to his people, God was bringing to pass that which had been longed for in the settling of New England, as it had been in the disappointed attempts to renovate old England, which in turn had seemed to be the logical end and outcome of the Reformation proper. So the revival of the 1740s was thought to be the "coming in of Glory of the Latter Days" (Bushman, 1970:129).

In one sense, to be sure, such sentiments can be read as "apolitical." But in a more profound sense they concerned the final transformation of society according to perceived scriptural norms and expectations. And insofar as those who thought themselves "saints" were drawn into appropriate activities and actions that would be congruent with this goal and would rise out of concern for it, these convictions could be none other than fundamentally political, that is to say, directed toward the creation of a new social and political order. Frequently it has been suggested that the Great Awakening represented the "democratizing of Puritanism"—or even Protestantism./14/ More properly, "democracy," or rule by the people, was a consequence of the assumption—or a translation into cultural terms of the religious conviction—that Christ had come to his people and empowered them in fundamental and final ways.

This decisive stage in the evolution of the relationship between scripture and society is nowhere more forcefully articulated or embodied than in the central indigenous figure of the Great Awakening, Jonathan Edwards (1703–1758), who, according to his lights, gave his life over to it. In adopting the renewal tradition begun and carried on by his grandfather, Solomon Stoddard, in the meticulous chronicling of his own anticipatory harvests of the 1730s, in the whole-hearted itinerating on behalf of the Great Awakening proper in the 1740s, in the criticism of its excesses yet defense of its essential authenticity, or in the attempts to yoke or link the New World Awakening with those reinvigorating Scottish and even continental churches through the Concert of Prayer. In

these ways, as a man of action, Jonathan Edwards stood wholly committed to the Great Awakening./15/

This activist side of Edwards and the political implications flowing
from it are summarized and explicitly expressed in his "An Humble
Attempt to promote Explicit Agreement and Visible Union of God's
People in Extraordinary Prayer for the revival of religion and the
advancement of Christ's Kingdom on Earth, pursuant to Scripture promises and Prophecies concerning the last Time," which was published in
Boston in 1747 (Edwards, 1977:307–436). It displayed the corporate
outcome that the Awakeners anticipated—finally, the coming of Christ
in his kingdom among the nations to inaugurate a millennial rule. In the
outworking of the power of prayer and the Spirit, "religion shall be
propagated, till the awakening reaches those that are in the highest stations, and till whole nations be awakened, and there be at length an
accession of many of the chief nations to the church of God" (Edwards,
1977:318). That the preface to this tract was signed by Awakening pastors in Boston, among them Thomas Foxcroft (1697–1769) and Joseph
Sewall (1688–1769), suggests both that Jonathan Edwards's views were
not idiosyncratic and that the implications of the Awakening for the
political life of the colonies were widely recognized.

No less should Edwards's more philosophical and reflective side be
recognized as rising from this problematic of the new life of the Spirit
made available in his time. In his writings philosophical reflection eventuated in the thoroughgoing repristination of Calvinism for which he
was celebrated. At the center of Edwards's innovative use of the Bible
was his adaptation and further development of typology as a strategy for
its interpretation./16/ That this was one of the most important among
several exegetical options for the seventeenth-century English Puritans
has already been noted. Toward the end of that century its position
among Puritan approaches to the Bible had been explored and thoroughly summarized by Samuel Mather in his sermon series published as
The Figures of Types of the Old Testament. Now Edwards decisively
extended typology. On the one hand, he paralleled (if not merged) types
of nature with those drawn from scripture. On the other, he dissolved
the strict type/antitype formula, so that post- and extra-New Testament
events (of history and even nature) might be construed as types of salvation events yet to come. The technical aspects of these extensions of the
subject are less significant for the immediate discussion than the extraordinary impetus this development gave to the attempt to pattern political
and social life according to biblical and biblically derived norms.

Jonathan Edwards was convinced that the scripture no less patented
New World society than it had Old World Israel. Edwards's obsession

with God's working to redeem the world in and through the mundane is nowhere more fully and precisely delineated than in his magnum opus, left unrevised and uncompleted at his death. *A History of the Work of Redemption* was precisely his literary codification of the religious cosmos within which the colonists understood themselves as coming into being as part of a dispensation that would consummate the new creation./17/

> It is reasonable to suppose that all revolutions from the beginning of the world to the end of it, are but the various parts of the same scheme, all conspiring to bring to pass the great event which the Creator and Governor of the world has ultimately in view; and that the scheme will not be finished, nor the design fully accomplished, and the great and ultimate event fully brought to pass till the end of the world, and that the last revolution is brought about.

> Let who will prevail now, let the enemies of the church exalt themselves as much as they will, these are the people that shall finally prevail. The last kingdom shall finally be theirs; the kingdom shall finally be given into their hands, and shall not be left to the other people. (Heimert and Miller: 32, 34)

To have centered this discussion so exclusively on essentially New England figures and materials should not be misleading. In the New England context there was a fuller, more self-conscious and sustained exploration of many subjects that came to be representative of other regions as well. In the middle colonies and eventually in the southern ones as well the Great Awakening had a similar effect, though at times without the extensive reflection and the theological self-consciousness that was fostered in New England./18/ The outcome was comparable— a popularizing of Protestant biblicism—though not rationalized at the level of theory. It was simply assumed by the Awakeners that the Bible spoke to the people directly, whether in Pennsylvania, inland Virginia, or Georgia. Further, the response to such speech, assumed the awakeners, should be action rooted in and based on scriptural norms. In sum, the biblicism of the Great Awakening was a central ingredient in the preparation of consciousness throughout the colonies to embrace a new future under biblical symbols. While not simply a political document, the Bible warranted actions of the people that would have an increasingly revolutionary import.

It is certainly a misrepresentation of Jonathan Edwards and the Great Awakening to see in them the direct expression either of an American nationalism or of a specific political program. Yet, at the same time we find here an energetic vivid reassertion of confidence in the providentially favored status and sure destiny of the colonists. When this confidence was linked to further developments and the expansion of the political life and resources of the colonies, the result was the cultural assumptions that made possible the founding of a new nation. The fusion of beliefs about American society and scriptural destiny, which Edwards voiced with exquisite clarity and power, marks among other things the decisive codification of the place and role of the Bible in the American political culture. It was a place and role that, while originating in the Protestant Reformation proper, was yet decisively shaped by English ideals and experience and was finally confirmed and perfected in the New World.

NOTES

/1/   The essay so described explores neither technical issues in biblical interpretation nor ways in which American Puritans derived specific political programs or policies from the Bible. There is a significant literature on these and related topics including such studies as Foster; Breen; Bercovitch, 1975. Our present subject is changes in the underlying assumptions about the relationship between the Bible and corporate life, including the specifically political aspects of such life, from the magisterial reformers (Luther and Calvin) through the Great Awakening in the American colonies (Jonathan Edwards).

/2/   On the reformers' historical reading and literal hermeneutics and the relation of these to their doctrines of faith and Christ see, for Luther, Althaus: 35–102; Preus: 188–247. For Zwingli, see Potter: 75–90, 172–73. For Calvin, see Dowey: 106–16; Frei: 19–37; and Wendel: 185–214.

/3/   Skinner's is the most thorough and lucid analysis of the political ideals of the Reformation, and much of the following discussion rests on his evidence. See also McNeill. For Luther and Zwingli, see the discussion and references in Ozment: 260–72. Breen has shown that in Puritanism the stress on the virtue of the ruler allowed for constant and critical appraisal of political authority.

/4/   This is not just an argument from silence. Luther and Calvin were quite content to evaluate governments according to their policies and religion and not according to their fundamental political organization. Calvin praised the monarch of England under Somerset's protectorate and deplored the reign of the Catholic Queen Mary. His guiding conviction was that ". . . Christ's spiritual kingdom and the civil jurisdiction are things completely distinct. . . . Spiritual freedom can perfectly exist along with civil bondage" (*Institutes*, IV.XX.1; see further Calvin, 1847:704–7).

/5/   For a discussion of the course of the Reformation in sixteenth-century England, see Dickens.

/6/   For an older but still useful discussion of this subject, see Haller, 1938.

/7/   Nuttall provides an early and influential discussion of how conservative Puritanism held common or related ground with more radical groups (see also Hill). On the general issue of how Puritanism related to political activity see Walzer.

/8/   For a general narrative of events in late seventeenth-century American Puritanism see Wertenbaker: chaps. V–X; for a recent interpretation of the impact of imperial policies on New England society see Lockridge.

/9/   See, for example, the report of the 1679 Synod of Boston, the "Reforming Synod," *The Necessity of Reformation.*

/10/   Sacvan Bercovitch has pointed out how the assertion of the federal status of America, linked to eschatological expectations, provided the Puritans with a rationale for hope in America's redemptive role in history despite the incongruities between their rhetoric and the reality of the growing pluralism and commercialism of seventeenth-century New England (see Bercovitch, 1975:100–108). Bernard Bailyn (32–33) shows how these ideas worked their way into eighteenth-century literature. The best discussion of declension rhetoric and its relation to social crises and the provincial mentality is Miller, 1953.

/11/   The sermons of this period are full of such language, which asserted New England's special status while condemning its failures in piety; see, for example, Danforth; Hubbard; Allin; Whiting.

/12/   The most complete discussion of the Great Awakening in New England is by Gaustad. For an examination of the prelude to the Awakening in a single colony see Bushman, 1967. Rutman (1970) is a useful introduction to the problem of interpreting the event. For readers oriented to the published materials of the Awakenings see Heimert and Miller.

/13/   On the phenomenon of separatism in eighteenth-century New England see Goen.

/14/   On the level of popular participation in political life as affected by the Great Awakening (which presupposed this understanding of scripture to society), see Heimert.

/15/   For Edwards's own writings on the Awakening, see Edwards, 1972. A recent biographical study focusing on Edwards as a pastor of the Awakening is that of Tracy.

/16/   For the centrality of typology in Edwards's thought, see Miller, 1948. Other discussions of this theme in broader settings include Brumm; Bercovitch, 1972; Lowance.

/17/   On Edwards's understanding of history, see Wilson, 1977:5–18.

/18/   Studies of the Great Awakening outside New England include Maxson; Gewehr. For an interesting study of the Awakening's impact on lay activity in Pennsylvania see Rothermund.

WORKS CONSULTED

Allin, James
    1679   *New England's Choicest Blessing.* Boston: n.p.

Althaus, Paul
    1966   *The Theology of Martin Luther,* translated by Robert C. Schultz. Philadelphia: Fortress.

Bailyn, Bernard
    1967   *The Ideological Origins of the American Revolution.* Cambridge, MA: Harvard University Press.

Ball, Bryan W.
    1975   *A Great Expectation.* Leiden: Brill.

Belcher, Joseph
    1701   *The Singular Happiness.* Boston: n.p.

Bercovitch, Sacvan
    1975   *The Puritan Origins of the American Self.* New Haven: Yale University Press.

Bercovitch, Sacvan, ed.
    1972   *Typology in Early American Literature.* Amherst, MA: University of Massachusetts Press.

Breen, T. H.
    1970   *The Character of the Good Ruler.* New Haven: Yale University Press.

Brumm, Ursula
    1970   *American Thought and Religious Typology.* New Brunswick, NJ: Rutgers University Press.

Bushman, Richard
    1967   *From Puritan to Yankee.* Cambridge, MA: Harvard University Press.

Bushman, Richard, ed.
    1970   *The Great Awakening.* New York: Atheneum.

Calvin, John
    1847   "To the Lord Protector of England," (1550) letter CCCXXXV of *The Zurich Letters*, edited by Hastings Robinson for the Parker Society. Cambridge: Cambridge University Press.
    1851   *Commentaries in the Epistles of Paul . . . Thessalonians*, translated by John Pringle. Edinburgh: Calvin Translation Society.
    1852   *Commentaries on the Book of the Prophet Daniel*, translated by Thomas Myers. Edinburgh: Calvin Translation Society.

Christianson, Paul
    1978   *Reformers and Babylon.* Toronto: University of Toronto Press.

Coolidge, John S.
    1970   *The Pauline Renaissance in England.* Oxford: Clarendon.

Danforth, Samuel
    1671   *A Briefe Recognition of New England's Errand into the Wilderness.* Cambridge, MA: n.p.

Dickens, A. G.
    1964   *The English Reformation.* New York: Scribner.

Dowey, Edward A., Jr.
    1952   *The Knowledge of God in Calvin's Theology.* New York: Columbia University Press.

Edwards, Jonathan
1972   *The Works of Jonathan Edwards*. Vol. IV, *The Great Awak-
               ening*, edited by C. C. Goen. New Haven: Yale University
               Press.
1977   *The Works of Jonathan Edwards*. Vol. V, *Apocalyptic Writ-
               ings*, edited by S. J. Stein. New Haven: Yale University Press.

Eisenstein, Elisabeth
1974   "The Advent of Printing and the Protestant Revolt," in *Transi-
               tion and Revolution*, edited by Robert M. Kingdon. Minneapo-
               lis: Burgess.

Foster, S.
1971   *Their Solitary Way*. New Haven: Yale University Press.

Frei, Hans
1974   *The Eclipse of Biblical Narrative*. New Haven: Yale Univer-
               sity Press.

Gaustad, Edwin S.
1957   *The Great Awakening in New England*. New York: Harper.

Gewehr, W. M.
1930   *The Great Awakening in Virginia*. Durham: Duke University
               Press.

Goen, C. C.
1962   *Revivalism and Separatism in New England*. New Haven:
               Yale University Press.

Graham, W. Fred
1978   *The Constructive Revolutionary*. Richmond: John Knox.

Greenslade, S. L., ed.
1963   *The Cambridge History of the Bible: The West from the Ref-
               ormation to the Present Day*. Cambridge: Cambridge Univer-
               sity Press.

Haller, William
1938   *The Rise of Puritanism*. New York: Columbia University
               Press.
1963   *The Elect Nation*. New York: Harper.

Haskins, G. L.
1960   *Law and Authority in Early Massachusetts*. New York: Mac-
               millan.

Heimert, Alan
1966   *Religion and the American Mind*. Cambridge, MA: Harvard
               University Press.

Heimert, Alan, and Perry Miller
1967   *The Great Awakenings*. Indianapolis: Bobbs-Merrill.

Hill, Christopher
1972   *The World Turned Upside Down*. New York: Viking.

Hubbard, William
1676   *The Happiness of a People . . . Attending Unto What Israel
               Ought to do*. Boston: n.p.

Lockridge, Kenneth A.
1981   *Settlement and Unsettlement in Early America.* Cambridge:
               Cambridge University Press.

Lowance, Mason
1980   *The Language of Canaan.* Cambridge, MA: Harvard Univer-
               sity Press.

Luther, Martin
1960   "Preface to the Complete Edition of Luther's Latin Writings,
               1545," translated by Lewis W. Spitz, in *Luther's Works*,
               Vol. 34, edited by Lewis W. Spitz, general editor, Helmut T.
               Lehmann. Philadelphia: Muhlenberg.

McNeill, John Thomas
1949   "The Democratic Element in Calvin's Thought," *Church
               History* 18.

Mather, Cotton
1690   *The Serviceable Man.* Boston: Samuel Green.
1692   *Midnight Cry.* Boston: n.p.
1710   *Theopolis Americana.* Boston: n.p.
1853   *Magnalia Christi Americana,* ed. Thomas Robbins, 2 vols.
               Hartford: S. Andrus & Son.

Mather, Samuel
1683   *The Figures of Types of the Old Testament.* Dublin: n.p.

Maxson, Charles H.
1958   *The Great Awakening in the Middle Colonies.* Gloucester,
               MA: Smith.

Middlekauff, Robert
1971   *The Mathers.* New York: Oxford.

Miller, Perry
1933   *Orthodoxy in Massachusetts.* Cambridge, MA: Harvard Uni-
               versity Press.
1953   *The New England Mind. From Colony to Province.* Cam-
               bridge, MA: Harvard University Press.
1956   *Errand into the Wilderness.* Cambridge, MA: Harvard Uni-
               versity Press.

Miller, Perry, ed.
1948   *Images on Shadows of Divine Things by Jonathan Edwards.*
               New Haven: Yale University Press.

Miller, Perry, and T. H. Johnson, eds.
1963   *The Puritans,* Vol. I. New York: Harper.

Morgan, Edmund S.
1963   *Visible Saints.* New York: New York University Press.
1965   *Puritan Political Ideas.* Indianapolis: Bobbs-Merrill.

Noyes, Nicholas
1698   *New-England's Duty and Interest.* Boston: Green and Allen.

Nuttall, Geoffrey
1957   *Visible Saints.* Oxford: Blackwell.

Old South Leaflets
    1891   General Series, no. 28. Boston: n.p.
    1894   General Series, no. 53. Boston: n.p.

Olsen, V. Norskov
    1973   *John Foxe and the Elizabethan Church.* Berkeley, CA: University of California Press.

Ozment, Steven
    1980   *The Age of Reform 1250–1550.* New Haven: Yale University Press.

Parker, T. H. L.
    1975   *John Calvin.* Philadelphia: Westminster.

Potter, G. R.
    1976   *Zwingli.* Cambridge: Cambridge University Press.

Preus, James Samuel
    1969   *From Shadow to Promise.* Cambridge, MA: Harvard University Press.

Rothermund, Dietmar
    1962   *The Laymen's Progress.* Philadelphia: University of Pennsylvania Press.

Rutman, Darrett
    1965   *Winthrop's Boston.* Chapel Hill: University of North Carolina Press.
    1970   *The Great Awakening: Event and Exegesis.* New York: Wiley.

Skinner, Quentin
    1978   *The Foundations of Modern Political Thought.* Vol. 2: *The Age of Reformation.* Cambridge: Cambridge University Press.

Solberg, W.
    1977   *Redeem the Time.* Cambridge, MA: Harvard University Press.

Spitz, Lewis W.
    1974   "Humanism and the Reformation," in *Transition and Revolution*, edited by Robert M. Kingdon. Minneapolis: Burgess.

Stoughton, William
    1670   *New England's True Interest.* Cambridge: S.C. and M.F.

Strauss, Gerald
    1978   *Luther's House of Learning.* Baltimore: Johns Hopkins University Press.

Synod of Boston
    1679   "Reforming Synod," *The Necessity of Reformation.* Boston: n.p.

Tracy, Patricia
    1980   *Jonathan Edwards, Pastor.* New York: Hill and Wang.

Walzer, Michael
    1965   *The Revolution of the Saints.* Cambridge, MA: Harvard University Press.

Wendel, Francois
1963   *Calvin*, translated by Philip Mairet. London: Collins.

Wertenbaker, Thomas Jefferson
1947   *The Puritan Oligarchy*, chaps. V–X. New York: Scribner.

Whiting, John
1686   *The Way of Israel's Welfare*. Boston: n.p.

Willard, Samuel
1700   *The Fountain Opened*. Boston: n.p.

Williams, G. H., et al., eds.
1975   *Thomas Hooker: Writings* . . . Cambridge, MA: Harvard University Press.

Wilson, John F.
1969   *Pulpit in Parliament*. Princeton: Princeton University Press.
1977   "Jonathan Edwards as Historian," *Church History* 46 (March).

II

The Bible in Revolutionary America

Mark A. Noll

Historians who wish to discuss the Bible and politics in Revolutionary America must first decide what they are talking about. The Bible we know, but how may its presence be noted in political history? The American Revolution is more elusive, but how could its history—whatever it actually was—relate to a religious text? In the first instance, do we look for political leaders who used the scriptures to strengthen personal piety, for statesmen who tried to imitate the morals of Jesus, or for dogmaticians who translated the results of exegesis into public policy? In the second, are we speaking of the Revolution as political processes formalized in the Declaration of Independence and the Constitution, as some sort of intracolonial struggle for power, or as the general spirit of the new nation? Both sides of the equation appear, at first glance, fraught with conceptual peril. But this confusion over definitions is not impenetrable. If we recognize that the Bible is a multifaceted book that was used in nearly as many ways in the late eighteenth century as it is in the late twentieth and that a fluid set of Revolutionary ideals dominated American political discourse long after the War for Independence was over, we are in a position to work through the superficial complexities of the issue. We can also divide the general question into more manageable inquiries, three of which provide the structure for this essay: Did America's founders read the Bible? Did biblical themes contribute significantly to the political theory of the age? Did the Bible figure in the public ethos that took shape during the early national period? The answers that emerge to these questions point to a complexity far more involved than mere confusion over definitions. For they show us that in the political history of the early United States the Bible was everywhere and nowhere, that the politics of Revolutionary America were distinctly biblical, yet quite untouched by the messages of scripture./1/

The Bible and the Founding Fathers

It should not be surprising that even the least orthodox of the founders of the nation paid some attention to scripture, for they lived at a time when to be an educated member of the Atlantic community was to know the Bible. It is useful to note this, however, since twentieth-century observers sometimes conclude from the obvious distaste that several of the founders displayed toward the hardier brands of evangelicalism that their entire generation was indifferent to the Bible. Nothing could be further from the truth.

To be sure, scripture did exert a greater influence among the secondary ranks of America's early political and cultural leaders than among the Revolutionary demigods. Many of these lesser lights self-consciously employed the Bible as a lens through which to view the self and the spiritual world. Patrick Henry of Virginia probably learned some of his effective rhetoric from the biblical expositions of revivalists, and he certainly infused his own public speech with scriptural content (Cohen). The same kind of influences may be traced, though somewhat less conclusively, in Massachusetts's Sam Adams (Williams). Several signers of the Declaration of Independence—including Connecticut's Roger Sherman and New Jersey's John Witherspoon—made lifelong efforts to order their personal lives according to their understanding of scripture (Collier: 325–29; Smylie, 1970). John Jay—United States ambassador, a great figure in the Revolutionary politics of New York, and the first Chief Justice of the Supreme Court—was a fervent Anglican who read the Bible regularly. Late in his life he wrote: "in settling my belief relative to the doctrines of Christianity, I adopted no articles from creeds, but such only as, on careful examination, I found to be confirmed by the Bible" (Pellew: 320). Jay was also one of the many from the Revolutionary generation who took part in establishing Bible societies in the early nineteenth century. It is indicative of the place of scripture in the private lives of many such statesmen that the founding president of the American Bible Society (1816), Elias Boudinot, had also been one of the first presidents of the Confederation Congress of the United States (1782–83) (Boyd: 106, 259).

Important as the Bible was for political leaders in the generation that established independence, it was an even more significant force for the next generation, whose task was to work out the meaning of the Revolution for an emerging American culture. Mason Weems, the mythologizer of Washington, not only immersed himself in the Bible but actually earned his living by selling it (Wills). Noah Webster, who is remembered for teaching Americans to spell, wanted most to be known for instructing the children of America in the Bible (Rollins: 117–18; Warfel: 401–15). The leaders of American higher education in the first generation after the adoption of the Constitution—whether Unitarian Levi Hedge at Harvard, Congregationalist Timothy Dwight at Yale, or Presbyterian Samuel Stanhope

Smith at Princeton—took for granted that scripture would be a cornerstone of the academic enterprise (Howe: 35; Cuningham: 240; Hudnut: 545–46). And this is to say nothing about the biblical fixations of the revivalists like Lyman Beecher and Charles G. Finney, who by the mid-1820s had eclipsed political leaders as the arbiters of American values.

By comparison with this ardent biblicism, the attention that the founding luminaries paid to scripture may seem trifling. Yet theirs was at most a relative indifference. George Washington and John Adams knew and respected scripture, and Adams at least read it on occasion (Boller: 39–43). From Adams late in his life even came the confession that "the Bible is the best book in the World. It contains more of my little Phylosophy than all the Libraries I have seen: and such Parts of it as I cannot reconcile to my little Phylosophy I postpone for future Investigation" (Cappon: II, 412). As the nation's first two presidents, Washington and Adams also promoted the Bible's public exposition by decreeing national days of fasting and thanksgiving. The third president, Thomas Jefferson, refused to call for such days, but still was willing to contribute to Bible societies (Jefferson: XIV, 14). Jefferson remained impressed throughout his life with the morals of Jesus and intrigued by the message of the New Testament, which he twice edited in order to remove the unreasonable parts (Mabee). James Madison, to whom we shall return, agreed with Jefferson that the government should not sanction national days of prayer, but he paid the Bible a higher compliment than his Virginia colleague. Rather than edit scripture, Madison during a formative period of his life studied it seriously as it was (Ketcham, 1960:72–73). The last of the great founders, Alexander Hamilton, both began and closed his American career as a devoted student of the Bible, even if he paid little attention to it during the middle part of his life (Adair and Harvey).

The conclusion to which this evidence points is that nearly everyone of consequence in America's early political history was, if not evangelically committed to scripture, at least conversant with its content. To one degree or another, the Bible was important for America's first great public representatives. But to say this is not necessarily to say that the Bible was important for early American politics. That conclusion must arise from a different sort of inquiry, which looks less to the details of individual biography and more to the content and derivation of public thought.

The Bible and Revolutionary Political Theory

Owing to the sophisticated labors of a whole host of recent historians, students of the Revolutionary period now have a compelling picture of the ideology, the popular political thought, which undergirded the struggle for independence and the creation of a new nation./2/ It would seem to be a simple procedure to ask if the Bible had anything to do with that ideology. One merely looks for political leaders or private Christians who came to hold Revolutionary principles as a consequence of studying specific passages of scripture or perhaps through a conscious effort to translate overarching biblical themes into political theory. To be sure, this would leave open the question whether the Bible was being understood correctly in Revolutionary America, but at least we would have identified a "biblical politics" in categories that made sense for the late eighteenth or the early nineteenth century. The question, however, turns out to be quite a bit more involved than that.

The Revolutionary ideas that moved Americans to revolt and that offered broad guidelines for the new nation are often styled "radical" or "real" Whig. They comprised both a political philosophy and a moral vision. As political theory they were rooted in the English Whig heritage of the late seventeenth and the eighteenth century with its commitments to parliamentary rights, the Protestant succession, and the traditional liberties of the British Constitution. By the late eighteenth century Whigs also shared with most advanced Western thinkers a belief in natural rights and in the social contract as the foundation of public order (see especially Bailyn, 1967:45). These abstract theories became an ideology with revolutionary potential when they were animated by "real" Whig pictures of good and evil. During the eighteenth century the actual political figures who were known as "real" or "radical" Whigs remained on the fringes of British politics, but their perceptions, especially of public authority, became crucial in America. What they transmitted across the Atlantic above all was a fundamental distrust of unchecked power, whether in the grasping hands of an arbitrary monarch, in the machinations of a venal Parliament, or in overweening aspirations of a state church. Unchecked power, the "real" Whigs held, nourished corruption, which in turn fed the maw of unrestrained power. Let authority get out of hand, and all the hard-won trophies of English liberty, every vestige of natural right—not to speak of the very rule of law itself—stood in mortal jeopardy. It was this powerful ideology that in the minds of American patriots transformed the blunders of Parliament into life-or-death crises. It explains, for example, how patriots could read Parliament's magnanimous extension of privileges to French Catholics by the Quebec Act of 1774 as an effort to subvert religious as well as political freedom in other colonies, or why the dispute over taxes on tea had such momentous consequences.

Another group of talented scholars has painstakingly traced the growth of "real" Whig convictions in British and European political traditions./3/

The Whig conception of politics grew out of the turbulent struggles between king and Parliament during the first half of the seventeenth century. A specifically dissenting voice was added from the Puritan efforts (1640–1660) to curb the monarchy and advance the cause of Parliament while perfecting the Protestant Reformation. Whig politics enjoyed its finest hour in the Glorious Revolution of 1688, which ousted the Catholic James II, installed the Protestant William and Mary on the throne, and elicited classic justifications of these actions by John Locke. Whig principles remained the theoretical basis for British politics throughout the eighteenth century, but even parliamentary leaders admitted that political in-fighting and petty grabs for power were the actual wellsprings of public policy throughout the period. Nonetheless, "radical" Whigs, who were excluded from ruling circles, continued to fear threats to freedom and contended that they were rampant in nominally Whig England. These "radical" Whigs were voices crying in the wilderness of Britain during the 1760s and 1770s, but in America they made straight the way for Revolution. Their picture of the world encouraged a nearly hysterical fear in America of Parliament's corrupt power, nerved a spirited defense of "traditional liberties," and called forth learned expositions of "unalienable rights."

The question remains, was this "real" Whig ideology biblical? The most influential interpreter of Revolutionary ideology, Bernard Bailyn, acknowledges that "the political and social theories of New England Puritanism and particularly . . . the ideas associated with covenant theology" contributed to "real" Whig thought (Bailyn, 1967:32). We have already observed that the nation's founders were conversant with scripture. And it was certainly common for many Christian patriots, especially ministers on days of fast or thanksgiving, to adduce texts from the Bible in support of the drive for independence./4/

Upon a closer inspection, these "biblical" elements in Revolutionary thought show little one way or the other. The founders may have read the Bible, but themes from scripture are conspicuously absent in the political discussions of the nation's early history./5/ As one might expect from the nature of the documents, biblical reasoning does not appear in the Declaration of Independence, the Constitution, or the new state charters. But it is also almost entirely absent from the places where it might be expected—the pamphlet literature advocating independence, the various state debates over the Constitution, the Democratic–Federalist wrangles of the 1790s, and the controversies surrounding embargo, the War of 1812, and the Hartford Convention during the Jefferson and Madison administrations. In short, the political figures who read the Bible in private rarely, if ever, betrayed that acquaintance in public.

Where ministers or lay people did bring the Bible into play, it was usually not for purposes of careful political reasoning. I have elsewhere described at length the creative ways in which patriotic ministers applied biblical texts to support their cause, regardless of how irrelevant to partisan political concerns such texts may hitherto have seemed to 1800 years of Christian exegesis (Noll, 1977:49–51, 1982a:41–42). Only a few examples are necessary to illustrate this. A Boston minister preached on Gal 5:12–13, especially the phrase, "ye have been called unto liberty," in 1765 to urge resistance to Parliament's Stamp Act (Bailyn, 1970:113, 140–43). After the war, a Connecticut minister took Deut 26:19 ("to make thee high above all nations . . . and that thou mayest be an holy people unto the Lord thy God, as he hath spoken") to be "allusively prophetic of the future prosperity and splendor of the United States" (Stiles: 403). Throughout the various armed conflicts of the Revolutionary period ministers applied the "Curse of Meroz" (from Judg 5:23) to those thought to be shirking their patriotic duties (Heimert: 332–34, 500–509). However much this use of the Bible may have communicated a sense of America's divine mission, it was hardly a serious effort to construct political theory from scripture.

All this, however, is still preliminary. After noting that leaders did not cite biblical chapter and verse in the expression of Revolutionary theory or that ministers often used fanciful exegesis in the heat of the moment, we still do not know whether major emphases of "real" Whig thought paralleled—or even reflected—biblical themes. Nor if they did, how the parallels or reflections came about.

Clearly, "real" Whig ideology shared some common emphases with broad themes of scripture, particularly as these had been developed by the Puritans (see Morgan). As did the "real" Whigs, so biblical writers suspected human nature (e.g., Jer 17:9, Rom 3:23). Scripture, particularly the Old Testament history of Israel, paralleled "radical" Whig convictions by linking virtue and social well-being. Sacred authors also spoke of the "reign" or "dominion" of sin (e.g., Rom 6:12, 14) much as "radical" Whigs bewailed the "tyranny" of corruption. Great concern for freedom—for the captive (e.g., Isa 61:1), in the truth (e.g., John 8:32), in Christ (e.g., Gal 5:1)—was a constant theme of both Testaments. As in the Whig picture, history appeared on the pages of the Bible as a cosmic struggle between good and evil. The extent of such parallels helps explain why it was so easy for so many ministers, particularly of Puritan stock, to read the Revolutionary War as a conflict between Christ and Antichrist (Hatch, 1977:86–87). It also may be the reason why so many Christians regarded the political tumults of the early nation as distinctly spiritual crises (Nash; Noll, 1979:86–89).

Yet there were other elements of Revolutionary ideology that did not slip as easily into Christian categories. Whigs, for example, often transformed the defense of freedom to worship into an idolatrous worship of freedom. By combining impatience with hierarchy and immense confidence in nature, they reduced the God of Christian revelation to the "Author of Nature." And Whigs retained moral blind spots—slavery, as an example—which *homines unius libri* like John Wesley or America's Samuel Hopkins could not tolerate.

These obvious inconsistencies between biblical and Whig values raise questions about the parallels. Were they merely haphazard similarities arising from the common intellectual heritage of Europe, or were they in fact true reflections of the biblical influence that all admitted had contributed to that heritage?

It is possible to offer historical answers here, but their results are at best problematic. To trace the "radical" Whig tradition to its sources cannot answer our question, for that effort reveals an extraordinarily diverse heritage (for a brief summary, see Robbins: 7–16). Bible-believing Puritans contributed to that tradition, as did the biblicist John Milton, defender of a free press. But many others had contributed to the "real" Whig heritage for reasons having nothing to do with scripture: doctrinaire republicans who detested monarchy of any kind, Scottish and Irish nationalists who hated the rule of Westminster, legal scholars who feared for the Common Law, latitudinarian Anglicans like Sir Isaac Newton who wanted to see the political order display the same harmony as the "laws" of nature, landowners whose property had been secured by the Glorious Revolution, and philosophers like John Locke who saw the state as a potential threat to natural rights or like Scotland's Francis Hutcheson who felt that the innate "moral sense" could dictate a just politics. And "radical" Whiggery also brought together theologically antithetical groups like Calvinist Dissenters and free-thinking deists who together chafed under the established Church of England. Examining the pedigree of "real" Whig thought makes it clear that the Bible is not a stranger to it, but it is equally evident that the Bible is not determinative.

A more fruitful strategy might be to examine the intellectual roots not of an entire tradition but of one influential founder. Here the obvious choice is James Madison, for he was not only the leading constitutionalist in early America but also the one founder who had undertaken serious theological and biblical study. Madison's association with Jefferson sometimes masks the tenacity of his own religious convictions, but he was in fact sincerely, if vaguely, religious and a defender of religion (Brant, 1941:I, 112–19). Madison's early experience—heartfelt, if formal, Anglicanism in his own home added to revulsion at the establishment persecution of Baptists and Presbyterians—shaped his entire life (Ketcham, 1960:67). He was an eager and adept student at Princeton under the Presbyterian stalwart, John Witherspoon, champion alike of Christian orthodoxy and political liberty. Madison spent several years in study during the early 1770s, part of which was devoted to examining scripture, reading divinity, and engaging in theological discussions of a remarkably sophisticated nature./6/ The Revolution, as it did for other young men at loose ends like Sam Adams, provided Madison with a cause, a preoccupation, and—almost immediately—a career. He became an influential political leader in the early republic but never lost his belief in the importance of religion or the need for the state to insure its free exercise. In addition, some of Madison's most influential political writing seems to contain ideas that parallel biblical themes.

Madison's famous *Tenth Federalist* has been an especially intriguing document in this regard. It was published on 23 November 1787 as part of the series coauthored with Alexander Hamilton and John Jay in support of the proposed Constitution. The *Tenth Federalist* sought to assuage fears that a popular government with the democratic elements contained in the new Constitution would lead to disaster—either when a dominant faction clawed its way to power through mob rule or when society dissolved into total anarchy. Madison conceded "the propensity of mankind, to fall into mutual animosities" and admitted that the "unfriendly passions" of humans, especially arising from "the various and unequal distribution of property," posed a serious threat to all democratic governments (*The Federalist*, 1961:131). He contended, however, that a large, far-flung republic, with democracy at work throughout the country in representative institutions, could overcome the corrosive power of faction precisely because its size and diversity would prevent a dangerous accumulation of power. This was, Madison urged, the very kind of government proposed by the new Constitution.

One of the perennial points of discussion concerning the *Tenth Federalist* is where Madison derived his view of human nature—as both corrupt yet capable of honorable activity. Here, it seems, might be a biblical view of human beings as both sinners and potential servants of God. James Smylie has argued persuasively that this is the case, that in fact Madison was expressing in the *Tenth Federalist* a theological view of humanity, derived from "the Calvinism" and "the 'common-sense' philosophy of his college mentor, John Witherspoon." Witherspoon, in turn, derived "his view of man first from the Bible" (Smylie, 1961:120, 121). In this reading, although Madison did not use the technical "theological terminology of his Princeton teacher" (Smylie, 1961:126), he was nonetheless expressing Witherspoon's perspective, especially when he contended that the "latent causes of faction are . . . sown in the nature of man" (*The Federalist*, 1961:131). According to Smylie, Madison's *Tenth Federalist* gave political shape to principles on human nature which, in their combination of realism concerning sin and confidence concerning God-given potential, anticipated some of the twentieth-century insights of theologian Reinhold Niebuhr (Smylie, 1961:131).

But here again the pursuit of a "biblical politics" runs into historical difficulties, for it is really not certain that Madison relied primarily on the Bible to shape his view of human nature, however much that view might seem consonant with biblical themes. In fact a whole chorus of learned commentators is at hand to show that Madison's view of human nature is only coincidentally related to the pages of scripture. Ralph Ketcham, who is a serious student of Madison's religious beliefs, feels that Madison's carefully balanced tension between confidence in self-government and skepticism concerning human nature came from his reading in the classics. Ketcham thinks Thucydides' unblushing depiction of human cruelty and Aristotle's political realism were especially important (Ketcham, 1958). Marvin Meyers, on the other hand, finds the key to Madison's thought in his general commitment to "the eighteenth-century liberal tradition . . . of natural rights and social compact, bills of rights and constitutional government," expressed specifically in a lifetime devotion to "freedom of conscience under nature's distant God." Meyers feels that Madison owed little to "abstract models of natural virtue or original sin" but drew instead from his study of history and the practical needs of the American situation (Meyers: xix, xxii). Still other scholars return to Madison's formal training. Douglass Adair has argued that Madison took his description of human nature and his analysis of faction from the political writings of David Hume (Adair). And Roy Branson suggests that it was not just Hume but the entire Scottish Enlightenment that shaped Madison's view of human nature (Branson).

Adair and Branson complicate the search for a Madisonian biblical politics when they draw attention to John Witherspoon as the mediator of ideas from Scotland. Witherspoon's own tangled intellectual history makes it more difficult to assess Madison's./7/ Witherspoon was an orthodox evangelical clergyman in Scotland before coming to America as president of Princeton in 1768. While in Scotland Witherspoon had made a career out of opposition to the Moderate party of the Kirk, the group that most enthusiastically supported the unfolding Scottish Enlightenment. In particular Witherspoon attacked the skeptical ideas of Hume as the inevitable conclusion to which Moderate principles led. Yet a strange transformation took place when Witherspoon crossed the Atlantic. As Princeton's professor of moral philosophy, Witherspoon was required to teach the principles of politics. But to guide this effort

Witherspoon turned instinctively to his erstwhile theological opponents, Hume and other philosophers of the Scottish Enlightenment. Thus, if it is from Witherspoon, as theologian, that Madison learned a biblical view of humanity, it was also from Witherspoon, as moral philosopher, that Madison gathered opinions about humankind which Witherspoon, as Scottish evangelical, had himself attacked as insufficiently biblical.

Taken together, these interpretations of Madison's thought point to a less than satisfactory search for a biblical politics. They show that Madison's political theory did contain parallels to some general biblical themes but also that it drew on the pre-Christian Greeks, mainstream eighteenth-century liberal thought, the specific suggestions of Hume, and the general outlines of the Scottish Enlightenment. It was also an approach to politics with a heady dose of pragmatism, growing from Madison's own efforts to understand the history of republics and to interpret that history for the needs of the American present. Even this founder, most propitiously situated to display a biblical politics, did so without clarity and with considerable ambiguity.

The search, in summary, for a biblical influence in Revolutionary political theory is inconclusive. We can say that some individuals who contributed to the development of "radical" Whig thought were deeply committed to the Bible. We can also say that at least one of the major architects of American political fundamentals, James Madison, respected the Bible and may have been influenced by its message to some degree. But what we cannot see are self-conscious connections between biblical themes and Revolutionary political theory. They may be there, but they remain hidden in the amorphous depths of eighteenth-century reasoning.

The Bible and Social Values in the Early United States

The role of the Bible in shaping popular social values in the early United States is much clearer than its part in forming Revolutionary political theory. Although the fate of public morality was often as uncertain in the 1780s and 1790s as the future of the country itself, by the second decade of the nineteenth century it was clear that the United States had survived its infancy and that its public ethos would be Protestant, evangelical, and biblical. In light of this "evangelical triumph" (Ahlstrom, 1972:387), this establishment of an "Evangelical Empire," (Marty: 4) it is not surprising that public life in the new nation also took on a biblical cast. Yet it is far from certain that even this development made something distinctly biblical out of the politics of early America.

The story of how, as Gordon Wood puts it, "evangelical Protestantism . . . seized control of much of the culture" (Wood, 1980:36), has many parts. It involved the revival of the nominally churched in settled areas of the country and the evangelization of the unchurched on the frontier. It included unprecedented efforts to spread the gospel at home and abroad and to hasten the moral reform of society. This process has been the subject of a full generation of serious scholarship./8/ Earlier studies concentrated on institutional renewal in New England and the Mid-Atlantic, particularly the creation of the great reform societies. These works sometimes implied that leaders of the Second Great Awakening harbored manipulative motives behind evangelical and reforming fronts. More recent work has shown the vitality of revival in the South and West as well as the pervasive connections between theological creativity, social reorganization, and evangelistic preaching. These later works usually acknowledge the integrity of evangelical efforts to control the self, regulate society, and renew the church in a disorderly age. Whatever interpretations are offered for these events, however, serious students of the period have amply demonstrated that the Bible was a crucial resource for those who sought to redeem the individual and sanctify the nation.

The leaders who transformed early America into an evangelical country did not feel compelled to repudiate the immediate past. In this lies the political significance of the Second Great Awakening. To a striking degree, the "Christianization" of American culture appropriated the themes of "real" Whig ideology for itself. This appropriation can be glimpsed in the generation of independence, as for example in the words of a theologically conservative Presbyterian minister whose plans for his denomination rested squarely on a "radical" Whig foundation:

> The United States have lately formed their several systems of civil government, so as to leave religion free, . . . and we have reason to hope religion will flourish also when civil powers leave it freely to be propagated, and practiced according to it's own free nature. The plan of church government which we have chosen, and we think derived from scripture, is a plan for liberty; the land we live in is a land of liberty; the time we live in is, especially, a time of liberty; and we cannot but desire . . . that many others . . . will revise their ecclesiastical principles, and see if they do not want something to make them fully consistent with christian liberty. (Green: 56)

Such "real" Whig churchmanship flourished at the turn of the century when, in the words of Nathan Hatch, a "cultural ferment over the meaning of freedom" embroiled church and social life alike (Hatch, 1980:545). In the early nineteenth century ecclesiastical elites and religious democrats battled each other for the mantle of Revolutionary ideals. It was a day when traditionalist Presbyterians attempted to secure civil and religious liberty through a decorous and philosophically supported appropriation of the Revolutionary heritage (Hood: 48–67). And it was a time when upstart despoilers of the ecclesiastical vineyard rested their arguments on the axiomatic truths of the Revolution. Thus, Barton Stone called his break from the Presbyterians a "declaration of independence," and the New England radical, Elias Smith, used Revolutionary language to advance his religious platform: "Let us be republicans indeed. Many are *republicans* as to *government*, and yet are but half republicans, being in matters of religion still bound to a catechism, creed, covenant or a superstitious priest. Venture to be as independent in things of religion, as those which respect the government in which you live" (Hatch, 1980:550, 548). These new leaders also self-consciously read the Bible through "real" Whig spectacles. For them the Revolution had secured the right to set aside all hierarchical and traditional interpretations of scripture in order to open the text for the individual and the individual alone (Hatch, 1982). Just a few years later, revivalists made capital out of Whig insistence on the rule of law as they sought to make God's righteous laws the law of the land (Walters; Griffin). And both the Revolutionary fear of tyranny and its special convictions about the place of America appeared in many of the Christian manifestoes of the 1830s, perhaps most notably in Lyman Beecher's *Plea for the West* (1835), a document combining exalted hopes for a Christian America and desperate forebodings concerning the enemies of freedom (Ahlstrom, 1972:459).

In short, the evangelicals who exerted such a great influence on American public values in the early national period regarded themselves as heirs of the Revolution. The popular faith of the early republic was evangelistic, moral, and biblical, but it was also American as defined by the "radical" Whig vocabulary of the Revolution.

The special energy that transformed these Revolutionary themes into Christian actions was the biblical vision of the millennium, the belief in a coming golden age characterized by the righteousness of the Old Testament and the Spirit-filled life of the New. Interpretations differed on details of how and when Christ would establish his millennial rule, but this did not stop many Americans from agreeing, as Timothy Smith summarizes, "that the Spirit of the Lord was mightily at work, ushering in the millennium through the hallowing of America" (Smith, 1979:22). As Smith has shown in several works (1957, 1979, 1980), this millennial vision was largely responsible for priming Christians for public action, for leading them to consider the liberties secured by the American Revolution as the forerunner of gospel liberty. Revivalists and reformers shared all of the "radical" Whigs' concern for public virtue, but little of the founders' squeamishness about supernatural faith. Spurred by the millennial hope and visions of a glorified America, evangelical Bible-believers worked to liberate the slave, purify the Sabbath, sanitize the diet, save the lost, educate the ignorant, care for the mentally ill, and sober the drunkard. With, again in Smith's words, "widespread reading of the Bible and growing reverence for its authority" (1979:24), the Revolution had labored and brought forth evangelical America.

Is this then where we find the biblical politics of Revolutionary America, in a perfectionistic vision of private and public righteousness? Again the answer is equivocal. Granted, the "biblical politics" of the early republic had transformed Whig convictions about the interdependence of personal and public virtue into Christian engines for evangelization and reform. And it infused the Whig view of history—a struggle between freedom and tyranny—with expectations of a millennial dawn. But the biblical politics of the early national period had an odd shape; it tolerated an immense gap. It had much to say about private responsibilities in public life and much to say about the ultimate state of society, but it had almost nothing to say about the way in which personal convictions and cosmic goals were to govern behavior in "the realms of the possible." For all their intense concern for bringing the Bible to bear on public life, the evangelicals of the early nineteenth century seemed almost oblivious to the fact that the Bible might be able to shed light on the political institutions, the economic and social superstructures, connecting personal righteousness and millennial hope.

Thus, on a whole host of overarching legislative, legal, constitutional, and national concerns, evangelicals had nothing political to offer. By 1820 the outlines of the great sectional controversy could be discerned. What did federalism mean for the rights of states? How could a solution be found to slavery that recognized both its economic and human dimensions? By the 1830s new waves of immigration began to pose troubling questions for the arbiters of Anglo-Protestant values, and industrialization had emerged as a tiny but dark cloud on the national horizon. Did the Catholic immigrant have a right to the American dream? Would wage-slavery become a blight on a scale with chattel servitude? To the extent that evangelicals recognized the seriousness of these issues, they did respond—but with moral indignation, bewilderment, atavistic nativism, self-serving interpretations of Revolutionary myths, and, to be sure, a flurry of biblical proof-texts. But it was no clearer than when northern abolitionist and southern slaver bombarded each other with passages from scripture that almost no one was treating the Bible as a source for political principles, as a source of insights for political strategies, or as an authoritative commentary on the nature and extent of God-given rights. Instead the Bible remained a book for private morality, public beneficence, and millennial hope. When believers in scripture did finally rise to these issues, the result was a debilitating clash of strategies, as in the divide over reforming procedures in the 1830s (Stewart: 93).

The absence of biblically based political theory in the early republic must be kept in perspective. The period from the start of the new century at least through the Civil War was not a creative one for political insights anywhere in America. James Madison's career illustrates this well, for historians regularly rate his service as president (1809–17) much less favorably than his earlier work on the Constitution. Although Henry Clay, Daniel Webster, John C. Calhoun, John Quincy Adams, and Andrew Jackson were statesmen of commanding ability, none of them was able to solve the problems inherent in the political legacies of the founders. If statesmen of this stature found it difficult to expound path-breaking political theory, it is little wonder that evangelical leaders—so active in battle for the Lord—experienced similar difficulties. In addition, it seemed to almost all those who forged the evangelical national culture that public advocacy—biblical preaching for conversion, biblical exhortations for reform, and biblical proclamation of the millennium—was enough. Enthusiastic over the movement of the Spirit, they thought they could remake society supernaturally, including its politics, without needing to construct theory from the ground up. Besides, they were satisfied with the Revolution.

Most Bible-believers in the early national period appear to have believed that the founders had settled major political questions once for all. Their own efforts to make American culture biblical took for granted the validity of that earlier political framework. They did not feel the need for a biblical political theory. It was enough that the message of scripture changed individual lives and provided hope for a millennial future. In contrast to the earlier generation of America's founding, when there was much political theory but only a shadowy Bible, the history of the early republic reveals a manifest scripture but only murky political theory.

Conclusions

The historical evidence offers a puzzling picture. In Revolutionary America the Bible was widely revered and studied among the cultural arbiters of the new nation, even among the least orthodox of the founders. Yet the Bible's direct political influence was extremely limited, the occasions when leaders turned to it for assistance in political reasoning extremely rare. Perhaps Puritan allegiance to scripture contributed in some ways to the roots of "real" Whig thought, but that contribution had become absorbed in the general thrust of radical ideology by the time of the American Revolution. Admittedly, the Bible was very important in the creation of a national ethic, even if the promoters of that ethic ignored the implied contradiction of grounding their manifestly scriptural preoccupations upon the incidentally biblical foundations of Revolutionary ideology. Thus it came about that the Bible was everywhere (in the national consciousness) and nowhere (in explicit political theory) during the early years of American politics, that the politics of Revolutionary America were distinctly biblical (because articulated by leaders who found inspiration in scripture and because taken for granted as the basis for national values) while at the same time quite untouched by the messages of scripture (because worked out *as politics* with almost no reference to the sacred page). It remains to attempt an explanation for this puzzle.

How could the Bible function as a private base, a political gloss, and a public glue all at once in early America? The most obvious answer is that just as Christians interact with culture in different ways (Niebuhr), so too they can read the Bible very differently. Philosopher Richard Mouw has recently suggested (1982) that American Protestants tend to read scripture in one or a combination of four ways: doctrinally (with emphasis on the construction of systematic Christian truths), morally (with emphasis on inspiration for proper learning), devotionally (with emphasis on the enhancement of personal piety), or culturally (with emphasis on guidelines for structuring institutions in "the world"). In Revolutionary America the Bible was being read doctrinally, morally, and devotionally, but almost never culturally. This explains how scripture could be so important for some aspects of a person's life (morally, say, for Jefferson, morally and devotionally for John Jay, devotionally, morally, and doctrinally for Lyman Beecher) without yet being important for political discourse.

To realize that the Bible was not being read culturally forces us to another conclusion: that early American leaders believed their cultural framework was simply a given that did not need to be questioned./9/ From a modern vantage point that cultural framework appears as a bewildering mosaic constructed of bits and pieces from the classical world, the Reformation, the Enlightenment, and the exigencies of life in America. But the leaders of the new nation appear to have regarded it as a unified whole sanctioned by time, the manifest triumphs of European civilization, and the Bible itself. Perry Miller (1955:55) and Sydney Ahlstrom (1979) have both observed that it was very difficult for Americans before the end of the nineteenth century to disentangle their thinking about the Bible from their general consideration of Western civilization. Leaders of the new United States illustrate the pertinence of this observation. Where they thought about the structures of society, they assumed that biblical values had something to do with them—however vague that something was and however much they might have disagreed among themselves about what that something entailed. The Bible simply did not exist as an independent variable when these leaders thought about culture, even if it had become an independent focus of authority on matters of Christian doctrine, questions of public morality, or issues of personal religion. To be sure, the Bible occupied a different place in the general thinking about politics during the Revolutionary period than it had in the social thought of Jonathan Edwards early in the century or in that of seventeenth-century Puritans or the leaders of the English Reformation. For one thing, members of the Atlantic community at the end of the eighteenth century, even the most dogmatic Bible students, deferred much more readily to reason and scientific proof—legacies of Newton and the Age of Light—than had their predecessors (for America, see Bozeman; Holifield; Hovenkamp). Still, the Bible continued to be used as if its values and themes melded easily and without strain into the major commitments of Western civilization. So long as this situation prevailed, so long as it did not occur to Bible readers that Western civilization and scriptural values could move in different directions, it was very difficult even for leaders devoted to scripture to conceive of the possibility that the Bible might have an independent role in constructing culture. And so long as that was the situation, the use of the Bible in the formation of political thought would be a rare and unexpected thing.

A final assessment concerning the Bible in Revolutionary America must depend upon one's view of the assumption that allegiance to the Bible and allegiance to Revolutionary ideology (the particular shape that Western political culture has assumed for America after independence) were pretty much the same thing. It is possible to argue that biblical values and the political convictions of the Revolution should be disentangled, both for analyzing the past and taking action in the present. Two contrasting groups make this case. On the one side, proponents of an American civil faith, like Sidney Mead (1975, 1976, 1977), trace many of the strains in our religious history to the retention of biblical particularism and look forward to the day when scriptural convictions no longer hinder the evolution of liberal democracy. On the other side are Christians who, following the example of the nineteenth-century Dutch theologian Abraham Kuyper, pose an antithesis between biblical values and the received values of the West, especially as expressed by the Enlightenment and the principles of European revolution. This point of view regards the confluence of biblical and Revolutionary values as a subversion of Christian testimony. Its adherents contend, however, that it is specifically the recognition of antithesis that makes it possible for Christians to survive within a pluralistic culture and to promote biblically rooted priniciples of justice in the public arena./10/ But far more common than either of these views has been the assumption that God and country can in fact march side by side, that biblical values and the political thought of the American Revolution deserve to be regarded as indistinguishable parts of a single whole. Historically considered, this assumption is filled with ambiguity and contradiction. Yet it remains very useful—for politicians invoking Transcendence to explain the essence of the nation as well as for those who periodically seek to turn America *back* to God—and so will probably remain, whatever the historians say.

NOTES

/1/   I would like to stress that this is an *essay* sketching a general argument for a broad topic. It is not a monograph with the type of documentary evidence appropriate for a monograph.

/2/   The crucial works here are Bailyn, 1967; Wood, 1969. A convenient summary of their work on the subject and that of many others is found in Shalhope.

/3/   The path-breaking American study is Robbins.

/4/   It is also true that familiarity with the Bible probably contributed to the conviction shared by many in the Revolutionary generation that the United States had been given extraordinary divine blessing and had been created to fulfill a divine mission. I have not discussed this aspect of the Bible's presence in Revolutionary America here because it is a subject that involves more the myths of popular perception than the specific convictions of political thought. For the barest indication of the vast literature on this theme, see the following works, all with substantial bibliography: Berens, 1978, 1979; Hatch, 1977; Noll, 1977:49–78, 1982a.

/5/   The one conspicuous exception to this generalization was the work of pacifists, especially Quakers, who were not at all reluctant to cite chapter and verse in support of their stand on the war (see Mekeel; Noll, 1977:126, 141–42).

/6/   It is indicative of Madison's convictions that in one of these discussions in 1777, with Presbyterian educator Samuel Stanhope Smith over human free will, Madison took the more traditional side (in this case roughly the position of Jonathan Edwards) while the clergyman Smith defended a view more in keeping with the optimism of the Enlightenment (Madison, 1962:I, 194–212, 253–57).

/7/   On Witherspoon's life, see Collins. There is a succinct statement concerning some of the contradictions of his career in Brant: 74–75. For Witherspoon's political opinions, see Witherspoon: III, 416–23, 430–72.

/8/   I have reviewed much of this work, with more extensive attention to recently published work, in Noll, 1982b.

/9/   I owe the germ of this idea to George Marsden of Calvin College, who made a similar, if more precise, analysis of eighteenth-century culture during an oral presentation at Malone College, Summer 1976.

/10/   This perspective expresses my own convictions and has shaped the point of view of this essay. On Kuyper, see Van Der Kroef; and for a contemporary statement of this approach, see Spykman.

WORKS CONSULTED

Adair, Douglass
    1974   "'That Politics May Be Reduced to a Science': David Hume, James Madison, and the Tenth Federalist." Pp. 93–106 in *Fame and the Founding Fathers: Essays by Douglass Adair.* Edited by Trevor Colbourn. New York: W. W. Norton.

Adair, Douglass, and Marvin Harvey
    1974   "Was Alexander Hamilton a Christian Statesman?" Pp. 141–59 in *Fame and the Founding Fathers: Essays by Douglass Adair.* Edited by Trevor Colbourn. New York: W. W. Norton.

Ahlstrom, Sydney E.
    1972   *A Religious History of the American People.* New Haven: Yale University Press.
    1979   Oral presentation at a conference on "The Bible in American Culture," Wheaton College, IL, 2 November 1979.

Bailyn, Bernard
    1967   *The Ideological Origins of the American Revolution.* Cambridge: Harvard University Press.
    1970   "Religion and Revolution: Three Biographical Studies." *Perspectives in American History* 4:83–169.

Berens, John F.
    1978   *Providence and Patriotism in Early America 1640–1815.* Charlottesville: University Press of Virginia.
    1979   "Religion and Revolution Reconsidered: Recent Literature on Religion and Nationalism in Eighteenth-Century America." *Canadian Review of Studies in Nationalism* 6:233–45.

Boller, Paul F., Jr.
    1963   *George Washington and Religion.* Dallas: Southern Methodist University Press.

Boyd, George Adams
    1952   *Elias Boudinot: Patriot and Statesman 1740–1821.* Princeton: Princeton University Press.

Bozeman, Theodore Dwight
    1977   *Protestants in an Age of Science: The Baconian Ideal and Antebellum American Religious Thought.* Chapel Hill: University of North Carolina Press.

Branson, Roy
    1979   "James Madison and the Scottish Enlightenment." *Journal of the History of Ideas* 40 (April-June): 235–50.

Brant, Irving
    1941   *James Madison: The Virginia Revolutionist 1751–1780.* Indianapolis: Bobbs-Merrill.

Cappon, Lester J., ed.
1959   *The Adams–Jefferson Letters*. Chapel Hill: University of
              North Carolina Press.

Cohen, Charles L.
1981   "The 'Liberty or Death' Speech: A Note on Religion and Revo-
              lutionary Rhetoric." *William and Mary Quarterly*, 3d ser. 38
              (October): 702–17.

Collier, Christopher
1971   *Roger Sherman's Connecticut: Yankee Politics and the Amer-
              ican Revolution*. Middleton, CT: Wesleyan University Press.

Collins, Varnum Lansing
1925   *President Witherspoon: A Biography*. Princeton: Princeton
              University Press.

Cuningham, Charles E.
1942   *Timothy Dwight 1752–1817*. New York: Macmillan.

The Federalist
1787–88 (1961) *The Federalist by Alexander Hamilton, James Madison, and
              John Jay*. Edited by Benjamin Fletcher Wright. Cambridge:
              Harvard University Press.

Green, Jacob
1781   *A View of A Christian Church, and Church Government . . .*
              Chatham, NJ: Shepard Kollock.

Griffin, Clifford S.
1960   *Their Brothers' Keepers: Moral Stewardship in the United
              States, 1800–1865*. New Brunswick, NJ: Rutgers University
              Press.

Hatch, Nathan O.
1977   *The Sacred Cause of Liberty: Republican Thought and the
              Millennium in Revolutionary New England*. New Haven:
              Yale University Press.
1980   "The Christian Movement and the Demand for a Theology of
              the People." *Journal of American History* 67 (December):
              545–67.
1982   "*Sola Scriptura* and *Novus Ordo Seclorum*." Pp. 59–78 in *The
              Bible in America: Essays in Cultural History*. Edited by
              Nathan O. Hatch and Mark A. Noll. New York: Oxford Uni-
              versity Press.

Heimert, Alan
1966   *Religion and the American Mind from the Great Awakening
              to the Revolution*. Cambridge: Harvard University Press.

Holifield, E. Brooks
1978   *The Gentlemen Theologians: American Theology in Southern
              Culture 1795–1860*. Durham, NC: Duke University Press.

Hood, Fred J.
1980   *Reformed America: The Middle and Southern States, 1783–
              1837*. University, AL: University of Alabama Press.

Hovenkamp, Herbert
1978   *Science and Religion in America 1800–1860*. Philadelphia:
               University of Pennsylvania Press.

Howe, Daniel Walker
1970   *The Unitarian Conscience: Harvard Moral Philosophy, 1805–
               1861*. Cambridge: Harvard University Press.

Hudnut, William H., III
1956   "Samuel Stanhope Smith: Enlightened Conservative." *Journal
               of the History of Ideas* 17 (October): 540–52.

Jefferson, Thomas
1905–7   *The Writings of Thomas Jefferson*. Edited by A. A. Lip-
               scomb. Washington, DC: Thomas Jefferson Memorial Associa-
               tion.

Ketcham, Ralph L.
1958   "James Madison and the Nature of Man." *Journal of the His-
               tory of Ideas* 19 (January): 62–76.
1960   "James Madison and Religion—A New Hypothesis." *Journal of
               the Presbyterian Historical Society* 38 (June): 65–90.

Mabee, Charles
1979   "Thomas Jefferson's Anti-Clerical Bible." *The Historical Mag-
               azine of the Protestant Episcopal Church* 48 (December):
               473–81.

Madison, James
1962   *The Papers of James Madison. Vol. I: 16 March 1751–16
               December 1779*. Edited by William T. Hutchinson and Wil-
               liam M. E. Rachal. Chicago: University of Chicago Press.

Marty, Martin E.
1970   *Righteous Empire: The Protestant Experience in America*.
               New York: Harper & Row.

Mead, Sidney E.
1975   *The Nation With the Soul of a Church*. New York: Harper &
               Row.
1976   "Christendom, Enlightenment, and the Revolution." In *Reli-
               gion and the American Revolution*. Edited by Jerald C.
               Brauer. Philadelphia: Fortress.
1977   *The Old Religion in the Brave New World: Reflections on the
               Relation Between Christendom and the Republic*. Berkeley:
               University of California Press.

Mekeel, Arthur J.
1979   *The Relation of the Quakers to the American Revolution*.
               Washington, DC: University Press of America.

Meyers, Marvin, ed.
1973   *The Mind of the Founder: Sources of the Political Thought
               of James Madison*. Indianapolis: Bobbs-Merrill.

Miller, Perry
1955   "The Garden of Eden and the Deacon's Meadow." *American
               Heritage* 7 (December): 54–61, 102.

Morgan, Edmund S.
1967   "The Puritan Ethic and the American Revolution." *William and Mary Quarterly*, 3d ser. 24 (January): 3–43.

Mouw, Richard J.
1982   "The Bible in Twentieth-Century Protestantism: A Preliminary Taxonomy." Pp. 139–62 in *The Bible in America: Essays in Cultural History*. Edited by Nathan O. Hatch amd Mark A. Noll. New York: Oxford University Press.

Nash, Gary B.
1965   "The American Clergy and the French Revolution." *William and Mary Quarterly*, 3d ser. 22 (July): 392–412.

Niebuhr, H. Richard
1951   *Christ and Culture*. New York: Harper & Row.

Noll, Mark A.
1977   *Christians in the American Revolution*. Grand Rapids: Eerdmans for the Christian University Press.
1979   "The Founding of Princeton Seminary." *Westminster Theological Journal* 42 (Fall): 72–110.
1982a   "The Image of the United States as a Biblical Nation, 1776–1865." Pp. 39–58 in *The Bible in America: Essays in Cultural History*. Edited by Nathan O. Hatch and Mark A. Noll. New York: Oxford University Press.
1982b   "Protestant Theology and Social Order in Antebellum America." *Religious Studies Review* 8 (April): 133–42.

Pellew, George
1890   *John Jay*. Boston: Houghton Mifflin.

Robbins, Caroline
1959   *The Eighteenth-Century Commonwealthman: Studies in the Transmission, Development and Circumstance of English Liberal Thought from the Restoration of Charles II until the War with the Thirteen Colonies*. Cambridge: Harvard University Press.

Rollins, Richard M.
1980   *The Long Journey of Noah Webster*. Philadelphia: University of Pennsylvania Press.

Shalhope, Robert E.
1972   "Toward a Republican Synthesis: The Emergence of an Understanding of Republicanism in American Historiography." *William and Mary Quarterly*, 3d ser. 29 (January): 49–80.

Smith, Timothy L.
1957   *Revivalism and Social Reform: American Protestantism on the Eve of the Civil War*. Nashville: Abingdon.
1979   "Righteousness and Hope: Christian Holiness and the Millennial Vision in America, 1800–1900." *American Quarterly* 31 (Spring): 22–45.
1980   "Afterword" to *Revivalism and Social Reform*. Baltimore: Johns Hopkins University Press.

Smylie, James H.
1961   "Madison and Witherspoon: Theological Roots of American Political Thought." *The Princeton University Library Chronicle* 22 (Spring): 118–32.
1970   "Presbyterian Clergy and Problems of 'Dominion' in the Revolutionary Generation." *Journal of Presbyterian History* 48 (Fall): 161–75.

Spykman, Gordon, ed.
1981   *Society, State and Schools: A Case for Structural and Confessional Pluralism.* Grand Rapids: Eerdmans.

Stewart, James Brewer
1976   *Holy Warriors: The Abolitionists and American Slavery.* New York: Hill & Wang.

Stiles, Ezra
1783 (1860)   *The United States Elevated to Glory and Honor.* . . . Pp. 399–520 in *The Pulpit of the American Revolution.* Edited by John Wingate Thornton. Boston: Gould & Lincoln.

Van Der Kroef, Justus M.
1948   "Abraham Kuyper and the Rise of Neo-Calvinism in the Netherlands." *Church History* 17 (December): 316–34.

Walters, Ronald G.
1978   *American Reformers 1815–1860.* New York: Hill & Wang.

Warfel, Harry R.
1936   *Noah Webster: Schoolmaster to America.* New York: Macmillan.

Williams, William Appelman
1960   "Samuel Adams: Calvinist, Mercantilist, Revolutionary." *Studies on the Left* 1:47–57.

Wills, Garry
1981   "Mason Weems, Bibliopolist." *American Heritage* 33 (February–March): 66–69.

Witherspoon, John
1802   "Lectures on Moral Philosophy." In *Works*, Vol. III. Philadelphia: William W. Woodward.

Wood, Gordon S.
1969   *The Creation of the American Republic 1776–1787.* Chapel Hill: University of North Carolina Press.
1980   "Evangelical America and Early Mormonism." *New York History* 61 (October): 359–86.

III

God's Judgment, Christ's Command:
Use of the Bible in Nineteenth-Century American Political Life

Louis Weeks

The Importance of the Bible in American Public Life:
The Jeremiad and Thanksgiving

"The Bible contains more real learning than all the volumes of men."
Alexander Campbell, founder of his own evangelical united front, warmed
to the task of providing a *Connected View of the Principles and Rules by
which the Living Oracles May Be Intelligibly and Certainly Interpreted*
(1835:292–300). He did not in 1835 hesitate to proclaim the authority of
scripture in matters political: "The best government on earth, call it
English or American, has within it the seeds of its own destruction. . . ."
Campbell said the unwillingness of English and American governments to
recognize the "maxims" of Christ's government, shown in the Bible,
resulted in the continuation of "ignorance, poverty, and crime. . . ."

Eager to promulgate his interpretations of the "Living Oracles" in
matters of sacrament and sanctity, Campbell did not stop to explain the
political implications of his claims. He made clear the warning that
should the United States continue to ignore the ethics of Christ, God's
judgment would be visited on the nation. Students of nineteenth-century
American political life can well inquire, if not in behalf of a Christian
theocracy as conceived by Campbell, at least in behalf of the facts of the
matter: How was the Bible used in the United States during that time?
The more basic question, however, queries occurrence before hermeneu-
tic: Was the Bible used in nineteenth-century American political life?

By one traditional reading, the answer definitely is an affirmative
one to the basic question. Yes, the Bible was used in American political
life throughout the century. Preachers, lay leaders in the various denominations, and politicians of almost every stripe made extensive use of the
scriptures. When John M. Mason spoke to the forming convocation for
the American Bible Society in 1816, he promised that contributions for
Bible printing would send the Holy Word to "desolate" families, "providing a radiating point of 'grace and truth' to a neighborhood of terror and

vice." The Bible in American life would be the means of "seeing the wilderness turned into a fruitful field, by the blessing of God . . ." (Dwight: 28). For the jubilee celebration of the American Bible Society, the Honorable Robert C. Winthrop, who followed Daniel Webster as senator from Massachusetts, bragged that the twenty-one million Bibles printed between 1816 and 1866 surpassed in importance all the "boasted achievements of mankind" (Dwight: 323). John Quincy Adams, John Jay, Salmon P. Chase, and Rutherford B. Hayes were just a few of the prominent politicians of the period who made significant contributions to the national society and served as officers in it. Hundreds more successful political leaders were active in local auxiliaries and made speeches testifying to the Bible's impact on American life (presumably including their own decision making).

Themes from the Bible, which had been applied to the church before being applied to the nation, continued to be popular throughout the century: "a city set upon a hill," "a light to the nations," "the servant of the Lord," "the chosen people," and "the mission of the nation" all made their way as expressions in the political life of the United States, still bearing biblical freight. Perhaps the nineteenth-century Americans did not "live in the Bible" as much as colonial leaders had done. The reader of comparative diaries does not so easily find extended references to relatives and friends as to characters with Bible personalities: "She became a Jezebel for me"; "I loved him as Jonathan loved David." Nevertheless, the Bible certainly guided much artistic expression and popular wisdom.

Following the extensive studies of Bodo, Cole, Foster, Griffin, Banner, and a host of other scholars, it can be shown that moral trusteeship in nineteenth-century America extended fearlessly into the political realm./1/ The ministers (and lay leaders, according to Foster, Griffin, and Banner) did not leave their Bibles at home when they ventured into the public arena in their united front. Charles G. Finney spoke for them all when he affirmed that the American Constitution and laws were borrowed from the Bible, not from Greece or Rome (Cole: 145). According to this reading of American politics, the Bible remained a norm of exceeding importance. Politicians knew when they followed it and when they strayed. If they did not quote it all the time, that was because in addressing public issues everyone of significance knew already the force of pertinent scripture. More precisely, for many issues in American life, to cite the Bible would have been to repeat the obvious./2/

An equal and almost opposite reading of the social history of the nineteenth century, however, argues that by the 1820s the Bible exerted little actual authority in matters political. Over the remaining decades of the century, it became less important, save in the national struggle regarding slavery and freedom for black people. This interpretation of the period Robert D. Cross characterized as a steady decline of the church's influence "on the conduct of life" (Garraty: II, 37).

Investigation of the texts of national party platforms between 1840, when political parties began making deliberate statements, and 1900, when the Christian century began, yields a powerful argument *ex silentio* that the Bible meant little in political affairs. None of the platforms provided by major parties relied upon the language of Zion, even though political parties saw platforms as avenues of communication with potential voters. The Liberty Party in 1844, to be sure, spoke in general terms of the need for people to be "their brothers' keepers." "That human brotherhood is a cardinal doctrine of the true Democracy, as well as of pure Christianity" the Liberty Party considered obvious to all. And when the Prohibition Party began fielding candidates for national office, leaders began to make claims for the "free use of the Bible, not as a ground of religious creeds, but as a textbook of purest morality. . . ." The one-issue fringes, important as they may have been for American politics, did not influence the more broadly based parties to follow suit (Porter and Johnson: 4, 79, passim).

When, on the few occasions presidents proclaimed days of "fasting and humiliation," in the tradition of the jeremiad, they received much criticism for their trouble. Numbers of public officials declared fast days during the War of 1812. Many took place locally, some at the state level. When President James Madison set 20 August 1812, as a day of national fasting, he managed to avoid specifically Christian (or Jewish) language, and he even recommended religious observances rather than requiring any. Nonetheless, religious leaders such as John Fiske of Massachusetts took a jaundiced view of such actions. When Madison proceeded to call another, for 12 January 1815, James Blythe of Kentucky bemoaned the lack of piety in Washington and excoriated the leaders. "The duty of today is to 'abhor ourselves, and repent in the dust and ashes,'" he preached. But he said the "duty of tomorrow" was to pledge not to "elevate to office any man who is profligate in his manner, or atheistic in his principles" (Gribbin: 20–22). "Religious people are urged to unanimity and exertion on this subject, by higher motives than any I can present; namely by the promise of God. 'But the judgment shall sit—And the kingdom, and dominion, and greatness of the kingdom under the whole heaven, shall be given to the people, of the saints of the most high, whose kingdom is an everlasting Kingdom . . .'" (Sonne: 120–24).

Abraham Lincoln, an insightful theologian in the presidency at a time of crisis, drew again on the jeremiad tradition in proclaiming nine separate calls for days of prayer. The first, 12 August 1861, was to be a day of "humble submission" to God's "chastisements." People were to "confess and deplore their sins and transgressions in the full conviction that the fear of the Lord is the beginning of wisdom" (Trueblood: 86). Another, called for the last Thursday in November 1863, came in response to Sarah Josepha Hale's campaign for an annual national Thanksgiving. In his proclamation, Lincoln accentuated the positive without sacrificing the ethical edge of his mature theology: "The year that is drawing toward its close has been filled with blessing of fruitful fields and healthful skies. . . . No human counsel hath devised, nor hath any mortal hand worked out these great things. They are the gracious gifts of the most high God, who, while dealing with us in anger for our sins, hath nevertheless remembered mercy . . ." (Linton and Linton: 92, 93).

Although some people protested any national religious celebration, many more objected the following year when Lincoln returned more explicitly to the jeremiad in proclaiming the first Thursday of August 1864 as a day of national humiliation and prayer. Forty-three democrats in Congress signed an address to the American people charging that the main problem confronting the nation was Lincoln's mismanagement of the war.

Soon the annual presidential proclamations setting aside a November Thursday became regularized, full of platitudes, and lacking reference to sins, penance, forgiveness, God's wrath, or ethical commitments. At least the nineteenth-century presidents, most of whom probably knew little of Deuteronomy 26, resisted the temptation to which subsequent presidents have succumbed: they did not move the holiday forward to allow merchants another week for Christmas commercialism. Nevertheless, American official theology relating to Thanksgiving became thin gruel quickly.

This second reading of the history, which views the use of the Bible as diminishing during the period under review, will tend to speak in terms of the process of secularization in America. Luckmann argues that privatization has been taking place in Western society through the decades. Religion has come to exercise little influence in matters public, and people have been drawn into an alternative, effective and secular identity. Churches have thus accommodated the process of internal secularization, thereby becoming marginal institutions. By implication, the Bible has become less and less relevant for public life. "The emerging social form of religions differs significantly from the older forms of religion which were characterized by the diffusion of the sacred cosmos through institutional specialization of religion" (Luckmann: 103). Luckmann's work has been supported by Talcott Parsons, Richardson, and a number of lesser-known scholars./3/

In sum, then, the answer to the basic question concerning the use of the Bible in American politics becomes a complicated one. Yes, the Bible was used. But no, it may have come to be infrequently and poorly used in official "theology." Even if trivialized and neglected in governmental documents, or perhaps intentionally avoided, the Bible and biblical themes remained important in addressing certain issues throughout the century.

Other essays focus upon the particular issues of minorities, the Civil War, and the rights of women—all issues of a consummate import during the century. We may look, though, at the speeches of a Theodore Parker even when he did not address those particular problems in American life. Parker used the scripture as he spoke of all political matters, and the ways in which he employed themes from the Bible begin the hermeneutical response: How did nineteenth-century Americans use the themes of scripture in matters political?

The Bible in American Political Discourse: The Example of Theodore Parker

In his heyday, Theodore Parker commanded public attention as did no other preacher in the United States. A dynamic and opinionated reformer and a biblical scholar at the same time, Parker naturally used biblical themes and allusions in assessing all social issues. So when he raised his voice on the subject of the Mexican War, or on the administration of the Fugitive Slave Law, Parker brought scripture to bear on those matters and set the expression for others to follow./4/

Addressing the assault by the United States on its southern neighbor, Parker invoked the biblical themes of peace and piety in dialectic fashion. In 1848, soon after the signing of the treaty of Guadalupe Hidalgo, Parker related for his congregation and for all who would listen a scathing rebuke of President Polk and those who had supported the war. He pointed to its cost in American lives and property, in Mexican lives and property, and other terms as well. His voice full of sarcasm, Parker spoke of the "effect on the morals of the people."

> O Christian America! O New England, child of the Puritans! Cradles in the wilderness, thy swaddling garments stained with martyrs' blood. . . . Come New England, take the old banners of thy conquering host, the standards borne at Monterey, Palo Alto. . . . bring them into thy churches, hang them up over the altar and pulpit, and let the little children, clad in white raiment and crowned with flowers, come and chant their lessons for the day. "Blessed are the pure in heart, for they shall see God. Blessed are the peacemakers for they shall be called the children of God." (Parker: 39)

Parker spoke of judgment and pharisaical hypocrisy as he called people to repentance for their sinfulness. Again, two years later, Parker responded to a governor's proclamation "to give thanks to God for our welfare" by preaching on the Fugitive Slave Law. He took for his text a favorite, Prov 14:34: "Righteousness exalteth a nation, but sin is a reproach to any people." He painted a rosy picture of New England in particular, of America in general, as he buttered the bread for toasting. Then he attacked the "despotic" ideas that threatened and pointed out their logic of destruction. Especially Parker decried the idea that people are bound to obey such a bad law as the one demanding return of fugitive slaves. "Then it was old Daniel's duty at Darius's command to give up his prayer; but he prayed three times a day with his windows up. . . ." Parker went on to cite Peter and John as examples of those who disobeyed the law to preach, and he named Amram and Jochebed as faithful to God's law in saving Moses. Turning to the core of the Christian gospel, Parker used irony again:

> There is another ancient case, mentioned in the Bible, in which the laws commanded one thing and conscience just the opposite. Here is the record of the law:—"Now both the chief priests and the Pharisees had given a commandment, that if any one knew where [Jesus] were, he should show it, that they might take him." Of course it became the official and legal business of each disciple who knew where Christ was, to make it known to the authorities. No doubt James and John could leave all and follow him, with others of the people who who knew not the law of Moses, and were accursed; nay, the women, Martha and Mary, could minister unto him of their substance, could wash his feet with tears, and wipe them with the hairs of their head. They did it gladly, of their own free will, and took pleasure therein, I make no doubt. There was no merit in that—"Any man can perform an agreeable duty." But there was found one disciple who could "perform a disagreeable duty." He went, perhaps "with alacrity," and betrayed his Saviour to the marshal of the district of Jerusalem, who was called a centurion. Had he no affection for Jesus? No doubt; but he could conquer his prejudices, while Mary and John could not.
>
> Judas Iscariot has rather a bad name in the Christian world: he is called "the son of perdition," in the New Testament, and his conduct is reckoned a "transgression;" nay, it is said the devil "entered into him," to cause this hideous sin. But all this it seems was a mistake; certainly, if we are to believe our republican lawyers and statesmen, Iscariot only fulfilled his "constitutional obligations." It was only "on that point," of betraying his Saviour, that the constitutional law required him to have anything to do with Jesus. He took his thirty pieces of silver—about fifteen dollars; a Yankee is to do it for ten, having fewer prejudices to conquer—it was his legal fee, for value received. True, the Christians thought it was "the wages of iniquity," and even the Pharisees—who commonly made the commandment of God of none effect by their traditions—dared not defile the temple with this "price of blood;" but it was honest money. It was as honest

a fee as any American commissioner or deputy will ever get for a similar service. How mistaken we are! Judas Iscariot is not a traitor; he was a great patriot; he conquered his prejudices, performed a disagreeable duty as an officer of "high morals and high principle;" he kept the law and the Constitution, and did all he could to "save the Union;" nay, he was a saint, "not a whit behind the chiefest apostles." "The law of God never commands us to disobey the law of man." Sancte Iscariote, ora pro nobis! (Parker: 116–18)

Parker's sermon-lecture on the "State of the Nation," which contrasted the laws of God with human laws, warned that America would receive punishment and even perish if such injustice became national "justice." People must heed Christ's commands given in the beatitudes and in the "Golden Rule of the Gospel." "Let us swear that we will keep the Justice of the eternal Law. Then are we all safe. We know not what a day may bring forth, but we know that eternity will bring everlasting peace . . ." (Parker: 131).

Parker's use of the themes of God's judgment, gospel law, and conditional blessing remains notable for at least two reasons. First, he treated the laws of God as both biblical and natural in both Old and New Testament expressions of them. Second, he included all within the scope of judgment, even himself. Parker extended the themes to encompass other issues as well—temperance, education, rights of labor, and penal reform. He stood most of the time in the camp generally labeled the "prophetic," as he considered the "nation under God" (Marty). Americans might be chosen especially by God, but it was for special service and for special duty. It meant Americans, including himself, bore special threats should they abuse in despotism any God-given favor.

In his knowledge of the Bible, as well as in his addressing all the public issues of the day, Parker proved an exceptional person. The reader cannot help noticing, however, that Parker used themes of judgment and ethics much as Campbell, Blythe, and Lincoln had done. Each called Americans to obedience with a warning, a conditional promise, and at least one ethical imperative. All these figures, and perhaps the Liberty and Prohibition parties as well, perceived any "American covenant" as conditional upon the people following the will of God and obeying the commands of Christ. Blessings from God did not just come in natural fashion without regard for those that received them. Americans were called to accountability. In structural terms, Parker and the others had not lost the mythic depth from which to engage in self-criticism—or societal critique, as some have charged (see Bellah: 58; Lacocque: 176).

In fact, the argument thus far supports recent findings that even the antebellum revival movements served to divide denominations and communities and led citizens to judge political institutions by moral and biblical criteria. John Hammond contends that converts sought to transform American institutions to conform with their religious ideals (1978:309).

Variations on the Judgment Theme

To extend the argument thoroughly is a task beyond the scope of this paper. But bits of evidence accumulate, indicating that the data are not altogether idiosyncratic. Thinkers and leaders even at the end of the century continued to summon images of the commands of Christ and of God's wrath against evildoers. One biographer has decided, for example, that William Jennings Bryan "believed that the foundations of moral law lay in the ethical teachings of Jesus" (Glad: 28). Bryan, according to this biography, possessed his amazing power at least in part from the invocation of biblical images of judgment and ethics. According to Bryan, Glad writes (29), Jesus Christ had obviated the need for philosophical systems and theological structures with his "one commandment" that condensed all ten and another "rule" to love neighbors as self. "The Nazarene . . . presented a plan for the solution of all the problems that now vex society or may hereafter arise."

Henry George provides a further example of the use of the Bible and biblical rhetoric in social and political criticism. When in 1880 he sought to move Americans to distribute the land in behalf of justice and efficiency, he used the image of Dives and Lazarus. By implication, he reasoned in *Progress and Poverty* (1880:8), the wealthy should heed Jesus' transparent parable and follow his teachings. Otherwise God would judge them unfit for Abraham's bosom. After the success of this book, George followed with *Social Problems* and made even more explicit use of the commands of Christ:

> We may go on forever merely raising fresh-air funds, and how great soever be the funds we raise, the need will only grow, and children— just such children as those of whom Christ said, "Take heed that ye despise not one of these little ones; for I say unto you, that in heaven their angels do always behold the face of my Father"—will die like flies, so long as poverty compels fathers and mothers to the life of the squalid tenement room. We may open "midnight missions" and support "Christian homes for destitute young girls," but what will they avail in the face of general conditions which render so many men unable to support a wife; which make young girls think it a privilege to be permitted to earn three dollars by eighty-one hours' work, and which can drive a mother to such despair that she will throw her babies from a wharf of our Christian city and then leap into the river herself! (1883:82)

Even the songs and literature of the day bore the stamp of divine judgment and gospel law. "The Battle Hymn of the Republic" did not preach a "sweet Jesus" altogether. No, "He is sifting out the hearts of men before the judgment seat." And one of the best sellers of the Gilded Age, Frank Norris's *The Octopus*, offered the opinion of many wheat farmers in the words of Mrs. Dyke, that "God will punish the gentlemen who run the railroad for being so hard and cruel" (II, 111).

What is more interesting, as the century progressed (if such a term be permitted) different kinds of people were using the themes of judgment and Christ's command from their perspectives. Black people moving north saw God's judgment falling upon the racist and oppressor, Christ's command inviting themselves to patience amid aspiration. Members of the Church of Jesus Christ of Latter-day Saints called upon the immediacy of that millennial judgment surely coming for the nonbelievers and those who persecuted Mormons, while they viewed Christ's commands as consonant with many Old Testament and newer revelations./5/

Labor organizers too, for the most part, depended heavily on biblical themes as they preached an evangel of solidarity. Familiar passages were quoted, sometimes paraphrased or recast in contemporary language, urging workers to unite. The labor historian Herbert Gutman has collected many such references. He declares that "prominent Gilded Age trade-unionists, labor reformers, and even radicals—with the notable exception of Samuel Gompers and [Daniel] DeLeon—shared a common faith in a just God, effused perfectionist doctrine, and warned of divine retribution against continuing injustice" (1966:137). More *outré* radicals, such as Mrs. P. C. Munger, wanted to bury the "dead leper" capitalist class with dynamite, "the last scientific fruit of the Holy Ghost." Much more commonly, the exodus and the ministry of the Nazarene were termed "labor movements" from which nineteenth-century movements could draw power. Gutman (1976:329) cites the dynamic appeals of George E. McNeill: "The influence of the teachings of the Carpenter's Son still tends to counteract the influence of Mammon. . . . We will find a new revelation of the Old Gospel, when the Golden Rule of Christ shall measure the relations of men in all their duties. . . . Then the new Pentecost will come, when every man shall have according to his need." The black pioneer organizer for the United Mine Workers, Richard L. Davis, characteristically used expressions of ethics and judgment taken from the Bible. Davis, twice elected to the UMW National Executive Board (1896, 1897), has been called "the most important" of the "Negro miners" of the period. "We are taught by the teachings of Holy Writ," Davis affirmed, "that in unity there is strength." He urged ethical compliance if not downright perfectionism on the basis of this authority: "Let us resolve to do better." As Herbert Gutman has shown (1976:131), Richard Davis under pressure resorted to a full dose of Pauline promises: "When Massillon, Ohio, miners threatened to quit the UMW, he reminded them of Paul's words in the New Testament: 'Except those abide in the ship, ye cannot be saved. . . . If her crew will only remain at their posts and not mutiny, I think she will make the harbor safely.'"

Different kinds of people in American life interpreted the judgment of God and the Christian ethic in various ways. As has been demonstrated already, the perspectives naturally included a measure of what might be called "self-serving hermeneutics." But for the most part, interpreters included themselves within the company of those being judged or commanded to obedience. Assessments of the changes that occurred in the understandings of both divine judgment and the "rule" of Christ might be studied in the way Shelton Smith followed *Changing Conceptions of Original Sin.* Their complexity, however, probably demands another mode of investigation. A study in a longitudinal fashion issue by issue would be required to reveal in clear terms the ways in which biblical themes functioned.

A Major Example of Bible-Based Legislation: The Sabbath Observance Laws

Americans grappled throughout the century with the interpretation of biblical teaching on the Sabbath, on the institution of it, and on the nature of Christ's commands regarding it. Citizens of the United States inherited from colonial times a strong tradition based upon the Puritan Sabbath. In the words of Winton Solberg, "a modified form of the Puritan Sabbath" existed in all the colonies, as a part of English life (79; cf. 27–80). Jonathan Edwards particularly had cited scripture several times in his classic defense of the institution. In the new nation, Timothy Dwight and Nathan Strong preached and published widely read sermons on the impingement of the "Fourth Commandment" on the lives of American citizens.

During the period under consideration, fully a hundred major works, not to mention reports and occasional papers, addressed the Sabbath issue pro and con. Essays and broadsides by Samuel Miller, Daniel Wilson, Nathaniel Emmons, Gardiner Spring, and Lyman Beecher all employed similar perspectives in defending the practice of legal protection of the Sabbath from profanation. All accentuated natural law and Christian duty in authorizing a restriction on commerce and entertainment on Sundays (Gilfallan: 150–55). It should also be noted that for upstanding Americans, attendance at church services on Sunday was fashionable and expected.

Travelers in the United States from Europe frequently commented on the difference between Sunday attention in the new country and the routine of their native lands (Fish: 62, 179).

One early and thorough treatment (1833) of the subject, by John Agnew, professor of languages at Washington College in Pennsylvania, emphasized the significance of the Genesis passages particularly. God instituted the Sabbath, according to Agnew (51), when the work of creation ceased. Gen 2:3 described "its original institution and present obligation." Agnew tried to refute the argument that God gave Sabbath observance only to the people of Israel and only at the time of their wilderness wanderings (Exod 16:21–30). Since the Sabbath was given to all people, not just to Moses and the children of Israel, it remained "binding on all who come to knowledge of it" (Agnew: 79). Therefore, "our constitution, as well as the Jews' was so made as to require the rest on the Sabbath" (Agnew: 83). For that reason Jesus commanded us to observe the Sabbath; it was "made for man."

Agnew as a Christian expressed no compunction about what he called the "change of day." "If there be a work which more gloriously displays the divine perfections, than that of creation, the presumption is, that the day of its completion will, henceforth, be the Sabbath" (Agnew: 100). The work of Christ's redemption, completed on the first day of the week, was such a display. "Christ entered his rest. . . ." That event accorded with Isaiah's proclamation of the coming of "a new heaven and a new earth" (Isa 65:17–18). Paul agreed (Eph 3:9, 10) "that the original creation merely prepared for the nobler work" (Agnew: 104). John too (Rev 1:10) showed that the "the Lord's Day" had become the new Sabbath. Agnew concluded his argument with some brief quotations from the "Fathers." Other biblical passages he deemed important in the argument included Num 15:32–36; Neh 10:31; 13:15–22; Jer 17:19–27; and Amos 8:5–10 (Agnew: 142).

Like support for Sabbath observance, resistance to Sunday laws in America also stemmed from colonial times and bore biblical authority. Roger Williams had balked at the regulations of the Puritan Sabbath because it inhibited the free worship of God and it contradicted the freedom of Christians in Christ. In the new nation, George Washington and other leaders had assured Jews that they would not be forced to work on Saturdays or to worship on Sundays in violation of their religious convictions. In an address in 1790 to the Hebrew Congregation in Newport, Washington quoted: "May the children of Abraham who dwell in this land continue to merit and enjoy the good will of the other inhabitants, while everyone shall sit in safety under his own vine and fig-tree, and there shall be none to make him afraid" (Blakely: 173).

Early concerted attacks on "open Sundays" in the new nation focused on the fact that post offices remained open on that day and mail was delivered. In 1810 Congress legislated both, and in 1825 it stipulated that offices should remain open all day. Evidently the primary weight of the argument now fell upon the legal doctrine of separation of church and state, although Griffin declares that Universalists and some Baptists opposed any such hint of establishment. The evangelicals, however, sought to have post offices closed on Sundays, so that employees could worship and so that commerce might be discouraged all the day long. They established in 1828 the General Union for Promoting and Observance of the Christian Sabbath. Eventually, Sunday mail delivery and the open post office ceased; but it is impossible to determine whether tradition or the Bible played the decisive role in the decision—or economic considerations./6/

During the Civil War, those who favored Sabbath observance chafed at the desecration of the Holy Sunday among the armies of the North and the South. Some even proposed that battles be suspended for divine worship on Sundays. In the opinion of one denominational leader, the army that broke the Sabbath more would receive a greater measure of God's wrath. On the other hand, if soldiers kept the Sabbath it "will prove a blessing and you will avert from your heads the wrath of God which comes on the land, because of the dishonor we, as a people, have placed on the day which He calls His own" (Weeks: 269).

The increasing complexity of industry, transportation, and recreational opportunities in American life in the latter decades of the century did not affect radically the force of the biblical arguments regarding Sabbath observance. Opponents of Sunday laws still quoted Jesus and the freedom passages from the gospel, cited the way he ate and healed that day, and they interpreted the command of Jesus to "render unto Caesar . . ." as pertaining to disestablishment. Proponents of Sabbath observance still argued from natural law, the exodus and wilderness experiences of Israel, the Decalogue, the practice of Jesus, and his commands to keep the law. More attention was given to the Sabbath psalms, however, and writers relied increasingly on Isaiah 58, where blessings and curses attendant upon the observance and the neglect of the Sabbath are described.

Increasing complexity in the religious sphere of American life profoundly affected the nature of the issue. The use of the Bible in addressing the matter became more complicated in that regard. Seventh-Day Adventists particularly took up the fight in favor of the Sabbath, but they opposed Sunday laws fiercely. Followers of William Miller, Hiram Edson, Joseph Bates, and Ellen White, as they organized a part of the adventist movement, began a concerted effort to free America from its enslavement to a pagan Lord's Day. They established the American Sabbath Tract Society, an institutional rebuttal to the Sabbath Union, which evangelicals had organized. And they emphasized Ellen White's formulation of the doctrine of "Investigative Judgment" and other "proved" teachings of scripture, the themes of conditional blessing from Old and New Testaments, and a great number of critical studies from history showing how Christians conflated pagan practice with theological reasoning.

One of the most complete statements against the efforts of the Sabbatarians came from W. H. Littlejohn, who collated all the pertinent passages from scripture, including the New Testament pericopes mentioning the "first day." He argued that Christians were not excused from the Sabbath, rather Christ commanded the Jewish Sabbath for all followers.

As Jewish people became more numerous in the United States, they moved quietly to gain space for the celebration of their holidays and Sabbaths. Rabbi Felsenthal, summarizing for a convocation on "Sunday Rest," explained that Jesus behaved and spoke as other progressive rabbis of his day, including many whose contributions made their way into the Talmud. He warned Christians not to force Jews to worship on Sunday, but he called upon God's blessing of the whole United States as it observed all Sabbaths (Atterbury: 128).

In the use of the Bible regarding Sabbath observance, advocates of Sunday laws became more sophisticated. They relied upon an increasing variety of texts as time passed. Though they continued to articulate the confluence of natural law and themes of judgment and ethics, they did not abandon the latter as they moved increasingly to emphasize natural law.

American society moved away from Sabbath observance as a legal category through most of the century. In part, religious demography contributed to the demise of the institution. But the biblical themes, the subject of the present study, remained rather constant. Important among them were the "law of God," "the blessing and the curse attendant upon adherence or disobedience," and the "commands of Christ." The complicated hermeneutics made "proofs" ever more difficult to follow.

Conclusion

Throughout the nineteenth century, themes from the Bible continued to be significant ingredients in American political life. Many leaders in the nation's life used the unequivocal expressions of covenant and mission. Some employed more profound and more conditional themes concerning the judgment of God and Christian ethics. At the same time an antiphonal movement toward religious privatization can be documented.

In general terms, as time passed more kinds of people took up the use of biblical themes. Social critics within the clergy, such as Theodore Parker, were joined subsequently by other types of persons in the public arena—labor organizers, blacks moving from a slave culture toward involvement in the politics of the United States, populists, and socialists, together with many others who sought to transform the life of the country. The use of the Bible by these different kinds of citizens became gradually more complex, so that study of the references and judgment about the role of the Bible become more difficult. One avenue of investigaton is the study of particular issues, and we have followed this approach in our examination of the debate about Sabbath observance, in which both proponents and opponents employed the Bible. But as the complexity of life increased, Americans became wary of such an ambiguous source of authority.

No wonder, then, Americans in public life were tempted to depend upon other authorities. When President William McKinley needed guidance on difficult matters of state, he simply prayed. And he evidently delighted in telling Methodist colleagues that God answered his prayers. A personal revelation convinced him that the United States should intervene in the Philippines "to educate . . . uplift and civilize them, and by God's grace to do the best we could for them as our fellow men for whom Christ died" (Faulkner: 252). Who needed the Bible when direct revelation was available?

NOTES

/1/   Consider Banner's insight on the limits of such trusteeship, however. Banner notes that when Ezra Stiles Ely published in 1828 an appeal for denominations and communities of Christians to back particular political candidates and to speak collectively on issues, his appeal met with a deafening silence.

/2/   But studies of Lincoln's use of the Bible indicate that he continued the practice. See Trueblood (52) for a recounting of Lincoln's witty words of solace in 1864, when only four hundred attended a rally and Lincoln quoted 1 Sam 2:2.

/3/   Richardson lauds the process, while the others take a more distanced perspective.

/4/   Parker also addressed the issues of black and white America, rights of women, and the Civil War in sophisticated Bible terms.

/5/   Investigation of the sectarian groups and their use of the Bible would comprise another topic altogether.

/6/   This essay has been written as the debate on the delivery of mail on Saturday
(the original Sabbath) takes place.

WORKS CONSULTED

Agnew, John H.
    1834   *A Manual on the Christian Sabbath Embracing a Considera-
                    tion of Its Perpetual Obligation, Change of Day, Utility and
                    Duties*. Philadelphia: Key and Biddle.

Atterbury, W. W., ed.
    1894   *The Sunday Problem: Its Present Day Aspects*. Papers pre-
                    sented at the International Congress on Sunday Rest, Chicago,
                    September 28–30, 1893. Boston: Jas. Earle.

Bacon, George
    1882   *The Sabbath Question*. New York: G. P. Putnam's Sons.

Banner, Lois W.
    1973   "Religious Benevolence as Social Control: A Critique of Inter-
                    pretation." *Journal of American History* 60:23–41.

Bellah, Robert N.
    1975   *The Broken Covenant: American Civil Religion in a Time of
                    Trial*. New York: Seabury.

Blakely, William A.
    1911   *American State Papers Bearing on Sunday Legislation*. Wash-
                    ington, DC: Religious Liberty Association.

Boardman, Fon W., Jr.
    1972   *America and the Gilded Age: 1876–1900*. New York: H. Z.
                    Walck.

Bodo, John R.
    1954   *The Protestant Clergy and Public Issues, 1812–1848*. Prince-
                    ton: University Press.

Campbell, Alexander
    1835   *Connected View of the Principles and Rules by which the
                    Living Oracles May Be Intelligibly and Certainly Inter-
                    preted*. . . . Bethany, VA: McKay and Ewing.

Cole, Charles C.
    1954   *The Social Ideas of the Northern Evangelists, 1820–1860*.
                    New York: Columbia University Press.

Dwight, Henry O.
    1916   *The Centennial History of the American Bible Society*. New
                    York: Macmillan.

Faulkner, Harold
    1959   *Politics, Reform and Expansion, 1890–1900*. New York: Har-
                    per and Brothers.

Fish, Carl R.
    1927   *The Rise of the Common Man, 1830–1850*. New York: Mac-
                    millan.

Foster, Charles I.
1960   *An Errand of Mercy: The Evangelical United Front, 1790–1837.* Chapel Hill: University of North Carolina Press.

Garraty, John A.
1970   *Interpreting American History: Conversations with Historians.* London: Macmillan.

George, Henry
1880   *Progress and Poverty.* New York: Appleton.
1883   *Social Problems.* New York: Robert Schaltrenbach Foundation.

Gilfallan, James
1862   *The Sabbath Viewed in the Light of Reason, Revelation, and History.* . . . New York: American Tract Society.

Glad, Paul W.
1960   *The Trumpet Soundeth.* Lincoln: University of Nebraska Press.

Gladden, Washington
1893   *Tools and the Man: Property and Industry Under the Christian Law.* Boston: Houghton, Mifflin.

Gribbin, William
1973   *The Churches Militant: The Way of 1812 and American Religion.* New Haven: Yale University Press.

Griffin, Clifford S.
1960   *Their Brothers' Keepers: Moral Stewardship in the United States, 1800–1865.* New Brunswick: Rutgers University Press.

Gutman, Herbert G.
1966   "Protestantism and the American Labor Movement: The Christian Spirit in the Gilded Age." *American Historical Review* 72:74–101.
1976   *Work, Culture, and Society in Industrializing America.* New York: Alfred A. Knopf.

Hammond, John L.
1978   "Revivals, Consensus, and American Political Culture." *Journal of the American Academy of Religion* 46:293–314.

Handy, Robert T.
1971   *A Christian America: Protestant Hopes and Historical Realities.* New York: Oxford University Press.

Hewitt, Emily, et al.
1971   "Models of Secularization in Contemporary Sociological Work." New York: Auburn Studies in Education.

Hudson, Winthrop S.
1973   *Nationalism and Religion in America.* New York: Harper & Row.

Kingsbury, Harmon
1840   *The Sabbath: A Brief History of the Laws, Petitions, Remonstrances and Reports.* . . . New York: Robert Carter.

Lacocque, André
1976   "A Continental View of the American Experience." Pp. 72–80 in *The American Religious Experience*. Edited by C. L. Manschreck and Barbara B. Zikmund. Chicago: Exploration Press.

Littlejohn, W. H.
1873   *The Constitutional Amendment*. Battle Creek, MI: Steam Press.

Linton, Ralph, and Adelin Linton
1949   *We Gather Together*. New York: Schuman.

Luckmann, Thomas
1967   *The Invisible Religion: The Problem of Religion in Modern Society*. New York: Macmillan.

Marty, Martin
1974   "Two Kinds of Two Kinds of Civil Religion." In *American Civil Religion*. Edited by R. E. Richey and D. G. Jones. New York: Harper & Row.

Mead, Sidney
1963   *The Lively Experiment: The Shaping of Christianity in America*. New York: Harper & Row.
1975   *The Nation with the Soul of a Church*. New York: Harper & Row.

Norris, Frank
1901   *The Octopus*. Garden City: Doubleday.

Parker, Theodore
1911   *Rights of Man*. Boston: American Unitarian Association.

Porter, Kirk H., and Donald B. Johnson
1966   *National Party Platforms 1840–1964*. Urbana: University of Illinois.

Richardson, Herbert
1967   *Toward An American Theology*. New York: Harper & Row.

Smith, Hilrie Shelton
1955   *Changing Conceptions of Original Sin*. New York: Scribner.

Solberg, Winton
1977   *Redeem the Time*. Cambridge: Harvard University Press.

Sonne, Nick H.
1939   *Liberal Kentucky, 1780–1828*. New York: Columbia University Press.

Trueblood, Elton
1973   *Abraham Lincoln: Theologian of American Anguish*. New York: Harper & Row.

Tuveson, Ernest L.
1968   *Redeemer Nation: The Idea of America's Millennial Role*. Chicago: University of Chicago Press.

Weeks, Louis
1981   "The Scriptures and Sabbath Observance in the South." *Journal of Presbyterian History* 59:267–83.

Part Two
THEMATIC PERSPECTIVES

IV

The Interaction of Biblical Religion and American Constitutional Law

Edward McGlynn Gaffney, Jr.

Introduction

In a seminal essay, Harold Berman has described the relationship between law and religion as an interaction, stating: "The principal affirmation is that law and religion are two different but interrelated aspects of social experience—in all societies, but especially in Western society, and still more especially in American society today. Despite the tensions between them, one cannot flourish without the other" (1974:11). Legal culture has shaped the form and content of major themes of biblical religion both in ancient and modern times. This article explores how biblical religion has contributed to the shaping of many of the human values protected by the American Constitution.

Three of the most significant values protected by this constitution are (1) freedom of expression, (2) associational freedom or the value of life in the community, and (3) limits on governmental authority. Each of these ideas has a long history. It is customary for students of American constitutional law to trace that history only back to the "founding fathers," generally without inquiring very closely about who they were, whether they truly represented "we, the people" (if people can be taken to refer to women, blacks, native Americans, and non-property-owning whites), and whether their economic interests shaped the document upon which we so depend for constitutional values (Beard; Jensen, 1940, 1950, 1974; R. Brown; McDonald; Lynd; Ferguson). Some students might dip into *The Federalist Papers*, but generally without any appreciation that they are reading partisan political propaganda or without even being aware that there were Anti-Federalists who roundly criticized the Constitution (Kenyon; Main, 1961, 1973; Wood: 475–99, 506–18). Some scholars acknowledge vaguely the influence of the Enlightenment, without becoming too specific about what is meant by that term; others relate particular ideas in the Constitution to a prominent seventeenth-century forerunner of the Enlightenment such as John Locke (Tribe: 12, 160, 428, 475, 948, 978) or to Charles Montesquieu (Tribe: 2, 427, 491) or Jean-Jacques Rousseau (Tribe: 428, 703). Still others have suggested that the Scottish philosophers of common sense such as Lord Kanes, Dugald Stewart, and Francis Hutcheson were more influential than Locke, Montesquieu, or Rousseau on the principal drafter of the Declaration of Independence, Thomas Jefferson (Koch, 1964).

It is not my purpose here to review any of the literature on the background of the American Constitution in the European Enlightenment, nor to trace the complex turnings over centuries that the ideas enshrined in the Constitution have traversed (see, e.g., Berman, 1977; Donahue). Rather, my purpose is simply to suggest that these ideas have a long lineage indeed and that among the ancestors of the ancient world who helped form these ideas are the authors of the Hebrew scriptures and the New Testament. I do so by exploring the biblical background of the three central constitutional values mentioned above and by pointing out a role that biblical religion might play in shaping American constitutional law in today's society.

Prolegomenon: A Distinction between the Church-State Relationship and the Interaction of Religion and Law

Some constitutional scholars have suggested that the First Amendment enjoys a certain priority or "firstness" not simply by virtue of its position within the Bill of Rights but also because the values it protects (religious freedom, freedom of speech, freedom of the press, freedom of assembly and association, and freedom to petition the government for redress of grievance) are quintessential to American society and hence are to be granted the status of preferred rights (Tribe: 564–990). In an essay exploring the interaction between religion and law it might seem obligatory to explore at length the linkage between biblical faith and the American understanding of freedom of religion protected under the two clauses in the First Amendment explicitly referring to religion, the clause prohibiting the federal establishment of a national religion (Antieau, Downey, and Roberts; Berns; Cord) and later, by virtue of the addition of the Fourteenth Amendment, prohibiting the establishment of a state religion (Howe), and the clause protecting the free exercise of religion.

A vast literature now exists concerning the relation between church and state in America referred to in these clauses. Members of the Supreme Court have detected a tension between the clauses. For example, Chief Justice Burger stated in the tax exemption case: "The Court has struggled to find a neutral course between the two Religion Clauses, both of which are cast in absolute terms, and either of which, if expanded to a logical extreme, would tend to clash with the other" (*Walz v. Tax Commission of City of New York*, 1970). In the same case Burger noted the "considerable inconsistency in the opinions of the Court" construing the religion clauses. The difficulties in construing the establishment clause in particular have been noted repeatedly by members of the Court throughout the past decade. In *Wolman v. Walter* (1977), Justice Powell referred in his concurring and dissenting opinion to a "tolerable . . . loss of analytical tidiness." In *Committee for Public Education and Religious Liberty v. Regan* (1980), Justice White stated candidly:

> Establishment Clause cases are not easy, they stir deep feelings, and we are divided among ourselves, perhaps reflecting the different views on this subject of the people of this country. What is certain is that our decisions have tended to avoid categorical imperatives and absolutist approaches at either end of the range of possible outcomes. This course sacrifices clarity and predictability for flexibility, but this promises to be the case until the continuing interaction between the courts and states produces a single, more-encompassing construction of the Establishment Clause.

Some scholars find this kind of admission in a majority opinion of the Court extraordinary but also an understatement of the "chaos and utter confusion of Supreme Court pronouncements in the Church–State area" (Scalia: 173).

I have already added to the literature on this theme, criticizing the Court's handling of *Meek v. Pittenger* and *Wolman v. Walter* (Gaffney, 1978) and its elaboration of the spurious principle that legislation can be invalidated if it tends to divide people politically along religious lines (Gaffney, 1980). For now it suffices to state that I do not regard the two religion clauses as inherently conflicting but as expressing in two related ways the same concern that the government may not monopolize religious value or impose its notion of religious value in a pluralistic society.

Neither clause suggests a hostility to religion (Louisell), nor do they in combination require a radical separation of legal and religious values (Berman, 1977:410). Tribe may have oversimplified the matter when he encapsulated the value protected by the religion clauses as the "rights of religious autonomy" (812), but he is correct in noting that:

> there are necessary relationships between government and religion; that government cannot be indifferent to religion in American life; and that, far from being hostile or even truly indifferent, it may, and sometimes must accommodate its institutions and programs to the religious interests of the people. . . . In much the same spirit, American courts have not thought the separation of church and state to require that religion be totally oblivious to government or politics; church and religious groups in the United States have long exerted powerful political pressures on state and national legislatures, on subjects as diverse as slavery, war, gambling, drinking, prostitution, marriage, and education. To view such religious activity as suspect, or to regard its political results as automatically tainted, might be inconsistent with first amendment freedoms of religious and political expression—and might not even succeed in keeping religious controversy out of public life, given

the "political ruptures caused by the alienation of segments of the religious community." (822, 866–67)

The main point here is that religion is a larger concept than one could ever learn from the few cases concerning public funds for private education or concerning prayer and religious instruction in public schools, which now represent virtually the only sort of legal materials in casebooks and treatises on American constitutional law. Hence, I leave to another day the discussion of the ways in which the institutions of church and state ought to be separate in American society. I focus here on the ways that biblical religion might legitimately be viewed as influencing the three central constitutional values mentioned earlier: freedom of expression, associational freedom, and limits on governmental power.

Freedom of Expression

It is not possible to review here all the complexities of the American system of freedom of expression. It should suffice to sketch an outline of that system—or non-system, as the case may be—by summarizing the writing on this theme by Thomas Emerson, the constitutional scholar who has contributed most significantly to this theme in recent times. Emerson began his 1966 essay on this theme with this lament: "No one concerned with freedom of expression in the United States can fail to be alarmed at the unsatisfactory state of First Amendment doctrine" (vii). In his essay Emerson analyzed the function of freedom of expression in a democratic society, practical difficulties in maintaining such a system, and the role of law in developing and supporting freedom of expression. He attempted a statement of general but sufficiently specific principles to guide courts in supporting a system of free expression and a formulation of detailed rules of law that should govern a variety of the problems relating to free expression in American society. He concluded with the hope that the working principles he had proposed would "furnish a rational and acceptable approach for giving significant meaning to the great and vital concept [of freedom of expression]" (117).

In *The System of Freedom of Expression* (1970) Emerson undertook to elaborate and to apply in concrete cases the ideas that he had set forth in his earlier essay. In the later volume Emerson described the complex mechanism of this system as a group of rights including "the right to form and hold beliefs and opinions on any subject, and to communicate ideas, opinions, and information through any medium . . . , the right to remain silent . . . , to hear the views of others and to listen to their version of the facts . . . , the right to inquire and, to a degree, the right of access to information" (1970:3). He observed that this group of rights is assured both to individual members of society and to groups assembled in associations. He noted further:

> Any system of freedom of expression must also embody principles through which exercise of these rights by one person or group may be reconciled with equal opportunity for other persons or groups to enjoy them. At the same time, the rights of all in freedom of expression must be reconciled with other individual and social interests. It is this process of reconciliation that has given rise to most of the controversial issues in the past and continues to be the major focus of attention today.
>
> Assurance of these rights to freedom of expression involves limitations upon the power of the state to interfere with or abridge them. (1970:3)

Not content with placing negative limits on governmental power, Emerson envisaged an affirmative role that the government could play in maintaining a system of free expression in modern society. According to Emerson, the state must minimally protect persons and groups from interference with their rights stemming from the government or from private parties. In addition, Emerson urges the state to provide a realistic administrative structure that would "develop a framework of doctrines, practices, and institutions which will take into account the actual forces at work and make possible the realistic achievements of the objectives sought." The most expansive role Emerson conceives for the state is that it "undertake positively to promote and encourage freedom of expression, as by furnishing facilities, eliminating distortions in the media of communication, or making information available" (1970:4).

It would, of course, be anachronistic to maintain that the system of freedom of expression that Emerson has described can be found within the pages of the Hebrew scriptures or the New Testament, for the ancient world did not know of the positive state referred to throughout Emerson's writings. It would, moreover, be naive to expect a fully developed system of freedom of expression in ancient Israel for an important theological reason that was avoided by Emerson when he stated: "No attempt is made in this essay to treat the provisions of the First Amendment which relate to freedom of religion" (1963:ix). The legal documents on which the covenant concept was based were suzerainty treaties, not parity treaties. One corollary of the impact of suzerainty treaties on law in Israel is that the word of Yahweh, the analogue of the emperor in the treaty tradition, is clearly in a privileged and exalted position. The role of the ambassador sent from the imperial court to remind the vassal of its treaty obligations apparently underlies the vocation and mission of the biblical prophet, who articulates not simply his own views of the matter but who can genuinely proclaim that he speaks in the name of Yahweh. The familiar introduction to the prophetic oracle, "Thus says Yahweh," derives, then, from a legal formula common in ancient Near Eastern treaty law. The formula serves not only to present the ambassador's credentials but also to warn the vassal that the curses found in the treaty can be invoked if the vassal does not turn away from its infidelity and return to the faithful observance of the stipulations of the covenant. For example, the vocation vision of Ezekiel (1:1–3:15) follows this ancient pattern of a messenger sent from the imperial court to a rebellious vassal people. As Lohfink states, "Ezekiel understood his task from the time of his vocation entirely within the framework of the covenant. This task is to bring into effect in Israel, in the name of God, the covenant law of God" (117; see also Zimmerli).

According to the covenant between Israel and Yahweh, then, the two parties are not to be thought of as equal partners bargaining over a commercial transaction or a business arrangement. Nevertheless, the biblical record reflects a remarkable commitment to the notions of freedom of speech that came centuries later to be protected in the American Bill of Rights. This commitment can be shown in two ways, by the boldness of proclamation in the prophetic preaching and by the pluralism of traditions retained within the canon of the Hebrew scriptures and the New Testament.

The covenant lawsuit (*rib*) was an important component of prophetic thinking (McCarthy: 38; Huffmon; Wright). A corollary of this theme is that the biblical prophet appears in the role of covenant mediator. J. A. Sanders has described this role succinctly:

> The prophet in ancient Israel was a spokesman for both his God and his people. He was an emissary or messenger from the divine court to the human marketplace, and from the marketplace to the heavenly presence. He was a mediator between God and man. As an Israelite his identity lay fully and completely with his people; but as a man called by God to be his prophet, his identity lay also in God over against the people. . . . The prophet was an emissary or messenger from his God to his people; he carried a message. This was a distinctive feature about the biblical prophet: his message was never limited to the head of government. He not only might bypass the king, instead of addressing him; but he also might actually disdain to recognize the king. (54, 57–58)

To be sure, the prophets did on occasion confront the heads of government. In one of the best known stories of confrontation with royal authority, the prophet Nathan, who had pronounced the oracle promising David a secure dynasty (2 Sam 7:1–17), used a parable to entice David into pronouncing a curse upon a rich man who had plundered his poor neighbor (2 Sam 12:1–4). The prophet then confronted the king

with the reality that he was the one upon whom the curse fell for ordering the assassination of his lover's husband. The pattern of the divine
emissary sent to chasten the rebellious vassal echoes through the passage:

> Yahweh the God of Israel says this, "I annointed you king over Israel,
> and I delivered you out of the hand of Saul; and I gave you your
> master's house, and your master's wives into your bosom, and gave
> you the house of Israel and of Judah; and if this were too little, I
> would add to you as much more. Why have you despised the word
> of Yahweh, to do what is evil in his sight? You have smitten Uriah
> the Hittite with the sword, and have taken his wife to be your wife,
> and have slain him with the sword of the Ammonites. Now therefore
> the sword shall never depart from your house, because you have
> despised me, and have taken the wife of Uriah the Hittite to be your
> wife." Thus says Yahweh, "Behold, I will raise up evil against you out
> of your own house; and I will take your wives before your eyes, and
> give them to your neighbor, and he shall lie with your wives in the
> sight of this sun." (2 Sam 12:7–12)

As the startling conclusion of the story demonstrates, sometimes regal
authority is amenable to correction. Thus, when David repents or turns
his conduct around, he can then hear from the prophet a word of conso-
lation and forgiveness (2 Sam 12:13–25).

Two further observations should be made about the boldness of the
preaching of the biblical prophets. First, as Sanders states, the vision they
see or the insight they possess "cannot be understood as [a] response to
extrasensory stimuli from the future but rather as divine judgment against
political misconduct" (65). If Isaiah would characterize the reformation of
Hezekiah (2 Kings 18) as a covenant with death (Isa 28:14–15), similarly
the radical abolitionists could in the 1830s burn the Constitution, which by
virtue of its compromise over slavery was regarded as a "covenant with
hell."

Second, the prophetic undertaking of pronouncing judgment on the
people was risky at best, for "bearers of unsavory news in antiquity were
often so identified with the content of their message that they were
killed for their labors" (Sanders: 65). Yet the final song about the 'ebed
Yahweh in Deutero-Isaiah proclaims in the face of such suffering: "Ours
were the sufferings he bore, ours the sorrows he carried. . . . He was
pierced through for our faults, crushed for our sins. On him lies a punishment that brings us peace, and through his wounds we are healed. . . .
By his sufferings shall my servant justify many, taking their faults on
himself" (Isa 5:3, 5, 11). It is important to recall that in its first stage of
reflection on the Hebrew scriptures the early Christian community came
to view the vocation and mission of Jesus primarily, though not exclusively, in terms of a biblical prophet confronting the powers that be and

calling as God's emissary for repentance (Mark 1:15; 9:4ff.; Acts 3:14; 7:52). It is likewise clear that the Servant Song from the Isaiah scroll was soon seen through Christian eyes as having been realized in the victorious passion and death of Jesus (Matt 26:28, 63, 67; 27:14, 29–31). And the followers of Jesus, gifted with his Spirit, were emboldened to speak out the proclamation of their faith in spite of sanctions threatened for such speech. In response to the warning of the authorities in Jerusalem to make no statements or to teach in the name of Jesus, Peter and John retorted: "You must judge whether in God's eyes it is right to listen to you and not to God. We cannot promise to stop proclaiming what we have seen and heard" (Acts 3:18–20). This sort of unabashed boldness was regarded by the early Christian community as a hallmark of authentic apostolic preaching (Acts 4:13, 29, 31; 2 Cor 10:2; Eph 3:12; Schlier; Rahner).

Second, one may conclude that freedom of expression is valued highly within biblical religion because the Bible preserves a variety of traditions, not all of which are easily reconciled. Indeed, the very existence of doublets and even triplets within the narratives in the Torah was a major literary clue that the final text we possess reflects different traditions, for which separate sources were posited in the documentary hypothesis. What is significant from the point of view of freedom of expression is that the exilic or postexilic Priestly editor of the Torah did not eliminate the preexisting Jahwist accounts of creation or of the flood from the final edition of Genesis. He included the J account of creation immediately after the P account and intertwined his account of the flood with the centuries-old J narrative. Similarly, the northern tribes knew all too well through years of bitter experience that royal power has a seamy side, manifest, for example, in governmental taxation and military conscription (1 Sam 8:10–18). This antimonarchical view is reflected throughout the remnants of the northern tradition (known as E, standing for the Elohist, or, in Sanders's view, for Ephraim) that survived the collapse of the northern kingdom at the hands of the Assyrians in 722 B.C.E. Once again, the crucial element from the perspective of freedom of expression is that the Deuteronomic historian into whose hands this material fell decided not to suppress or censor the viewpoint despite its seeming conflict with the promise to David and his royal successors of an everlasting dynasty (2 Samuel 7) but to preserve the E tradition, and he incorporated it into his narrative (Sanders: 23). And the final editors of the Hebrew scriptures likewise decided to include within the canon disconsonant voices on matters of such moment to us as whether there is any meaningful way of speaking of life after death, as is manifest in a synoptic reading of the *Wisdom of Solomon* and *Qoheleth* (Lohfink: 138–69).

The editors of the New Testament were likewise committed to a general principle of freedom of expression. The very fact that significant theological differences on questions such as the person and mission of Jesus, the content of the Lord's Prayer, and the words of institution at the Last Supper can be spotted at a glance when parallel texts of the first three Gospels are compared gave rise to their nickname, the Synoptics. The conflict between Peter and Paul over the Christian mission to the Gentiles is not covered up or swept under the rug but is reported graphically. Paul and James clearly do not agree on the nature of justification in their sharply differing emphases on faith and works. The relation between Christians and the emperor is portrayed very differently in Romans 13 and Revelation 13 (Stringfellow), and the debate over whether the polity of the church should be congregational, presbyterial, or episcopal finds its roots within the pluralism of styles of church governance found within the text of the New Testament (Küng). To be sure, this diversity has yielded the question of the canon within the canon, manifested, for example, in Luther's low regard for James or in Ernst Käsemann's dim view of the Captivity Epistles and the Pastorals because of their tendency to "early Catholicism." But the point remains that freedom of expression is reflected in the very composition of the New Testament canon.

Biblical religion, then, cannot be viewed simply as an ancient prototype of repression and uniformity that is contrary to the model of free expression so cherished in our liberal democracy. On the contrary, the bold speech and the variety of beliefs witnessed to in the biblical record makes the Bible one of the significant ancient sources of freedom of expression. Viewed in this way, the Bible can continue to serve modern American society by providing the motivation to believing members of that society to speak their minds courageously but without hubris on a variety of social issues concerning which the voice of religious conscience is entirely appropriate.

The failure of religious bodies to voice their concerns on such matters can be justified neither on the basis of biblical religion nor on the basis of a correct reading of the First Amendment. In a major case setting constitutional standards concerning libel, Justice Brennan wrote that the First Amendment bespeaks "a profound national commitment to the principle that debate on public issues should be uninhibited, robust, and wide-open, and it may well include vehement, caustic, and sometimes unpleasantly sharp attacks on government and public officials" (*New York Times v. Sullivan*, 1964). The religious voice need not be vehement or caustic; indeed, it need not always be critical of government. But it may not be stifled or muffled merely because religiously grounded. Christians, moreover, must never forget that the church in Nazi Germany was to a shameful degree guilty of silent complicity in the lawless and illegitimate exercise of authority that led to the Holocaust.

I have already focused on the convictions of the radical abolitionists that slavery be ended immediately. It remains only to add that this view, as well as their stubborn insistence that they would be heard, was grounded in the biblical model of freedom of expression.

This model should not be mistaken by adherents to biblical religion as a promise of success. By the same token, the caution that we may fail to change society should not be confused with a counsel of timidity or with failure of nerve. In our world we may have grown too accustomed to the futility of bold speech attempting to curb the excess of governmental authority, described by Senator William Fulbright as "the arrogance of power." The Nathan-David story referred to above serves as a timely reminder that such bold speech can on occasion yield similar results in our society. For example, Senator Sam Ervin appeared equally at home in citing the Bible and the Constitution as he confronted the evidence of excessive presidential power that came to the attention of the Watergate Commission. The analogy with the biblical story, however, ends there, for the subsequent resignation of President Nixon was rewarded by President Ford with a plenary pardon that in biblical terms is meaningless because it was not preceded by genuine repentance, even if the only court reviewing the Nixon pardon deemed it efficacious in constitutional terms on the nonbiblical view that the president's pardoning power is absolute (*Murphy v. Ford*, 1975).

Finally, religious believers are familiar both with the requirements of the First Commandment and with the dubious accretions of Byzantine court etiquette that many religious bodies have adopted as part of their style of address and communication. For both of these reasons, they should be equipped to recognize idolatry and pomposity when they see it, even if, like Justice Stewart on pornography, they might have a hard time defining it. Thus, when Harold J. Berman notes that one of the significant features of the religious character of American law making is the way that it employs formal ritual, the religious voice from the back of the secular temple might be heard to voice three concerns. First, the ritualization of law giving may yield the expectation that lawgivers, executive magistrates, and judges be given more homage than is due them in a democracy. Norman O. Brown has remarked, "An end to idolatry is never easy" (114). Religious believers ought not to make it any harder in the secular order by failing to object to ritual pomposity. Second, one should not trust magistrates accustomed to ritual adulation to ritualize radical dissent from their authority; and one should trust them still less to execute the self-destruction of their power to control a system perceived by many in our country as oppressive and unjust. Since open criticism and vigorous protest are so vital in our democracy, our legislators and magistrates should not be set on too lofty a pedestal. Third, the prohibition against idolatry should train reflexes within believers to refrain not only from hero worship but also from adulation of the text. For example, even if biblical believers did not know much about the narrow world view of Justice George Sutherland, they should instinctively reject Sutherland's claim that the American Constitution is a "divinely inspired instrument." And they should likewise recognize as puffery and nonsense the exaltation of the text proclaimed in 1913 by a Wall Street lawyer named Henry R. Estabrook:

> Our great and sacred Constitution, serene and inviolable, stretches its beneficent powers over our land . . . like the outstretched arm of God himself . . . the people of the United States . . . ordained and established one Supreme Court—the most rational, considerate, discerning, veracious, impersonal power—the most candid, unaffected, conscientious, incorruptible power. . . . O Marvellous Constitution! Magic Parchment! Transforming Word! Maker, Monitor, Guardian of Mankind! (Bickel: 15)

Freedom of Association

The preamble of the Constitution states that it is "we, the people" who establish the constitutional order. Despite this grand promise, one of the major flaws of the document is its individualistic character. Laurence Tribe, for example, has characterized the Constitution as "insufficiently sensitive to the social dimension of humanity and of the communal dimension of society" (700). Perhaps the atomistic bias of Enlightenment thinking is responsible for the individualism of the Constitution. In any event, the biblical concept of a covenanted people has pointed the American mythos in a different direction. And that direction has received at least some form of judicial recognition in the cases that speak of a constitutional right to freedom of association.

Although this freedom is not specified in so many words in the Bill of Rights, it has been recognized by the Supreme Court as a corollary of the rights explicitly protected by the First Amendment. The theory that has developed since the leading case in this area, *NAACP v. Alabama ex rel. Patterson* (1958), is that the First Amendment protects not only an individual's right to freedom of speech or assembly or right to petition the government for redress of grievance, but also concerted activity by a group to exercise these freedoms.

By articulating an independent right to freedom of association, the Court has ensured that the First Amendment guarantees will not be reduced to exclusively solipsistic concerns. Communities, as well as persons, are the objects of constitutional safeguards. As Tocqueville observed over a century ago, the "most natural privilege of man, next to the right of acting for himself, is that of combining his exertions with those of his fellow creatures and of acting in common with them" (196). Or as Mark DeWolfe Howe wrote, many forms of private organizations in our society are thought of as entitled "to lead their own free lives and [to] exercise within the area of their competence an authority so effective as to justify labelling it . . . sovereign" (91).

The central message that emerges from Supreme Court decisions articulating a right to freedom of association is that this freedom insulates private groups from unreasonable governmental interference with their internal affairs. Among the voluntary associations that the Court has protected in this way are labor organizations, political parties, civil rights groups, the leadership of religious bodies, and the management of banks and corporations.

Freedom of association, however, remains a muted theme in constitutional doctrine. As Tribe puts it:

> [A]rdent believers in the richness and diversity of a pluralist society, where a variety of voluntary private associations and groups operate simultaneously to maximize opportunities for self-realization and minimize the strength of centralized power, will find little comfort in the freedom of association as it has evolved under the umbrella of the first amendment. (702)

Through the process of judicial interpretation elaborating the doctrine of freedom of association, the excessive individualism of the American Constitution has begun to be corrected. Some commentators urge that this process culminate in a clear statement that "whatever action a person can pursue as an individual, freedom of association must ensure that he can pursue with others" (Raggi: 15). Constitutional doctrine has not yet, however, developed to this extent.

For this very reason, biblical religion can serve as an important corrective to American constitutional law. Although concerned intensely with persons, the Bible does not view them as isolated atoms, but as interrelated, socially connected parts of a whole, or as members of a community (Giblet: 43). To return to the ancient Near Eastern treaty tradition, the concept of a covenant implies the gathering of the people in solemn assembly (*qahal*) for an annual ceremony of covenant renewal. This feature of the covenant concept colors the narrative of the Sinai theophany in Exodus 19, which precedes the giving of the law, and it is clearly the background for the covenant renewal ceremony at Shechem narrated in Joshua 24. The social character of the gathered people is a major theme in Deuteronomy, the book that served as a primary source for the self-understanding of the early Christians as "the church of God" (*ekklesia tou theou*). This theme is aptly summarized in the teaching of the Second Vatican Council in the Dogmatic Constitution on the Church:

> At all times and among every people, God has given welcome to whosoever fears Him and does what is right. It has pleased God, however, to make men [and women] holy and save them not merely as individuals without any mutual bounds, but by making them into a single people. . . . (Abbott: 24–25)

Without some notion of a community with a significant story binding it together and giving it common purpose and meaning, it is doubtful that the courts will be able to articulate any substantive answer to the profound question, "Who is a member of our community?" I am not proposing that Exodus and Deuteronomy should be treated as a hidden amendment to the American Constitution. But reflection on Israelite law would lend support to conclusions dramatically different from those reached by the Supreme Court, for example, in cases involving aliens and even American natives born of alien parents. The legal tradition of the northern tribes, for example, includes the injunction: "You shall not oppress an alien; you know well how it feels to be an alien, since you were once aliens yourselves in the land of Egypt" (Exod 23:9). When refugees from these tribes fled to the south, they found safe harbor in Judah, and their legal code (including the provision protecting refugees) was honored. Thus Deuteronomy contains explicit directions to include the alien, the orphan, and the widow within the extended family or community that was gathered for the joyful annual celebrations of the Feast of Weeks in the summer and the Feast of Tents or Booths in the autumn (Deut 16:11, 14). This inclusion of the foreigner in familial and communal merrymaking stands in sharp contrast to the forced exclusion of Japanese noncitizens and of American citizens of Japanese ancestry (the Issei and Nisei) not only from the homes of their friends and neighbors but also from their own hearth and home and our judicially sanctioned placement of these people in concentration camps known euphemistically as "relocation centers" (*Korematsu v. United States*, 1944; *Hirabayashi v. United States*, 1944). It was a mark of Chief Justice Earl Warren's modesty and greatness that he came to regret the role he had played as California's Attorney General in this shameful episode of nativistic prejudice. According to the law students who used to visit Justice Hugo Black, the author of the *Korematsu* and *Hirabayashi* decisions, like Harry Truman on the bombing of Nagasaki and Hiroshima, he never lost any sleep about the wisdom of his wartime decision.

The tender story of Ruth demonstrated not only that the God of Israel rewards the spirit of self-sacrifice even where practiced by a foreigner but that marriage to a foreigner was possible under ancient Hebrew law. Once again, the American legal experience has something to learn from the parallel biblical precedent, for we prohibited racial miscegenation for centuries in this country before the Supreme Court finally decided in 1967 to hear a case involving this issue (*Loving v. Virginia*). It is likewise significant that one of the regrets that Chief Justice Warren expressed concerning his judicial career was the "passive virtue" of denying certiorari in a number of pre-*Loving* cases, the effect of which was to send people to jail for the offense of interracial marriage.

Finally, the inability of the courts to resolve the question of life in community on any substantive basis is reflected in the shift from *Furman v. Georgia* (1971), banning capital punishment as cruel and unusual, to *Gregg v. Georgia* (1976), allowing capital punishment where specific procedures for identifying those deemed worthy of execution have been followed. In short, the courts have exalted process values over the substantive value of life in community.

The lack of a sense of communal or shared value led in the Enlightenment to the exaltation of personal freedom and each person's preference (MacIntyre). A view of American history that takes biblical religion into account as one of its shaping forces might yield a greater sense of common origins, purpose, and destiny. Without such a view it seems unlikely that freedom of association will develop much further as a theme of American constitutional law.

Limited Government

However idiosyncratic in spots, Laurence Tribe's treatise on American constitutional law provides the most comprehensive effort yet undertaken to reach a systematic understanding of the text of the Constitution and its development through judicial interpretation. In his effort to organize constitutional doctrine in a coherent and genetic fashion, Tribe has developed seven analytic models of understanding: the model of separation of powers (among the branches of government and between the levels of government, state and federal), the model of implied limitations on government (contractual liberty), the model of settled expectations (no uncompensated takings), the model of governmental regularity (procedural fairness), the model of preferred rights (liberty beyond contract), the model of equal protection, and the model of structural justice. Although analytically distinct categories, these models coalesce in the sense that they all bespeak in one way or another the ways that Americans have limited governmental authority by structuring and controlling it.

As was suggested above with respect to freedom of expression, it would be anachronistic and naive to search the ancient scriptures of Israel and the Christian community for texts proving or disproving the way that our Constitution goes about the task of allocating and limiting governmental power. On the other hand, it would be myopic to assume that the notion of limits on governmental authority had a pedigree no longer than the Enlightenment. To be sure, Enlightenment thought helped powerfully to topple autocratic and oppressive forms of government in Europe at a time when emperors and kings were presumed to enjoy their royal prerogatives as a matter of divine right. A recent cartoon in the *Journal of the American Bar Association* portrays such a monarch complaining that "divine rights aren't what they used to be." Believers in biblical religion can laugh at the cartoon as heartily as anyone who thinks that the Enlightenment brought down the power of kings, but they would simply add: "Divine rights of kings weren't ever what most European kings thought they were." I explore here several ways in which the Bible has contributed to the limitation of governmental authority.

The biblical tradition places severe limits on the nature of kingly authority. For centuries the people existed without it, depending on the charismatic leaders known as the judges to gather the loosely confederated tribes together when their survival was threatened. When monarchy was introduced into Israel in the person of Saul, it was not without its critics, as the antimonarchical tradition referred to above amply demonstrates (1 Samuel 8:1–22; 10:18–25; 12; 15). Saul, David, and Solomon, the only three kings to govern a united Israel, are not remembered as lawgivers, as were other potentates in the ancient Near East such as Ur-Nammu, Lipit-Ishtar, or Hammurabi. Instead, the whole of the Torah is regarded as the gift of Yahweh through his prophet Moses. The later biblical prophets, moreover, felt empowered both to challenge and to ignore royal authority. Both these prophets and the historical writing of the Deuteronomist view the destruction of the northern kingdom by the Assyrians in the eighth century and the destruction of the southern kingdom by the Babylonians in the sixth century as the consequences of the infidelities of the people and the monarch to the stipulations of their covenant with Yahweh. In the Second Temple Period there was no attempt to revive the institution of the monarchy. This remains the case for the entire period of Israel's history after the destruction of the Temple by the Romans in 70 C.E., including, of course, the post-1947 period of the modern state of Israel.

There appears to be a fairly solid consensus in New Testament scholarship that the preaching of Jesus is consistent with this Hebrew view of limited governmental authority (Yoder; Cassidy). To summarize this preaching, the reign of God that Jesus announced was not coterminous with the political power of Caesar (John 18:33–37; 19:14–16). Jesus explicitly rejected the formal title of "king" and the messianic expectations people had of him that would give him political power over the nations (John 6:15; Luke 4:5–8, citing Deut 6:13). Although he fomented no revolution against Roman rule, the famous logion on the temple tax should be construed to mean that one should give to Caesar only that which is his due (Mark 12:16–17; see Acts 10:25–26). And the only throne over which the title "king" rightly occurs is the place of his non-violent resistance to lawless Roman rule, the cross (Mark 15:26–27).

The biblical traditions on limited governmental authority cannot be used to support the particular allocations of power made in the American constitution. But these traditions can serve as a powerful motivating force for persons to challenge such authority whenever it exceeds the bounds of legitimacy. For example, the civil rights movement of the 1960s derived much of its strength not only from Martin Luther King's ethic of love but also from the view that illegitimate authority supporting an unjust system of legal segregation and racial oppression had to be resisted in the name of a higher justice. People who "sat in" to challenge the morality of the Jim Crow laws and who challenged the legitimacy of their arrest under loitering ordinances used to bolster these laws found biblical warrant for their acts of disobedience in the example of the Hebrew midwives resisting the decrees of the pharaoh (Exod 1:15–22) and in the political model of the entire exodus event as an act of insurrection against a duly constituted monarch (Cox).

Similar convictions motivated various acts of resistance to the government's prosecution of a lengthy, costly, and undeclared war in Southeast Asia. The very fact that many of these acts were illegal was undoubtedly due in some measure to the refusal of the justices of the Supreme Court throughout the entire Vietnam era to review the merits of any of the major legal challenges to that war (*Ashton v. United States*, 1967; *Mora v. McNamara*, 1968; *Luftig v. McNamara*, 1968; *Velvel v. Nixon*, 1970; *Massachusetts v. Laird*, 1970). On the premise that it is reasonable to believe that judges read the newspapers or watched television during the Vietnam era, one might expect that they would have had some moral feelings about the rightness or wrongness of the conduct of the war in Southeast Asia. If so, then like Melville's Captain Vere modern justices let legal formalism take priority over questions of conscience. Unlike Vere, the Court thought it could avoid responsibility by deciding not to decide. Like Billy Budd, many persons went to their death as a result (Cover: 2–6, 250–52).

Furthermore, the charge that legal formalism was allowed to override questions of conscience applies not only to the conscience of the judges but also to the consciences of those who were compelled to fight the war, many of whom became its casualties or in some other way its tragic victims. In *United States v. Seeger* (1965) the Court rewrote the congressional enactment concerning the conscientious objector exemption to conscription for military service, extending the exemption to those whose objection is grounded in a belief structure that serves as the functional equivalent of orthodox belief in God (secular humanism as a religion). Justice Clark cited as authority for this conclusion the theologian Paul Tillich on the notion of God as the ground of our being, the Anglican bishop John Robinson on the modern breakdown of belief in a God "up there" or "out there," and the passage from the Second Vatican Council on respect for the world religions. The American Civil Liberties Union did not suggest that this theology for draft boards constituted an impermissible establishment of religion. Five years later the Court added another judicial gloss to the conscription statute, teaching in *Welsh v. United States* (1970) that the conscientious objector status must be available to "all those whose consciences, spurred by deeply held *moral, ethical*, or religious beliefs, would give them no rest or peace if they allowed themselves to become a part of an instrument of war" (emphasis added).

In *Gillette v. United States* (1971) and *Negre v. Larsen* (1971) the Court was presented with the moral question that most troubled young men facing the draft or those already inducted into military service during the Vietnam era, the problem of selective conscientious objection. While this time the Court took its role as constitutional adjudicator more seriously, it reached the establishment clause issue only to dismiss it casually: the Court asserted that in limiting the conscientious objector status to those "opposed to war in any form," Congress had not given any preference to those whose objections arise out of a pacifist context over those whose convictions were grounded in a just war theory.

Justice Black was not heard to murmur in dissent his ringing conclusion in *Welsh* cited above. Nor did Justice Marshall, who wrote the opinion for the Court in *Gillette*, ever explain autobiographically how a great champion of civil rights could come to believe that a fundamental civil liberty, a "preferred freedom," that of free exercise of religion, could be overridden easily by an argument from administrative inconvenience. (How could General Hershey run the Selective Service System if his draft boards had to cope with people who were religiously opposed not to every war that ever had been fought but only to the one in which they were asked to become involved?) Justice Brennan, who applied the standards of "overriding governmental interest" and of "least restricting alternative" to the category of religious discrimination in the welfare benefit termination case (*Shervert v. Verner*, 1963), issued not even a gentle concurrence reminding his brethren that they had forgotten the relevant standards.

Justice Douglas, long comfortable with the role of sole dissenter, was the only one who thought it apt to cite the teachings of the church of which Louis Negre was a member. Stating explicitly his reliance on an *amicus* brief written by John Noonan, Douglas unmasked the legal position of the Court and set forth some of the details about the case which made it clear that a person had been forced by our legal system to choose between obedience to his country and the higher duty to his God made known in the official and authoritative teaching of his church. The documents of Vatican II, deemed relevant in *Seeger* in support of secular humanism, were cited by none of the Justices in *Gillette* or *Negre*. Had one of them thought it appropriate, we might now read in the U.S. Reports the only passage in which the Council issued a condemnation: "Any act of war aimed indiscriminately at the destruction of entire cities of extensive areas along with their population is a crime against God and man himself. It merits unequivocal and unhesitating condemnation" (*Pastoral Constitution on the Church in the Modern World*, Art. 80; see Abbott: 294).

Another significant feature of limited government is the expectation of procedural fairness. This value also has ancient precedents in biblical law, which provided that judges be impartial (Exod 23:8; Deut 16:18–20), required two or more consistent witnesses in a criminal proceeding (Deut 16:15; cf. Matt 18:20), allowed cross-examination of adverse witnesses as a means of detecting perjury (Dan 13:48–62), and provided in some instances for appeal of a verdict from a biased tribunal (Deut 17:8–13). The prophet Amos, as we have already noted, denounced the breakdown of procedural justice in the city gates and formulated a standard that was later to be recognized, if sporadically and inconsistently, in American constitutional law as a requirement under the Equal Protection clause of the Fourteenth Amendment that access to justice should not be premised on the wealth or poverty of the applicant (Amos 5:7, 10–12).

As with the texts on the monarchy and resistance to it, none of these biblical precedents dictates the outcome of cases in which access to the courts is determined under current standards of American constitutional law, or what will happen to a litigant who makes it to court in today's society. But attention to the biblical ideal of equal justice under law, which forms the inscription over the main door to the Supreme Court, would urge greater consistency than the Court has thus far provided in

Equal Protection cases dealing with access to the court. At least it would give us an additional ground for wondering why poor people should be entitled to go to court for a divorce (*Boddie v. Connecticut*, 1971) but not for a bankruptcy (*United States v. Kras*, 1973).

The ancient biblical narratives of resistance to governmental authority and ancient precedents for fairness of governmental procedures do not and should not—*pace* the fundamentalists of the New Right—directly control how America should be governed today. By the same token, however, these biblical traditions cannot be eliminated from the way that America tells her tale—*pace* the dogmatic secularists—without a significant loss of cultural identity and purpose. To refer again to the treaty traditions of the ancient Near East, a curse on those who would undo our covenant with one another. To paraphrase Shakespeare, a plague on the houses of the two contentious factions that know not how to interrelate law and religion or who are manifestly hostile to the interaction.

Conclusion: The Danger of the Naked Public Square and the Duty of Learning to Sing the Ballad of the Exiles in a Foreign Culture

Richard John Neuhaus has suggested that the cultural crisis of our society consists chiefly in the exclusion of "the popularly accessible and vibrant belief systems and worldviews of our society . . . from the public arena in which the decisions are made about how the society should be ordered" (1979:12). He cites Daniel Bell's judgment at the conclusion of *The Cultural Contradictions of Capitalism* that the answer to this crisis must include a more public role for religion. He continues:

> Specifically with regard to law, there is nothing in store but a continuing and deepening crisis of legitimacy if courts persist in systematically ruling out of order the moral traditions in which western law has developed and which bear, for the overwhelming majority of the American people, this society's sense of right and wrong. There is in store a continuing and deepening crisis unless a transcendent moral purpose is reasserted by which the state can be brought under critical judgment, unless it is made clear once again that the state is not the source but the servant of the law. With apologies to Spinoza, transcendence abhors a vacuum. Today there is such a vacuum in the public space of American law and politics. Unless it is democratically filled by the living moral traditions of the American people, it will surely be filled, as has so tragically happened elsewhere, by the pretensions of the modern state. (1979:12)

Elsewhere Neuhaus has written that "the naked public square is a dangerous place" because there is "no absolute, no transcendent prohibition against evil" (1981:22).

In a similar vein John Coleman, a sociologist at Berkeley, has called for "a renewed public role for the symbolic imagery of the Judeo-Christian ethic of fraternity [and sorority], mutuality, conscience, human dignity and responsible participation in shaping the goals and choices of society" (193). He does so in part because his reading of American history has led him to the conclusion that "the strongest American voices for a compassionate, just community always appealed in public to religious imagery and sentiments" (193). But he does so also because he is persuaded as a sociologist that:

> the American religious ethic and rhetoric contain rich, polyvalent symbolic power to command commitments of emotional depth, when compared to "secular" language, especially when the latter is governed by the Enlightenment ideals of conceptual clarity and analytic rigor. Secular Enlightenment language remains exceedingly "thin" as a symbol system. I do not think that, sociologically, a genuine sense of vivid *communitas*, in Victor Turner's sense of the term, is possible on the basis of a non-religious symbol system. Yet, it is just such a renewed commitment to an ethic of solidarity in community which over-rides individual interest which seems of paramount necessity in American culture and life today. (193)

Both Neuhaus and Coleman are aware of the difficulties associated with the use of religious language in the content of social ethics. Neuhaus suggests that religious belief should not be thought of as privileged in a pluralistic society, nor invulnerable to public challenge and critical reason. "So long as religion persists in its divisive and self-protective ways," he writes, "it will be justly dismissed from the public arena as dangerously 'sectarian'" (1979:13). Coleman acknowledges both "the perennial need for philosophy as ancillary to theological vision and reflective ethics" and the possibility that the "more powerfully evocative language of the Bible can become exclusive, divisive in public discourse and overly particularistic" (193–94). Even these tendencies, however, do not suffice to justify the exclusion of the biblical heritage from the shaping of public policy, including American constitutional law. As Coleman puts it:

> Every language is particular. Every language stands within a very particular tradition of interpretation. Every language is caught in the conflict of interpretations. To prefer a speciously "neutral" language of secular humanism to the biblical language seems to me either to be naive about the pretended neutrality and universality of the secular language or to give up on the claims of the Judaeo-Christian heritage to be illuminative of the human situation. (194)

As I mentioned at the outset, I do not view the Bible as a detailed blueprint for American society. I can now add that the Constitution itself, when

viewed within the history of ideas sketched here, can provide the mediating language needed to work out a new kind of covenant for Americans
in today's world. As I have suggested above, the Constitution can correct
religion where its insights or its adherents falter. Conversely, I have also
argued that the Bible can, as Coleman suggests, provide a much richer
symbol system, which is needed to overcome deficiencies in the Constitution such as its individualistic bias.

In the light of these convictions I would like to conclude with a few
comments on Psalm 137, which bespeaks the difficulty of singing jubilant
Israelite hymns in a foreign culture. According to this psalm, the
Hebrew music makers wept at the suggestion that they must play the
joyful songs of Zion to entertain their captors (vv. 1–4). The ancient
covenantal pattern of blessing and curse recurs in the remainder of the
psalm, which contains first a curse on the psalmist should he fail to honor
the memory of Jerusalem, the "greatest of his joys" (vv. 5–6), and then a
blessing on those who would destroy the power of imperial Babylon and
return the homesick exiles to the place associated with divine justice, the
land where Israel can sing the praises of God's law, full-throated and
without embarrassment (vv. 7–9).

This ballad of the exiles might appear strange to us for at least two
reasons. First, many religious or at least "pious" people are not accustomed to cursing in their worship services or to cursing at all, let alone
cursing themselves, but this psalm is a vigorous self-imprecation for
failure to remember one's religious heritage. Second, the irreligious may
be similarly unaccustomed to being the object of divine blessing, especially when the benediction is chanted over them for their role in restor-
ing religious values. For example, Cyrus the Persian, who liberated the
Hebrews from their Babylonian captors in 535 B.C.E., was undoubtedly
uncomfortable with the notion that he was the servant of the Lord of
Israel; yet that is how Israel remembers him (Isa 41:1–7, 25–29; 45:1–6;
48:12–16).

Strange as this psalm may sound to our ears, it contains an important
statement for our society—a society that needs to be renewed in its ability to allow people to recall their religious stories and to sing their religious songs and needs to be warned of the dangers of obliterating religious consciousness or of pronouncing this consciousness irrelevant to the
public order and off limits in matters legal and political. In short, we
need to learn to sing the ballads of exiles in a foreign land, weeping with
those who weep, laughing with those who laugh, and occasionally danc-
ing for joy, confident in our expectation that we are going home, that
one day we and our world will be free at last to bask together in the
glory of the children of God (Rom 8:21).

WORKS CONSULTED

Abbott, Walter, ed.
1964   *The Documents of Vatican II.* New York: Herder and Herder.

Antieau, Chester, Arthur Downey, and Edward Roberts
1963   *Freedom from Federal Establishment: Formation and Early History of the First Amendment Religion Clauses.* Milwaukee: Bruce.

Beard, Charles
1913   *An Economic Interpretation of the Constitution.* New York: Macmillan.

Berman, Harold J.
1974   *The Interaction of Law and Religion.* Nashville: Abingdon.
1977   "Origins of Western Legal Science." *Harvard Law Review* 90:894–943.

Berns, Walter
1976   *The First Amendment and the Future of American Democracy.* New York: Basic Books.

Bickel, Alexander M.
1970   *The Supreme Court and the Idea of Progress.* New York: Harper & Row.

Brown, Norman O.
1966   *Love's Body.* New York: Vintage.

Brown, Robert E.
1956   *Charles Beard and the Constitution: A Critical Analysis of "An Economic Interpretation of the Constitution."* Princeton: Princeton University Press.

Cassidy, Richard
1978   *Jesus, Politics, and Society: A Study of Luke's Gospel.* Maryknoll, NY: Orbis Books.

Coleman, John
1980   *An American Strategic Theology.* Paramus, NJ: Paulist Press.

Cord, Robert L.
1982   *Separation of Church and State: Historical Fact and Current Fiction.* New York: Lambeth.

Cover, Robert M.
1975   *Justice Accused: Antislavery and the Judicial Process.* New Haven: Yale University Press.

Cox, Harvey
1965   *The Secular City: Secularization and Urbanization in Theological Perspective.* New York: Macmillan.

Donahue, Charles
1980   "The Interaction of Law and Religion in the Middle Ages." *Mercer Law Review* 31:466–76.

Emerson, Thomas I.
1966   *Toward a General Theory of the First Amendment.* New York: Random House.
1970   *The System of Freedom of Expression.* New York: Random House.

Ferguson, E. James
1969   "The Nationalists of 1781–1783 and the Economic Interpretation of the Constitution." *Journal of American History* 56:241–61.

Gaffney, Edward McGlynn, Jr.
1978   "*Meek, Wolman* and the 'Fear of Imaginable but Totally Implausible Evils' in the Funding of Nonpublic Education." Pp. 75–93 in *Freedom and Education: Pierce v. Society of Sisters Reconsidered.* Edited by Donald P. Kommers and Michael J. Wahoske. Notre Dame: Center for Civil Rights.
1980   "Political Divisiveness along Religious Lines: The Entanglement of the Court in Sloppy History and Bad Public Policy." *St. Louis University Law Review* 24:205–36.

Giblet, Jacques
1961   *The God of Israel, The God of Christians: The Great Themes of Scripture.* New York: Desclee.

Howe, Mark DeWolfe
1965   *The Garden and the Wilderness: Religion and Government in American Constitutional History.* Chicago: University of Chicago Press.

Huffmon, Herbert B.
1959   "The Covenant Lawsuit and the Prophets." *JBL* 78:286–95.

Jensen, Merrill
1940   *The Articles of Confederation: An Interpretation of the Social-Constitutional History of the American Revolution, 1774–1781.* Madison: University of Wisconsin Press.
1950   *The New Nation: A History of the United States during the Confederation, 1781–1789.* New York: Knopf.
1974   *The American Revolution within America.* New York: New York University Press.

Kenyon, Cecelia M.
1955   "Men of Little Faith: The Anti-Federalists on the Nature of Representative Government." *William and Mary Quarterly* 3d Series 12:3–43.

Koch, Adrienne
1964   *The Philosophy of Thomas Jefferson.* Chicago: Quadrangle Books.

Küng, Hans
1967   *The Church.* New York: Sheed and Ward.

Lohfink, Norbert
1968   *The Christian Meaning of the Old Testament.* Milwaukee, WI: Bruce.

Louisell, David
    1976   "Does the Constitution Require a Purely Secular Society?"
                      Catholic University Law Review 26:20–34.

Lynd, Staughton
    1967   *Class Conflict, Slavery, and the United States Constitution.*
                      Indianapolis: Bobbs-Merrill.

McCarthy, Dennis J.
    1972   *Old Testament Covenant: A Survey of Current Opinions.*
                      Richmond: John Knox.

McDonald, Forrest
    1958   *We, the People: The Economic Origins of the Constitution.*
                      Chicago: University of Chicago Press.

MacIntyre, Alasdair
    1981   *After Virtue.* Notre Dame: University of Notre Dame Press.

Main, Jackson Turner
    1961   *The Anti-Federalists: Critics of the Constitution, 1781–1788.*
                      Chapel Hill: University of North Carolina Press.
    1973   *Political Parties before the Constitution.* Chapel Hill: Univer-
                      sity of North Carolina Press.

Neuhaus, Richard John
    1979   "Law and the Rightness of things." *Valparaiso University Law
                      Review* 14:1–13.
    1981   "From Sacred to Profane America—And Back Again." *Catho-
                      lic Mind* 79:10–23.

Raggi, Reena
    1977   "An Independent Right to Freedom of Association." *Harvard
                      Civil Rights–Civil Liberties Law Review* 12:1–30.

Rahner, Karl
    1971   *Theological Investigations,* vol. 7. New York: Herder and
                      Herder.

Sanders, James A.
    1972   *Torah and Canon.* Philadelphia: Fortress.

Scalia, Antonin
    1981   "On Making It Look Easy by Doing It Wrong: A Critical View
                      of the Justice Department." Pp. 178–85 in *Private Schools and
                      the Public Good.* Edited by Edward McGlynn Gaffney, Jr.
                      Notre Dame: University of Notre Dame Press.

Schlier, Heinrich
    1967   "parresia." Pp. 871–76 in *Theological Dictionary of the New
                      Testament,* vol. 5. Grand Rapids: Eerdmans.

Stringfellow, William
    1977   *Conscience and Obedience: The Politics of Romans 13 and
                      Revelation 13 in the Light of the Second Coming.* Waco, TX:
                      Word Books.

Tocqueville, Alexis de
    1945   *Democracy in America.* New York: Alfred A. Knopf.

Tribe, Laurence H.
1978   *American Constitutional Law*. Mineola, NY: Foundation Press.

Wood, Gordon S.
1969   *The Creation of the American Republic, 1776–1787*. Chapel Hill: University of North Carolina Press.

Wright, George Ernest
1962   "The Lawsuit of God: A Form-Critical Study of Deuteronomy 32." Pp. 26–67 in *Israel's Prophetic Heritage: Essays in Honor of James Muilenburg*. New York: Harper & Row.

Yoder, John Howard
1972   *The Politics of Jesus*. Grand Rapids, MI: Eerdmans.

Zimmerli, Walther
1965   *The Law and the Prophets*. Oxford: Basil Blackwell.

V

Jesus and Economics:
A Century of Reflection

Max L. Stackhouse

Some Orienting Observations

It is often considered proper to state conclusions at the end of a study. Yet many introductions offer an overview of the main lines of argument as well as a statement of the context to which the study is addressed. In these "orienting observations" I will attempt to summarize some of the results of this excursion into a body of neglected literature and to set the context for my subsequent, more detailed account of modern Christian thinking about ethics and economic systems. The literature of modern theological–ethical teachings about economic justice reveals six persistent motifs.

1. The tendencies toward a polarization of those who see Christianity as potentially compatible with revolutionary communism and those who see Christianity as realizable within the context of commercial capitalism is not new. It simply is not the case that those fascinated with the more radical forms of liberation theology, which derives primarily from Third World contexts and uses Marxist categories in its analysis of current social conditions, have created something fresh (see Dunn). To be sure, the contexts and application of both biblical motifs and of "scientific socialist" concepts are new, but the channels of thought and strategies for action—some promising, some rather obviously dead ends—have been pursued before.

Similarly, the kinds of arguments that one finds today in G. Gilder's *Wealth and Poverty*, a book that has recently become something of a handbook of the neo-conservatives in the United States, one wherein the author explicitly speaks of a "theology of capitalism," are but echoes of arguments that are also a curious mixture of the promising and the perilous.

The adage of Santayana surely stands: "Those who forget the past are doomed to repeat it." It does not appear that we are in a day of fresh religious or ethical thinking about economic matters, but in a day of the repristinization of old themes repackaged for contemporary consumption.

If there is one aspect of contemporary thought that has changed in this area, it is that much of the contemporary debate is being conducted by Catholic authors. Previous discussion, in America at least, was almost exclusively Protestant. In spite of earlier encyclicals on modern economics, this area is rather new to the wider reaches of Catholic thinking, just as present questions of bioethics seem new to many Protestants. But in both cases the channels of thought cut by one tradition are being echoed at present in a new key by the other with relatively little knowledge of the subleties previously worked out. In Catholic authors as diverse as Michael Harrington (1973) and Michael Novak (1980), we find American examples of what one can also see in the liberation theologian Gustavo Gutièrrez (1973) and the religious educator Bruno Manno (Manno and Jegen)—the "protestantization" of Catholicism on economic questions.

2. The body of literature that reflects on these matters, which displays remarkable consistency, can be dated from the 1850s, 1860s, and 1870s to the present. It begins in rather tentative early efforts, reaches considerable sophistication from the 1890s to World War II, is refined in the struggles against fascism and Stalinism on one side and the failures of capitalism which brought the depression on the other, and exists as a rather pale echo in the present.

The nineteenth century, in much theological literature, is commonly supposed to have ended with World War I, after which new chapters of intellectual and social life were entered. In terms of the basic contours of economic thought, and especially of religious and ethical reflection on it, that is simply not the case. It may well be that American participation in that war drew a rather isolationist America into world politics in a new way. It may be that both the defeat of the kaiser in Germany with the subsequent establishment of a (very frail) constitutional democracy at Weimar and the return of the Russian troops from the German front just in time to participate in dethroning the czar are landmarks in the overthrow of the last bastions of Caesarism in terms of direct *political* continuities with the ancient regimes of Europe. And it may also be the case that, in intellectual thought, the rising influence of Freud in *psychology*, of the phenomenologists and the Vienna Circle in *philosophy*, of neo-orthodoxy in *theology*, and of the theory of relativity in *physics* brought a transformation of scholarly reflection in many areas just on the heels of World War I. But comparable revolutions did *not* take place at the same time in *economic* thought, in religious and ethical reflection upon it, or in the basic orientations toward political economy. Even the social welfare provisions of the 1930s are more a reflection of the continuity than of the disruption of an emerging tradition alert to similar efforts in Laborite England and Bismark's Germany in the previous half century./1/

Whatever changes have in fact taken place in economic life, whatever moves have been made in Europe or America to strengthen or dismantle the welfare state and a mixed economy, and however they are ethically applauded or condemned, the categories for understanding these changes, both descriptively and normatively, have not been substantially altered. The "century of reflection" implied in the title of this essay thus refers to a rather elongated period that lasts at least from the 1850s to the present.

That should not surprise us. In the last half of the nineteenth century the full force of the industrial revolution expanded from England and came to grand visibility on the continent, where it had slowly developed previously. It belatedly engulfed America under the stimulus of the Civil War and penetrated (often through European colonialism) to every corner of the globe. The basic legal structures by which great corporations could be formed were already established (see Davis), and the frontier in America was already closing. Henceforth economic development would be by intensification of the technological means of extraction, production, distribution, and consumption, through the expansion of the corporation system centered in the cities rather than by the expansion of territory and the exertions of settlers who brought virgin lands under the plow. Traditional economies, and the long-standing patterning of the classes based on them, were eroded or exploded by these developments. Subsequent economic developments, until today, were dealt with by the developing social sciences, by moral reflection, and by political policy, as well as by industrial planners, on grounds first cultivated by the intellectuals of several ideological stripes who confronted these transformations before the end of the last century.

3. The primary moral response to these developments during this elongated century has been through efforts to apply "the teachings of Jesus" to economic structures. This is not to say that other ethical resources were not brought to bear on the crises experienced. On the contrary, many aspects of classical natural law theory were utilized; also, and most to the point in the context of the present book, were biblical materials from the prophets of the Old Testament. Further normative concepts were drawn from both medieval and Reformation theology. Nor can we forget the impact of the utilitarians in moral theory or the evolutionary ethical theories of progressive development from Darwinian social thought generally. Still, both particular biblical texts and frequently repeated themes from the Synoptic Gospels are, more than any other set of sources, the touchstones of the modern religious-ethical

perspective on economic life. Such accents are characteristic of Protestant ways of working on social issues. These accents have indelibly
stamped our ethos, although that fact is not widely recognized. Many
Catholic, Jewish, secular, and non-Western authors, disinterested in or
ignorant of the specific religious context in which the Amercan economic
ethos developed, are thus seldom equipped to interpret the last century
of reflection in this area or to see its import./2/

As we shall see, different authors drew on different biblical materials
and wedded the results to economic life differently. Some (e.g., Stelzle)
turned to Jesus because they advocated a Christian engagement with
economics out of a pastoral concern for those victimized by the raw
edges of the new economic systems. Others (e.g., Gladden), following the
earlier traditions of Locke, believed that what could be worked out sci-
entifically as the moral basis for political economy is best grasped by
those who have neither the leisure nor the learning for scientific reflections but who understand the sublime ethical principles of Jesus. In some
versions, the Continental rather than the Anglo-American Enlightenment
was taken as the model of interpretation. Following the lead of the
nineteenth-century neo-Kantians, authors of this stripe (e.g., Harnack
and Herrmann) took universalistic principles of "autonomous" ethics,
also seen as exemplified by Jesus, as the clue to all significant religious
knowledge. Still others see in the nineteenth- and twentieth-century
quests for the historical Jesus the recovery of the most authentic and
revolutionary message the world has ever known, relieved of the obfus-
cation by which the church and its dogmatists had long obscured it. This
accent led to a vision of the kingdom of God that entailed progress
toward a noncompetitive sharing of material resources in a cooperative
New Jerusalem for all.

It is surely not unimportant in this connection that a profoundly personal pietism had tended to dominate in the immediately preceding
period of western religious life. The predominance of Lutheran Pietism
in Germany, of evangelicalism in England, and of revivalism on the
American frontier had all pressed Protestantism toward an individualism
that had challenged previous Christian thought and needed challenging
itself in view of the new social complexities the faith was facing (Niebuhr: esp. chap. III). In any case, it was clear that those who became
engaged in moral reflection about economics knew that new, massive,
modern structures had emerged in the "Christian West" and that they
had been at least partially prompted by, especially, Protestant branches
of Christianity that had a very high estimate of the continued import of
the Bible. Whether one wanted to secure the new developments, curtail
them, or rechannel them, one had to legitimate the desired direction by

appeal to the core of the Christian tradition. Sooner or later modern economics, including political economy, had to be shown to be compatible or incompatible with Christ. It is ironic that, when continuity with these roots was lost by some ecumenical Protestants, sharp cricitism has been voiced against mainstream Protestantism from evangelical and Roman Catholic authors who have drawn from biblical materials (see, e.g., Rifkin; Byron; R. Webber).

4. The turn to biblical resources entailed two rejections and one limit that give the whole body of this American literature on economics a common stamp. First, "possessive individualism" of the sort celebrated by those following the lead of Adam Smith or by subsequent voices (such as Ludwig von Mises and F. S. Hayak) was rejected. The understanding of the human as a rational calculator of costs and benefits does not fit with a Christian anthropology. And the understanding of society in terms of automatic and progressive harmonies resulting from the efficient pursuit of private interests does not fit with a Christian interpretation of history. These perspectives failed to understand that the law of life is love, that sin deflects the rational capacities, and that egocentrism destroys social harmony. Further, these theories were used to defend varieties of corporation building that did not, empirically, sustain the individualism advocated (see Sutton et al.).

Second, atheistic and antireligious collectivism was rejected. Frequently this entailed explicit repudiation of the techniques, the ideology, and the secular social theories, as well as the violence, of the French Revolution. As the books of Rousseau had been burned by Protestants in the streets of Geneva when he advocated a "totalistic" society, so most authors rejected the visions (if not always the tools) of Compte and Marx. In the twentieth century they rejected vehemently Lenin and even more strongly Hitler. The "secular," "materialist" perspectives that these figures represent were viewed as being anti-God and destructive of a Christian respect for human persons. In each case the vision of a "natural" group (class, nation, or race) was thought to be the clue to the political-economic future of humanity. Religious writers saw this as an antipersonal collectivism, which would inevitably rethrone tyranny. Collectivism, whether defended on romantic or "scientific" grounds, was viewed as a threat to pluralism and the responsibility of the individual. This, it is said in a thousand ways, does not comport with Christian theology.

As will be seen below, all the representative Christian authors who wrote on economic ethics, whatever they drew from Adam Smith, Karl Marx, or their heirs, finally and fundamentally rejected both the prototypical models of individualistic, commercial capitalism and the collectivist political economy of communism. In most cases they rejected these for the reason that both views rest on an interpretation of *homo econo-micus* that holds that humanity is basically driven by material interest, rationally calculated. While accepting that insight as a partial truth, theologians and ethicists of the Christian community have repudiated that view on both normative and descriptive grounds, whatever power it may have still among secular academics, managers, commissars, and ordinary believers. Christians saw the power of this reality as a testimony to the reality of sin. But sin is not final.

In fact, say the religious authors, people are driven by cultural norms and values as much as by material interests, and hence the nature and character of predominant norms and values are of paramount import. They offer clues to a reality beyond the fact of sin. Drawing on biblical resources, they also drew a limitation. They argued that, while ethics—indeed explicitly religious ethics—is necessary to sound econom-ics, there are questions of a purely technical sort in economics that can-not be answered by a biblically based perspective. They were well aware of problems that had developed in the relations between theology and ethics on one hand and the natural sciences on the other in Christian history, whenever the ancient divines attempted to prescribe the con-tours of scientific work on the basis of religious and ethical doctrines alone. They were not about to repeat these same errors in the newer social sciences, particularly economics. Hence, one seldom finds detailed discussion of technical economic questions such as would be proper, say, to a university course on economic measurements. Instead, one finds most treatments of economics set in the context of a more general inter-pretation of society. The focus is on Christian principles applied to the logic of social relations, of which one aspect is economics. The purpose is to clarify the normative boundaries and general ends of economic activ-ity, with considerable space left for specific technical questions in eco-nomic thought and action.

As a consequence, one finds a rather wide spectrum of positions that have been advocated by particular authors and in church materials. These served as bases for both advocacy movements and scholarly work, carried out under the titles of Christian Socialism, Social Gospel, Reli-gion and Labor, Christianity and Economics, Christianity and Industry, Ethics of Wealth, Applied Christianity, etc. Indeed, by 1900 the body of literature under these and related headings had reached such proportions in the United States that the Library of Congress introduced the term "Christian Sociology" as a major heading to include these topics in its cataloguing system.

5. From the middle of the nineteenth century to the present, class analysis has been a common feature of Christian writing. One encounters

arguments to the effect that God has special concern for the poor and the downtrodden, and occasional arguments appear that society requires a leisure class to preserve and cultivate the arts and the sciences. But more pronounced is the resounding presumption that God favors the middle classes. (It is classes, not class; some stratification according to ability, effort, level of responsibility and value to the community is regularly presupposed.) If people are poor and suffering, something is wrong with either them or the social system that oppresses them. Something has to change so that they can become a part of the rather broadly construed middle classes. To be sure, the nineteenth- and early twentieth-century thinkers would agree with the contemporary slogan of Liberation Theology: God is on the side of the oppressed. But they held this to be so because they also presupposed that all should be included in the middle classes. Some, although not many, also believed that some who were poor were in fact poor because of moral deficiency. But even the struggle against alcoholism among working-class people soon took on the character of a crusade against the liquor merchants who exploited the poor. Prohibition was the result.

Similarly, some authors argued that, if people are so rich that they are no longer subject to the vicissitudes of life that daily affect their neighbors, if they are isolated from the needs of common humanity, and if they can utilize their wealth to distort the structures of the common life for private ends, something is wrong either with them or with the structure of the social system that allows such uncontrolled special privilege. Indeed, in some authors there is much less a critique of capitalism than a sharp moral critique of capitalists. This critical attitude worked itself out in "trust busting" and progressive income tax structures./3/

6. The original thinking in this area was done by "learned clergy," whether they were situated in ecclesiastical, seminary, or university settings—and in the latter setting whether in theology, sociology, or economics departments. The categories they constructed dominated large segments of religious training in Protestant circles and academic life generally until quite recently. Contemporary religious leadership, especially at the pastoral level, seems ignorant of this tradition and much confused about the contribution Christian thinking can make to economic life. The churches of which they are a part often pass resolutions in direct continuity with the earlier traditions, but clergy seldom pay much attention.

One can attribute this recent break with the tradition and current ignorance about it to several possible causes. For one thing, in the heat of the battles against Hitler and the cold war against Stalinism, the focus of religious thinking about public issues shifted from purely economic

questions to more political ones. As the adage puts it: It is hard to concentrate when you are up to your knees in crocodiles. At the same time,
the institutionalization at the hands of the New Deal of much that had
been advocated by the older tradition of economic reform predisposed
those who had a persistent interest in economic questions to turn to political channels to accomplish their ends. So did newer issues, including
civil rights, the Vietnam War, and equal rights for women. Thus, politics, expressed in a confidence in state policies to realize economic righteousness, began to dominate "Christian sociology."

Second, the enormous growth of the influence of psychology began
to displace some of the earlier emphasis on sociological issues in theological education. Pastoral care in the ecumenical churches and techniques
for conversion in the evangelical ones tended to become the definition of
"applied Christianity" as the state assumed wider welfare functions.

In addition, new techniques and perspectives on biblical studies
undercut the perceived reliability of turning to the New Testament for
ethical guidance in public affairs. Under the impact of the Bultmannian
revolution in historical studies of the Bible, the "mind of Christ" seemed
much more difficult to perceive than had been previously thought, the
historical Jesus much harder to know, and the relevance of the kergyma
to any social issue more difficult to state. The discontinuity between the
culture of the early church and modern culture was accented to the
degree that many wondered whether biblical materials have much continuity with present modes of thinking at all.

Further, economics in practice and economics as a social science
developed in geometric ratios of increasing complexity so that it seemed
much less amenable to social, philosophical, ethical, and religious analysis. The skyscraping towers of industry and finance began to dwarf the
steeples of the churches; and the heavily mathematical econometric
models programmed into the computers did not seem to leave much
space for the inclusion of "humanistic" variables.

Ecumenically and socially oriented ecclesiastical bodies drew on the
intellectual capital that had been built up during the first three quarters
of our elongated century to advocate an enormous agenda of action on
particular social issues, but these bodies rarely attempted to cultivate the
body of scholarship or a "public theology" that could discerningly guide
action. The rising influence of non-Protestant groups also made the
efforts less compelling. "Actionism" became a temptation of many
"praxis-oriented" advocates of "social Christianity." Simultaneously, the
fantastic growth of the secular university system disinclined scholars who
were interested in economics from turning to any "Christian sources."
Instead, economics became increasingly the "science of the American

dream," cut off from normative issues. (Indeed, when figures such as John Kenneth Galbraith want to be particularly acerb in destroying an opponent, for example, they call the opponent's view "theological.") Yet ironically "denominational sectarianism" and "confessionalism" seem to me, a noneconomist, to be more rampant among economic theorists that among religious groups.

In brief, our study of the use of biblical resources in contemporary reflection on ethics and economics will have to take place in the context of a century-long tradition, now in decline by neglect, that involves a spectrum of beliefs about the core of Christ's teachings and about various non-laissez-faire and non-collectivist understandings of economic life, usually under the code word "Christian sociology." To carry out this study, we will focus first on key figures who articulated the most common assumptions about what we can derive from Christian beliefs on economic questions in the modern world. In the next section we will survey several new international developments whereby essential definitions were refined. Finally, we will point to new voices who are resurrecting old questions and perspectives and briefly inquire what can and should be made of this tradition today.

The Early Sources

Timothy Smith's notable book, *Revivalism and Social Reform* (esp. 215ff.), shows that the roots of the American reexamination of economic ethics are in the revivals of the pre–Civil War period. The origins of "social Christianity" in its modern forms were distinctly influenced by the new burst of evangelicalism. Some branches of the older Calvinism had begun to petrify, and the newer movements claimed to be more closely related to what the early church and the Reformation had been about. Although doctrinal disputes preoccupied much revivalistic attention—specifically regarding the new threat of Unitarianism on the one hand and Arminianism on the other—the social disputes focused on the question of property. Calvinism had entered into a somewhat uncomfortable alliance with philosophical modes of thought from the English Enlightenment—particularly Locke. This alliance produced both new shapes of democratic constitutional government and an interpretation of private property that was nearly absolute. But in the ante-bellum revival movements, the absoluteness of property was challenged, particularly by the question of whether Christians could hold other people in slavery as property. From Boston to Iowa City, from 1840 on, revivals were being held that included powerful preaching against slavery and against the individualistic doctrines of property that enslaved human souls. As Smith shows, dozens of books and hundreds of articles grew out of this movement pitting "the principles of Jesus" against slavery. The authors literally dared Southern theologians to try to prove the justice of their system, as several, on biblical grounds, were inclined to do.

Since there is evidence of slavery in the Bible, a weighty question was soon brought to the forefront of the discussion: Which parts of the Bible are normative for all times, and which parts reflect the temporal outlook of a particular period of history? (The same question was also being forced in the natural sciences by the increased study of fossil evidence, but that discussion is outside our present concern.) To ask the question is to open the door to a historical interpretation of scripture. The question also invites the analysis of present historical conditions in comparison with and in contrast to the ancient ones. It opens the way for the discernment of new principles from scripture because new social conditions force new questions that previous ages may not have seen clearly. It leads to the application of newly discerned enduring principles to changing conditions in fresh ways. Indeed, it makes synthesizing biblically based ethical principles with continuously modified social analysis a perennial requirement.

If authors of this period did not quite accept Ranke's aphorism, "Every age is immediate to God," they did accept the idea that there are "epochs" in human history and that each "age" has its own vocation under God. In proto-fundamentalist circles, this led to the periodization that we now associate with the Scofield Reference Bible (and to the creationist, anti-evolutionary "catastrophism" of Louis Agassiz). Among the antislavery evangelicals, whether new Calvinist or Arminian, the "epoch" idea led to the view that the challenge of this particular age was on the social-economic front, especially vis-à-vis the new shapes of industrial life. Many believed, as Walter Rauschenbusch and several others were to articulate more fully in the next generation, that under the impact of "free church protestantism" political life had been democratized; legal institutions had established equality as a governing principle (especially with the abolition of slavery); public education had made accessible to many what had once been the privilege of a few; and patriarchal authoritarianism in family life had been abolished as a moral norm, if not as a fact. But now, under the influence of the "robber barons," a new, exploitative industrial feudalism was on the rise and threatening the gains that had been made in these other areas of life. That was the challenge of these days, of this epoch.

Once the door was open to challenge the absolute doctrine of "the natural rights of property," both secular Enlightenment theories of property, in the tradition of Locke, and decadent Calvinist theories, which saw personal wealth as a sign of special divine favor, came under increased criticism./4/

In 1851 Stephen Colwell, a trustee of Princeton Theological Seminary, wrote *New Themes for the Protestant Clergy*. Published only three years after the *Communist Manifesto* and alert to non-Marxist socialist thought in Europe, this little volume argued that "the whole socialist movement . . . [is] one of the greatest events of this age. . . . The works of socialists have exposed this hideous skeleton of selfishness—they have pursued it with unfaltering hatred; and this constitutes our main obligation to them" (Colwell: 15). Such an unveiling of the soft underbelly of American prosperity, Colwell argued, is to be met by a new application of Christian principles—stewardship, fellowship, compassion, justice, and honesty—to the economic order.

Colwell anticipated the flood of criticism that was to flow soon after the Civil War, in part because this war itself brought more and more people into the rapid industrialism it evoked. New cycles of boom and bust, new relationships of labor and management, new concentrations of wealth transformed the American dreams of yeoman farmers from crops and neighbors to factories and unions. Because we sometimes remember the frontier days of the Wild West as typical of the post–Civil War years, we forget that the cities were growing faster than the frontier. Between 1860 and 1890 the urban population quadrupled, while the rural population only doubled. In the words of Arthur Schlesinger (225), "the city took supreme command," and that meant industry, trade, commerce, corporations, and labor.

Parallel to these empirical changes, theory was also changing: the clergy increasingly rejected the presuppositions of classical, laissez-faire economics. In a highly significant study of this period, C. H. Hopkins says, "They regarded unrestricted competition as an arrogant contradiction of Christian ethics and the unhuman treatment accorded the laborer as a violation of the fundamental Protestant conceptions of the nature of man" (25). In 1866, the Reverend G. H. Boardman saw an affront both to Christian principles and to good science in Adam Smith's theory that individualism and selfishness could produce good results if only the providential laws of the market were given a free hand (98). Two years later, the Reverend John Bascom of Williams College argued that the logic of Smith's work would lead to the polarization and fixation of class divisions (686).

Scattered sermons, periodical essays, and whole journals began to wrestle with these issues. Lyman Atwater's essay of 1872, "The Labor Question and its Economic and Christian Aspects," was widely quoted for years. He argued for profit sharing and claimed that the industrialist "is bound by every Christian and moral obligation to give the laborer a fair and righteous share of the rewards of production" (491–92). And, as Hopkins points out (36), Joseph Cook of Boston, Richard Newton of New York, and dozens of less-known writers were arguing the same themes in the *Methodist Quarterly Review*, the *Baptist Standard*, and the *Sunday Afternoon*.

Specific academic developments were to have their influence also. Henry C. Carey wrote the first scholarly American treatise on sociology, with a pronounced emphasis on economic matters, between 1858 and 1860, entitled *The Principles of Social Science* (3 vols.). William Graham Sumner introduced the first course in sociology in America at Yale in 1876, and Lester F. Ward, a disciple of Comte, wrote the first textbook in this area within five years. Teaching expanded until Albion Small, trained as a theologian, instituted the first department of sociology at Chicago, in 1893.

These American efforts were fed by European writings. In 1866 Sir John Robert Seeley published *Ecce Homo*, a work widely read and reviewed in America. He argued that the true meaning of Jesus was to be found in his purpose for the church, and the purpose of the church was the improvement of social morality. John Ruskin's *Unto This Last* (1866) had an even more pronounced influence. His work is filled with invective against the modern economic system, and he prescribes a return to the golden age of agrarian harmony with nature. This work was quoted for nearly half a century and had an impact on subsequent thinkers from Mahatma Gandhi to E. F. Schumacher, the author of the much-discussed *Small Is Beautiful* (1973). In his account of the development of these socioeconomic themes in American Christian thought, however, Francis Greenwood Peabody, the first professor of Christian Social Ethics in this land, points out that "by a strange perversion . . . [the] prophetic denunciations have outlived [the] positive teachings . . ." (71). Similar treatment would soon be accorded Maurice and Kingsley, as these two celebrated Christian Fabians would rise as major leaders on the British scene.

German radical Christians were also widely quoted. From the 1848 revolution on, a series of voices attempted to apply the "principles of Jesus" to economic matters. Rudolf Todt, Pastor Stoecker, and later Goere Nathusius, Kuetter, and the Swiss-German Ragaz became deeply involved in seeking the bases for a Christian interpretation of the economic issues of the day, often with specific reference to Marxist thought as it was growing among the laboring classes of Europe. Their efforts eventuated in the formation, by 1889, of the Evangelical Social Congress, which was to sponsor yearly international conferences on Christianity and social issues. They drew into that circle leading figures from France and Italy who also shared comparable concerns (Peabody: chaps. I, II). It was in some ways the Christian effort to form a Christian, democratic, "non-Marxist Internationale," committed to social change and economic justice.

What all these diverse voices proclaimed is this: "We have come to the end of a great era of mere individualism in religion, in politics, in economics. . . . Adam Smith and Jean-Jacques Rousseau were the prophets of that age" (Dombrowski: 17). That age is now over! But they did not believe that Marx provided the clue to the new age. Instead, a new Christian ethic was needed.

Near the end of the nineteenth century, the number of major figures who were pursuing analogous courses in America was large. Washington Gladden, nationally famous pastor and president of the Missionary Society; Richard T. Ely, who founded the American Economic Association; W. D. P. Bliss, who edited the famous *Encyclopedia of Social Reform*: and literally scores of other figures were able to publish hundreds of books on "Christian Sociology" in which the primary focus was on the transformation of the economy on the basis of the "principles of Jesus."

While the newer social sciences provided the analysis of the empirical situation, a distinctive understanding of the teachings and principles of Jesus provided the normative orientation. The focus is Jesus Christ, understood as the one living in continuity with the Law and the prophets. He is viewed also as the crucified and resurrected Lord who is the source of the historically imminent power of the kingdom of God, the clue to hope and change. Jesus is the initiator of a new era of social relations, which in every age challenges the principalities and powers that tend to rule every society.

The starting point for their understanding of Jesus, it should be said clearly, was in neither biblical scholarship nor theology as a systematic science of faith. Rather, their starting point was the crisis of the age, the experienced disjunctions of life. To sort out and guide the people of God in this crisis, these writers quite naturally turned to biblical ethics. In so doing they echoed a tendency in Protestantism since the days of Wyclif, Hus, Calvin, and the left wing of the Reformation. They were, each and every one, alert to the new modes of biblical scholarship being worked out by E. Renan, J. Weiss, and the new modes of historical criticism. They also knew the work being done in church history by Harnack and in systematics by Ritschl. But such authors as these were appropriated primarily as they helped to provide resources for the articulation and application of ethical principles to the life situation in which the American "Christian sociologists" found themselves.

By the beginning of the twentieth century, much that had been developed in more scattered efforts could be stated in less ad hoc fashion. Indeed, a certain conventional spectrum of opinion was worked out within which most of the writers for the next thirty years could be placed. To illustrate both the major accents in this area and the poles of the spectrum, I take two books that summarize the work of the preceding several decades: Shailer Mathews's *The Social Teaching of Jesus* (1897) and Walter Rauschenbusch's *Christianity and The Social Crisis* (1907). The former is more "personalistically" focused, the second more "socioeconomically" focused.

Biblical Themes in Shailer Mathews's Dispositional Fraternalism

Mathews begins with an analysis of "Christian sociology." What is intended by the term and what not? He is quite clear that there is no "Christian method of sociological investigation" (1897:1). "The process of investigating social forces and results . . . can no more have an ethical— still less religious—character than the study of a crystal . . ." (1897:1–2). But whenever a scientific investigator attempts to formulate the results of investigation, to speak of the significance of what is found, ethics and religiously conditioned orientations are inevitable. Thus, in the same sense that we can speak of Aristotelian science or Baconian science, since they went beyond mere observation and generalized about the significance of what they found, so we can speak of "Christian sociology." The particular bits of information are arranged in a particular way to offer a more holistic interpretation of what is at stake in the information.

It is manifestly clear, Mathews argued, that Jesus gave no systematized social teachings, any more than he gave a systematic theology (1897:3–4). Further, much of what we have understood about the New Testament since the Reformation has been individualistically and spiritually centered. The salvation of individual souls "and not a new society has been the objective point of most preaching" (Mathews, 1897:5). No less serious problems attached to the "sociology" side of the term Christian sociology. That discipline is plagued by "the impatient and over-zealous publication of certain doctrines," which are based "largely on hasty thinking and hopes" (1897:6).

Nevertheless, as a skilled geologist, working from the perspective of the general principles of geology, can infer certain deep structures of the earth by careful examination of certain outcroppings, so Christian sociology can interpret social outcroppings from the perspective of the general principles of humanity as a form of socially related moral and spiritual being. The latter, Mathews asserts, has been taught more acutely by

Jesus Christ than even by Plato, Thomas, Kant, or Hegel and, indeed, has had more impact on the world (1897:9). To ignore that is simply intellectual dishonesty.

But "Christian sociology," as Mathews sees it, corrects previous errors. Christian anthropology is the clue to sociology, and the Christian understanding of human nature is first of all person-centered. An undeniable regard for the concrete person stands at the center of Christian teaching. Two features attend *this* "individualism." First, the whole gospel presumes that to be human is to be "essentially body *and* soul, flesh *and* spirit. . . . Jesus does not regard the body as necessarily evil" (1897:23, with references to Matt 10:28; Mark 10:8 and 12:25; and John 6:51–53). Second, this "physio-psychological being" is capable of merging "its life with that of similar beings—that is its capacity for social life. . . . [Yet] sociability does not mean the extinction of individuality. . . . There are attracting and correlating powers of the personality that reach out to others and form . . . a new substance that is essentially a unity derived through union. To disregard the promptings and needs of this social part of the personality is to invite an intellectual and moral death whose earliest symptoms are sin and abnormality of all sorts" (1897:27–28).

To secure this view of "Christian personhood in a unity of fellowship" as the basis for Christian social teachings, Mathews explores (1897:30ff.) the biblical images of the vine and branches, the mansion and rooms, the companionship of being yoke-fellows (John 15:1–2; John 17:23; and Matt 11:27–30). Indeed, to call Jesus Son of God and Son of Man and to claim that he is our brother is to establish a fraternal baseline for all our thinking. So great and essential was this relational understanding of human nature that dominated the New Testament, that "the whole significance of Jesus as a mere ethical teacher is overtopped by it." Jesus was viewed as "the incarnate God—the perfect realization of this capacity for union" (1897:31).

On this basis, it is possible for the ethics of society to be understood in a deeper sense. It had to do with actualizing the union as far as possible within the limits of history, a union that preserves and enhances and does not negate the particular person, just as membership in a healthy, closely knit family does not inhibit but cultivates each member while recognizing the sometimes sharp differences in ability, need, authority, and capacity to contribute to the whole. The vision of this "fraternal" union, to which Mathews gives distinctly ethical articulation in the terms kingdom of God and righteousness of God by carefully examining all the New Testament references to such terms, provides the model of the "ideal society." It is the basis for the quest for a new social order. The new social order, as a spiritual fellowship among humans and between

God and humans, that expresses itself "in social relations may at once be established potentially in the midst of that other social order, which is based upon a disregard of the normal religious and social capacities of men, and which becomes of necessity self-destructive and in tendency anarchistic" (1897:77).

In this effort, Mathews is concerned that there are two common misuses and misunderstandings of such terms as the kingdom of God. One is the "apocalyptic-eschatological" view in which a catastrophic end of the world is expected and only the few elect are rapturously and immediately to be taken into heaven. Mathews acknowledges that there are moments of urgency in the New Testament, but he does not find in his reading the foreboding attitude to the future that this view demands. Instead, he points to those passages about the kingdom where it is seen as already among the people (Luke 17; 20f.); where the analogy is drawn to the growth of the seed in the field (Matt 13:24–43); where some have to struggle mightily in order to gain entrance (Matt 11:12–15); and where the kingdom has different results among different people (Mark 4:3–4), as balanced against a lopsided apocalyptic view. Neither is the kingdom to be understood as a violent revolution toward a monolithic political-economic order. Political enthusiasts of all ages have so misunderstood the image, he points out (1897:44). Instead, Jesus "refuses the tempting suggestion to become a new Caesar (Matt 4:8–10); later his disciples are warned against the leaven of Herod—that is, of an overweening political ambition (Mark 8:15); he flees from those who would force him into politics (John 6:15) . . ." (1897:45). Instead, the kingdom has to do with the moral vision of a loving, sharing, familial social order initiated by God and to be carried out in a life of freedom, by choice and moral commitment by all who would become a brother or a sister of Christ.

On this basis, Mathews offers an interpretation of the decisive arenas in which Christians are to live out their divine mandate and make concrete the vision given to them (1897:16ff., 90–91). The monogamous family is, to him, the obvious starting point. It is to be based on the unitive sharing and equality of the sexes, although it can take several particular shapes in concrete lives. In Mathews's view, scripture does not offer blueprints for society or prescribe particular decisions but defines basic boundaries within which humans must practically work out the implication of governing principles. Similarly, in politics Jesus cannot be called a socialist, a monarchist, or a democrat in the modern senses with clarity. All we can surmise is that the community of faith is not to become identical with the coercive structures of government and that both anarchy and tyranny are wrong (1897:107ff.). All political systems are to be evaluated by their capacities to avoid these perils and to sustain all persons in community.

Mathews treats the decisive third area, economics, in a comparable way. He recognizes that in many aspects the New Testament can be easily misunderstood. Jesus is portrayed as speaking out harshly against the wealthy. In sayings such as that of the camel and the needle's eye (Matt 18:24), in parables such as that of the beggar Lazarus (Luke 16–19f.), and in responses to questions such as that of the rich young ruler (Luke 12:33), "it would seem as if the renunciaion of wealth was one of the conditions of joining the new society" (1897:137).

> It would not be at all strange, therefore, if from these teachings and facts men should have concluded that the pursuit of wealth was unchristian and wealth itself an evil rather than a good. And so men have thought at all times since the days of Jesus. The preaching of the church against wealth has been equalled only by its zeal to obtain it. . . . [Nevertheless,] through the centuries in which the leaven of Jesus has been working in society, wealth has enormously increased . . . ; the poor have always been present, and the Christian church has always endeavored, with more or less wisdom, to do them good. They are God's poor. (1897:138–39)

A more balanced reading of the scriptures, in Mathews's view, however, reveals that what Jesus' critique of wealth is fundamentally about is "his recognition of the relativity of goods" (1897:143). More important than material wealth is the making of our lives a part of other lives. Thus, the question is not wealth itself but whether or not it is used for the establishment of genuine personhood and loving relationships. This, he argues (1897:144), is "the only possible interpretation which can be placed on that otherwise extraordinary parable of the unjust steward" (Luke 16:1ff.). The questions Jesus poses to us are not "Are you wealthy?" or "Are you poor?" The questions are "What shall it profit a man if he gain the whole world and yet lose himself?" (Luke 9:25) and "Have you done the will of my father?" (1897:156). The point is that we cannot serve two masters. The struggle for fortune more often than not breaks down that sense of dependence that binds person to person and all to God.

> In the same proportion as the semblance of independence increases is there danger that a man will forget that he is always an integral part of society and that he can be truly a man only as he is dependent upon God and in sympathy with his fellows. . . . This is the secret of Jesus' command to trust the Heavenly Father for clothes and food (Matt 6:31f.). These things are not evil, but if once regarded as the highest good, they will inevitably lead to a selfish competition for personal advantage at the cost of generous impulses and faith. (1897:146)

All this, Mathews says, brings Jesus close to the moral impulses that lie behind much modern talk of socialism.

> If wealth is not for purely individual enjoyment, but is to be used for
> the good of society . . . , it is not a long step to the belief that any
> form of private property is anti-fraternal and that society itself can
> best administer economic matters for the good of its members. Some-
> thing like corroboration is given such an interpretation of Jesus' posi-
> tion by the fact that the company of his followers had a common
> purse (John 12:19; 13:6), and that the members of the primitive Jeru-
> salem church "had all things in common" (Acts 2:44f.; 4:32–37).
> (1897:151)

But Mathews does not think that, in the final analysis, the case can be
made that Jesus was a socialist. "It is futile to attempt to discover modern socialism in the words of Jesus. There is, it is true, nothing incompatible with such a system were it once proved to be the means best
adapted to furthering the true spirit of brotherliness . . ." (1898:151). But
the same could be said for other systems.

Further, those who argue that Jesus identified completely with the
poor, those who call for the abolition of private property or press every
social policy toward material equality, simply have not read the gospel
carefully. It is true that no man ever "had a deeper sympathy with the poor
and unfortunate" and that Jesus "felt profoundly the misery and injustice
which spring from the irresponsible power of the wealthy. . . ." But "it is a
mistake to think of early Christians as altogether from the poorest classes.
They were from the well-to-do and even from the wealthy classes as
well. . . . If Jesus were homeless, the houses of the rich were continually at
his service. If his head was sometimes wet with the dews of heaven, he
knew also what it was to have poured on him costly ointment. The rich
man Zacchaeus was welcomed quite as heartily by him as his fellow citizen
the beggar, Bartimaeus" (1897:147). "When his friends saw fit to criticize a
woman who had anointed him, on the ground that the cost of the ointment
might much better have been given to the poor, Jesus rebukes them"
(1897:154). Nor can the story of Ananias and Sapphira properly be taken as
a socialism that entails social ownership of the means of production. Their
fate is sealed not by their failure to share all their property, for others in
good standing in the community clearly did not do so. The problem was
"their lying to the effect that they had so done" (1897:153). Indeed, in his
Gospel Matthew uses some of his sharpest words for those who pretend to
identify with the poor by asceticism or rhetoric to gain spiritual and moral
status but carefully and dishonestly reserve secure deposits of wealth for
their own future. This is a quite different matter, in Mathews's view, from
a call for absolute equality. It simply cannot be argued on biblical grounds
that Jesus demands equality in material things. "There are men to whom
one talent could be entrusted, and those to whom five and ten (Matt 25:4–
30; Luke 19:12–27)" (1897:177).

In summarizing his views, Mathews argues (1897:156–57) that the key point is this ethical principle that all wealth is to be fraternally gained and used. It is, in this sense, "a public trust—a principle that is made no less true from the fact that its application to various problems of any age must be left to the age itself." Jesus neither "forbids trusts nor advises them; . . . he neither forbids trade unions, strikes and lock-outs, nor advises them; he was neither socialist nor individualist . . . ; [he was] friend neither of the working man nor the rich man as such. He was the Son of Man, not the son of a class of men." Nevertheless, his denunciation is unsparing of those who become wealthy "at the expense of souls; who find in capital no incentive to further fraternity; who endeavor so to use wealth as to make themselves independent of social obligations and to grow fat with that which should be shared with society." The conditions of the motivations and dispositions, the quality of will and social affection, are the core of Jesus' message, in Mathews's view.

Shailer Mathews's mild fraternalism represents one persistent wing of Christian teaching about economics and its sociopolitical implications that has been present in social thought for some 130 years. It is less anti-capitalism than it is anti-greed. It is social in the sense that persons, the dignity and value of whom Jesus taught, require one another to be whole. It is economic in the sense that the biblical view of incarnation requires attention to material as well as spiritual means of sustenance. And it is thoroughly political, in the sense that it points toward a way of approaching life in community. The gospel thus seeks to extend the spirit of love, understood in familial, fraternal, relational terms, into the ethos of the times.

Walter Rauschenbusch's Prophetic Socialism

If Shailer Mathews's perspective on Jesus and economics may be called dispositional and familial, Walter Rauschenbusch's may be called radical and prophetic. Such a distinction may be made in spite of the facts that each regularly quotes the other and that it is possible to read pages from either without being sure which one wrote those pages. But while Rauschenbush has many accents that are found also in Mathews, he has another side, which I will stress here. The difference arises not only because Rauschenbusch summarized and echoed the more radical voices of the previous half century but also because he explicitly connected his view of Jesus and economic justice with the message of the prophets of the Old Testament. Thus, his use of the Bible differs from that of Mathews. "A comprehension of the essential purpose and spirit of the prophets," wrote Rauschenbusch, "is necessary for a comprehension of the purpose and spirit of Jesus and of genuine Christianity. In Jesus and the primitive Church, the prophetic spirit rose from the dead. . . . The real meaning of his life and the real direction of his purposes can be understood only in that historical connection" (1907:3).

All "natural" religions tend to worship "powers" and tend to get "in tune" with them by ritualistic actions. The preferred powers may be the powers of nature, the powers of fertility and sexual potency, or the powers that govern peoples by force or wealth. But the prophets from Moses to Amos, Hosea, Isaiah, Jeremiah, and Micah are all heralds of the fundamental truth "that religion and ethics are inseparable, and that ethical conduct is the supreme and sufficient act" (Rauschenbusch, 1907:7). The prophets do not worship powers or cultivate cultic precision, but they bring the plumb line of godly justice to measure them. Further, they seldom focus on the private morality of personal life, or even on the family: the "twin-evil against which the prophets launched the condemnation of Jehova was injustice and oppression" (1907:8). This too, argues Rauschenbusch (1907:64), is the central message of John the Baptist, the figure in the New Testament whereby the explicit link is made between the ancient prophetic tradition and Jesus. Indeed, "the Christian movement began with John the Baptist. All the Evangelists so understood it (Mark 1; Matt 3; Luke 3; John 1)." "In joining hands with John, Jesus clasped hands with the entire succession of the prophets with whom he classed John. . . . [Thus, Jesus] was not merely an initiator, but a consummator. . . . He embodied the prophetic stream of faith and hope" (1907:53–54). But whereas the prophets had spoken of and to the righteousness of Israel, Jesus did away with the nationalistic features of the prophetic tradition. His message extended the core of the prophetic message further than the prophets could have imagined. Indeed it became "universal in scope, an affair of all humanity," "revolutionary" in intent (1907:62, 85ff.).

It would be a serious mistake, argues Rauschenbusch frequently, to understand Jesus *simply* as a revolutionary reformer or a moral teacher or heir of the prophets. He was, as all the church has confessed, the Son of God, the crucified and resurrected Lord, the savior of souls, the Christ, the inaugurator of a new humanity. But it is precisely as these that he made the visions of the prophets concrete and bore within him the germs of a new social and political order, which the devotees of Christ have regularly and repeatedly attempted to avoid.

There are several reasons for this neglect, some quite understandable, some less so. "The early Christians did not belong to the literary class with whom the impluse to record its doings on paper is more or less instinctive." Hence, our records are incomplete. Moreover, given the Roman suspicion of any issues that appeared to be social or political, there was good cause for "not publishing them freely" (1907:95). Paul expected "an immediate spiritualization of the entire Cosmos," and his influence came to dominate those branches of the church that emerged triumphant in the Mediterranean basin (1907:104). In addition, the apocalyptic hope for the immediate return of Christ led some away from interest in "worldly" matters. Yet even in these records are elements that, properly seen, have direct implications for our understanding of Christian attitudes on socioeconomic questions. The eschatological apocalypticism that we see at several points in the New Testament, for instance, clearly implies "an overthrow of the present world powers" and the constant seeking for new possibilities by the discernment of the signs of the times (1907:110ff.).

At the same time, subsequent Christians have not seen the revolutionary aspects of the gospel that are present in the New Testament because they were often so allied by class background, inclination, and training that they could focus only on the spiritual, the individualistic, and otherworldly features of the New Testament witness. Even otherwise highly respected contemporary scholars, judged Rauschenbusch (1907:46), are subject to this charge. Supported by personal or official alliances between ecclesiasticism and privilege and cut off from the masses, Christians through history have repeatedly turned to speculative reflection, ascetical disengagement, personalistic pietism, or ritualistic ceremonialism—the means by which the social-ethical dimensions of Jesus' teaching have been successfully overlooked (1907:143ff.). Even if "upper class philosophers might permit themselves very noble and liberal sentiments . . . , there was no connection between them and the masses, and their sentiments ended in perfumed smoke" (1907:152).

Nevertheless, a "volatile spirit has always gone out from organized Christianity . . . , [rousing the faithful] to love freedom and justice in their fellowmen" (1907:150). It is endemic to the spirit of Christ, even where it is not fully conscious or partially repressed.

> Has it not lifted woman to equality and companionship with man, secured the sanctity and stability of marriage, changed parental despotism to parental service and eliminated unnatural vice, the abandonment of children, blood revenge, and the robbery of the shipwrecked from the (formerly approved) customs of nations? Has it not abolished slavery, mitigated war, covered all lands with a network of charities to uplift the poor and the fallen, fostered the institutions of education, aided the progress of civil liberty and social justice, and diffused a softening tenderness throughout human life? (1907:147)

Insofar as these have become features of western civilization under the influence of Christianity, it must be acknowledged that the positive effects of the church in its social witness have been less due to the conscious intents of the organized church or its ecclesiastically preoccupied official thinkers than due to its indirect and diffuse influences (1907:150). There is something in the message and spirit of Jesus that cannot be entirely subverted. And at the present, when the possibilities are at hand for Christians to speak out and to organize, when the earlier privileged alliances of magistrates and clergy have been broken, when modern biblical studies bring us into closer contact with the person and context of Jesus, and when contemporary social sciences open new doors to the analysis of society and its institutions, we have the possibility of making the indirect and diffuse influences of the New Testament direct and intentional. That is the task of Christian sociology and the church generally today, argued Rauschenbusch (1907:208ff.).

When we do turn to the application of the teachings of Jesus to contemporary social life in a direct way, we cannot avoid seeing fundamental discrepancies. The governing social aim of Jesus was "the kingdom of God." Rauschenbusch pointed out, as did Mathews, that this concept has been subject to numerous interpretations and misinterpretations. It clearly is not dependent on human force or divine catastrophe, but "after all this has been said, it still remained a social hope. . . . It is still a collective conception" (1907:65). It is a vision particularly marked by a transformed attitude toward economics.

Jesus taught, "Ye cannot serve God and Mammon." In making this statement, he was not merely pointing out a danger to the soul: "in his desire to create a true human society he encountered riches as a prime divisive force in actual life" (1907:75). When Jesus confronted the rich young man and bade him get rid of his wealth, the advice was partly for the good of the young man's soul. "But Jesus immediately rises from this concrete case to the general assertion that it is hard for any rich man to enter the Kingdom of God" (1907:75). It does no good to try to make the case that the real problem was that the young man *trusted* too much in wealth for his own spiritual good. That interpretation is neither warranted by the best Greek textual evidence we have nor by a thorough reading of the whole corpus of Jesus' saying about wealth. "It gives a touch of cheerful enjoyment to exegetical studies to watch the athletic exercises of interpreters when they confront these sayings of Jesus about wealth. . . . There is a manifest solicitude to help the rich man through [the needle's eye]." In spite of the some thirty-six interpretations of such sort, as Rauschenbusch notes (1907:77–78), the clear meaning cannot quite be obscured: "It is hard to get riches with justice, to keep them with equality, and to spend them with love." The social, and not merely the individual, meanings cannot be avoided.

The parable of the steward (Luke 16) presents a similar case, in which a passage has "often been so allegorized that the application to the rich has almost evaporated" (1907:80)./5/ But when the Pharisees of all ages scoff at such teachings, they must confront the story of Dives and Lazarus, by which Jesus replies to such scoffing. The story is not intended to give information about the future life; it is about the treatment of the brothers of Dives. It has to do with the "gulf that separates the social classes" (1907:84).

As a corollary to his views about the wealthy, the prophetic Christ of Rauschenbusch is portrayed as the explicit ally of poor and working people. Jesus was a man of the common people, and he never deserted their cause as so many others have done.

> He had worked as a carpenter for years, and there was nothing in his thinking to neutralize the sense of class solidarity which grows up under such circumstances. The common people heard him gladly because he said what was in their hearts. His triumphal entry into Jerusalem was a poor man's procession; the coats from their backs were his tapestry. . . . During the last days in Jerusalem he was constantly walking into the lion's cage. . . . It was the fear of the people which protected him while he bearded the powers that be. His midnight arrest, his hasty trial, the anxious efforts to work on the feelings of the crowd against him, were all a tribute to his standing with the common people. (1907:84)

Clearly, the intention of Jesus—indeed, the intention for Jesus recognized by Mary before Jesus himself was teaching—was that through him God would "put down the proud and exalt them of low degree . . . , fill the hungry with good things and send the rich empty away" (Luke 1:52–53). "The first would be last and the last would be first" (Mark 10:31). The poor and the hungry and sad were to be satisfied and comforted; the meek who had been shouldered aside by the ruthless would get their chance to inherit the earth, and conflict and persecution would be inevitable in the process (Matt 5:1–12).

In Rauschenbusch's treatment of Jesus in these and other passages we can see aspects of Christian sociology that were not present in any striking degree in the thought of Mathews. Rauschenbusch saw class analysis as a useful tool in biblical exegesis, and he was more directly and explicitly convinced that Jesus had rather distinct guidelines for social arrangements—and not only a concern for persons—plus a command to love. For Rauschenbusch, the positive guideline was toward democratization of the economic order. This was already a theme in *Christianity and the Social Crisis* and in *Christianizing the Social Order*. Rauschenbusch spelled out his social theory on these lines more explicitly. Through its earlier, indirect work, argued Rauschenbusch

(1912, esp. parts III, IV, and V), the spirit of Christ has gradually and painfully brought about the relative socialization of the church, the family, the school, the political order. In each of these arenas of life, people give according to ability and take according to need. Equality and mutual solidarity are governing principles. Things are held in common and disposed of by democratic means. For these gains we are indebted to those who grasp and fought for the prophetic Jesus in earlier ages. However, he argues, all these are now under threat of distortion or destruction by the new autocracies of the capitalist corporations aided and abetted by the "bloody law of tooth and claw" celebrated by social Darwinism and competitive economic theory. Indeed, the new autocrats attempt to crush the labor movements, which are a modern corollary of the early church. The present distribution of wealth, income, influence, and power, together with the governing principles, values, and goals of the economic order, are direct affronts to all that Christ lived, taught, and died for. Jesus was, without question, for the democratization of the economic order.

Rauschenbusch was more willing to plunge into the actual analysis of existing social conditions than Mathews. He held that Jesus was quite alert to the actual political and economic dynamics of his day, and that Christians, in their preaching and teaching as heirs of Jesus, ought to be so also. The entire middle section of *Christianity and the Social Crisis* and most of *Christianizing the Social Order* analyzed in a detailed, if sometimes journalistic, way the rise of the labor unions and the resistance to them, taxation policies, income distribution, the ecological consequences of industrial pollution, urban land use, corruption, police practices, the status of women and minorities, and the exploitation of the poor by gambling and drug (primarily alcohol) interests. Further, Rauschenbusch traced the negative influence of these on the four "socialized," "democratized," "partially redeemed," indeed, "communistic" institutions—the church, the home, the school, and the state.

To avoid misunderstanding, it is necessary to make clear what he means by "communistic." He means by the "communism of the state" the collective institutions

> by which the people administer their common property and attend to their common interests. It is safe to say that at least a fourth of the land in the modern city is owned by the city and communistically used for free streets and free parks. Our modern State is the outcome of a long development toward communism. Warfare and military defense were formerly the private affair of the nobles; they are now the business of the entire nation. Roads and bridges used to be owned largely by private persons or corporations, and toll charged for their use; they are now communistic with rare exceptions. Putting out fires

> used to be left to private enterprise; today our fire departments are
> communistic. Schools used to be private; they are now public. . . .
> The right of jurisdiction was formerly often an appurtenance of the
> great landowners; it is now controlled by the people. The public
> spirit and foresight of one of the greatest of all Americans, Benjamin
> Franklin, early made the postal service of our country a communistic
> institution of ever increasing magnitude. . . . In no case in which
> communistic ownership has firmly established itself is there any
> desire to recede from it. . . . The water-works in most of our cities
> are owned and operated by the community, and there is never more
> than local and temporary dissatisfaction. . . . On the other hand, the
> clamor of public complaint about the gas, the electric power and
> light, the railway service, which are commonly supplied by private
> companies, is incessant and increasing. (1912:391-92)

Such gains, he held, are proper outgrowths of the spirit of Christ in
our social history. In brief, Rauschenbusch believed that the drive
toward social solidarity implied by Jesus' doctrine of the kingdom of
God comports well with modern tendencies to establish democratically
controlled, communitarian, "socialist" power over those industrial realities that are decisive for the welfare of the common people.

The Spectrum Institutionalized

Mathews and Rauschenbusch present foci representing a certain
range of views that had been under discussion for half a dozen decades
before they wrote. Other notable figures, such as Washington Gladden
and Francis Greenwood Peabody, both closer to Mathews's personalism,
and W. D. P. Bliss and George D. Herron, both closer to Rauschenbusch's socialism, occupied distinguished places in the spectrum. These
figures saw one another as allies, not as enemies, in spite of numerous
disagreements on exegetical and social-analytical grounds. What united
them was, on the one side, a fundamental confidence that trust in Jesus
and his teachings would reveal the clue to economic ethics and, on the
other side, the common perception that commercial greed and the modern "science" of utilitarian economics did not, and constitutionally could
not, grasp either the actual character of human nature or the ethical
principles necessary for the humane reconstruction of the economic
order in American life. These authors drew from both capitalist and
socialist economic theorists, but always selectively. Their efforts to establish on a biblical basis a "Christian sociology" that was really a fundamentally reordered political-economic system thus clarified the basic
boundaries within which the Christian discussion of economic ethics had
been and subsequently would be carried on. They all believed that God
intended and Jesus taught that people are to be, economically, "persons
in community." Some authors put the focus on personhood, others on

communitarianism; none entirely obscured the other point of reference.

One could draw an analogy between this discussion and early church debates about how it is that Jesus Christ is "fully God" and "fully human." The main point of the doctrine seems to be that something essential about the nature of the savior is lost if he is viewed only as one or the other or if one aspect becomes merely an addendum to the other. Nor can some third reality be posited that is neither divine nor human, or that makes him distinct from either humanity or God.

One could similarly formulate the logic of "Christian sociology." Something essential about the nature of economic life, upon which the concrete existence of millions depends, is lost if only private interest *or* only collective structure is regarded. Neither one can be seen as merely the implication of the other. And it is nonsense to posit some third way that has no place for either personalism or communitarianism. The figures mentioned above, in conversation with the best social theories available to them, as the early church fathers were in conversation with the best forms of Greek and Roman philosophy available to them, and equally fully committed to the biblical witness as the source and the norm for their efforts, articulated a doctrine of "person in community" that attempted to establish decisive boundaries for modern Christian thinking about economic life. These boundaries did not describe how to conduct every strategy or how to make every decision within the boundaries. Disagreement within the spectrum is likely to continue. Yet these writers indicate where and when Christians are likely to fall outside the permitted spectrum by lurching too far in one direction or another. If private interest and individualistic economic calculation are accented rather than social harmony, economic chaos results. If the accent is on collective action and class or national solidarity without remainder, the inevitable result is economic czarism. In either case, "the wages of sin is death."

At the time this doctrine was being developed, two parallel movements within the churches and one in academic life were also under way. All three were to play a distinctive role in the institutionalization of this doctrine. One of these was the Sunday school movement; the second was the missions movement. Both were indigenously American but had analogues in Europe. The third development, the academic one, originated in European thought and had its earliest development there before being taken up by American religious thinkers. This was the redefinition in sociology begun by Max Weber and carried further by Ernst Troeltsch and R. H. Tawney. It involved new directions in social science beyond the traditions of Smith or the theories or Marx, and its effect was to change the social-scientific baseline upon which Christian sociology depended. We will examine these three movements in order.

1. *The Sunday school movement.* Those who developed the doctrines of Christian sociology were deeply engaged in the life of the churches. Many were pastors, more were seminary professors, and all were committed to the propagation of the doctrines among the laity. Most preached in local churches and wrote for Christian education journals. Very quickly they seized upon the opportunity to use their influence in the Sunday school programs, which had grown up for both youth and adults during the nineteenth century, to propagate their new doctrine. They wanted to get their message to the people, and they were less inclined to speak directly to the public authorities than to trust a convinced laity who would, through Christian citizenship, bring about the desired transformations of economic life. "Not by power, nor by might, but by every word that proceeds out of the mouth of the Lord" (Zech 4:6).

The Sunday School Times had already asked Charles Stelzle to write a series of articles on economic issues by 1900. The new economic doctrine was taken as the main subject matter of a nationwide program of adult literature for the next decade. The various denominations utilized this material in somewhat different fashions, but the content and format are remarkably similar throughout the literature. Series No. 1 of the 1910 program, for instance (edited by Josiah Strong), correlated the biblical texts chosen for nationwide study in adult Sunday school classes with commentaries on the socioeconomic conditions of modern life, and it suggested strategies for lay people to actualize Christ's way in their own world of work and political economy. (This material was also used in study groups of the YMCA and as weekly devotional meditations in more than five hundred social service agencies.) The topics discussed, seriatim, read like a somewhat quaint version of what became known later as the New Deal and the agenda of ecumenical Protestant pronouncment from 1908 to today.

The series began with an analysis of the "Scripture Basis" for "The Ethics of Work." With multiple references to biblical texts, God was represented as a creative worker. Humans are required to work; Christ is a worker, the apostles and St. Paul also; work is enjoined for all Christians. This means that when some are too rich to have to work, when others are too lazy to work, and when some are willing to work but are thrown into unemployment, the principles of the Bible are violated. Nor can wage earning or industrial production be considered the only arenas of work. Thousands of "wives of workingmen and farmers . . . work very hard, but are not wage-earners." Further, we "need more artistic and creative" labor. Merely routine manual labor, especially with long hours, stunts the human ability to follow Christ. In typical fashion, a series of suggested questions were also presented for discussion: "Should the State provide every man the opportunity to work?" "Should there be a leisure class and working class?" etc. (Strong: 3–4).

From this starting point regarding the economic life, the series moved to the consideration of child labor, which "the whole spirit of Christianity forbids . . . ," and to the role of "Women in Industry" (Strong: 4–9). The biblical texts, Strong pointed out, call attention to the heroines of the scriptures, who in special circumstances rose to leadership. Strong then argued that the modern industrial order is a special circumstance, for "with machinery the world's work is becoming less and less a matter of muscle and more and more a matter of brain. Under the new conditions, man's superior physical strength counts for nothing in many occupations, while the finer nervous organization of women [provides] precisely the conditions of success." After tracing the negative effects of unequal pay for women, and the possible negative consequences for family life if the internal structure of family living were not reconstituted, the series turned to the general problem of wealth and capital. With copious reference to biblical materials and to contemporary statistics regarding growing discrepancies between the classes, strong emphasis was placed on the social basis and hence the social obligation of all wealth. The series further called for political control over unconstrained corporatism (Strong: 22–23), supported the development of trade unions (Strong: 26ff.) and advised how to implement health and safety standards in industry (Strong: 89–92).

In a similar fashion, problems of housing, public utilities, civic corruption, and socialism as a solution were discussed. Special attention was also given to the "Race Question," to "Labor Conditions," to "Prison Reform," and to "Immigration Policies" on the domestic front, while the discussion of foreign relations took up the problems of "Colonialism," "International Arbitration," and "Peace." Throughout these pages, capitalist and socialist literature in economics was used, both subject to the core doctrine which Mathews and Rauschenbusch had helped articulate.

The agenda is not new, and it was not new then. Its pithy brevity reflects more than a half century of ad hoc writings and several decades of efforts at systematic statement. The principles it enunciated and the methods of study used set the contours and the agenda for much populist work in Christian social ethics until the present.

2. *The Missionary movement and the origins of ecumenism in America.* In the vigorously developing mission societies of the nineteenth century as well as in the Sunday school movement, the economic doctrine that I have called "person in community" became institutionalized. Although much of the missionary effort was driven by the evangelical

impluse to convert individual souls to Christ, and although there were constant temptations to make the mission stations outposts for political and economic as well as cultural imperialism, it is clear that the missions movement tended to undercut hard-line divisions between denominations and to give the whole church a more cosmopolitan perspective. As Shailer Mathews was to write in his autobiography several years later, many involved in the mission movements

> never realized that evangelization was only one aspect of the inter-penetration of Western and Eastern cultures, but the psychology of a generation stirred to religious enthusiasm by the call to transform a world was changed. Within it there was no surreptitious imperialism. . . . What would have been the result if industrialism, militarism and science had been the only forms of the [new international contact] . . . is not difficult to imagine. But thousands of young men and women . . . interpreted the ideals of the West to peoples who have known only exploitation. (1936:34–35)

And among these ideals were the reforms implied in the doctrines of Christian sociology.

The impulse to missions prompted the formation of a number of "homeland missions" in America. Numerous such societies had been formed soon after the Civil War to aid the newly freed blacks, and by the late nineteenth century nearly every major city had at least one City Missionary Society. Many had several, and to coordinate work the Baptists, Presbyterians, Congregationalists, Methodists, and Disciples (sometimes with the cooperation also of Episcopalians and Lutherans) frequently combined to form interdenominational committees. The advocates of Christian sociology saw in these constituencies a way of transcending the artificial divisions of dogma which kept the Body of Christ apart and through cooperative work on social and economic problems a way of uniting the churches around the new doctrine.

The path from these early committees to a genuine ecumenicalism is long, slow, and complex. But there is no doubt that the origins of the ecumenical movement in America are in the homeland missionary societies of the late nineteenth century or that the Christian response to economic changes, on the bases sketched in this paper, brought about the core agreements that made the Federal Council of Churches, consisting of some thirty Protestant denominations, possible by 1908. The Federal Council's first major pronouncement, indeed, was the "Social Creed," slightly modified in 1912 and again in 1932, but basically unchanged since (see Hopkins: 306–17; Ward, 1961). It began by stressing the authority of the New Testament and of Jesus for dealing with economic and social matters: "The problems of modern industry can be interpreted and solved only by the teachings of the New Testament, and Jesus Christ is the final authority in the social as well as in the individual life." The statement continued by declaring that the church was confronted by "the most significant crisis . . . of its long career" and then proceeded to address that crisis by putting the Federal Council and its member churches on record as favoring a lengthy list of social reforms. Not all were economic; some were political and some not; some were closer to the traditional themes of biblical social criticism than others. The list included equal rights for all, an end to child labor, women's rights in the work place, the end of poverty, health conservation, safer working conditions, accident insurance and pensions for workers, a shortening of working hours along with a living wage for all, unions and employer-employee bargaining to settle industrial disputes, and protection of the individual and society alike from the liquor traffic. Ending the list was a call for "the application of Christian principles to the acquisition and use of property, and for the most equitable division of the product of industry that can be ultimately devised." "The final message," concluded the statement with phrase directly from the earlier Christian sociologists, "is redemption, the redemption of the *individual* in the *world*. . . . There is no redemption of either without the redemption of the other" (Ward, 1961:317).

Within a decade, comparable statements had been ratified by the particular denominational bodies in official actions and became the official stances of mainstream Christianity. Robert Moats Miller (1958) has traced the actions of the Methodists, the Northern Baptists, the Presbyterian Church, U.S.A., the Congregationalists, the Episcopalians, the Disciples, the Reformed Church, the Evangelical Synod of North America, and the Unitarians. All argued that property rights are not sacred when they lead to the violation of basic human rights, and all shared the conviction that a just society required the substitution of a "cooperative commonwealth" for industrial autocracy, possessive individualism, and a competitive capitalism driven by greed.

It is not possible, within the confines of this paper, to trace with accuracy the degree to which these religious voices determined the formation of the "New Deal." What is clear is that when the pressures of the depression of the 1930s struck America, it was the specific policies advocated by these church leaders that became the policies of the nation, with very little reference to the religious character of the perspective on social issues as they had actually developed.

The early figures had brought about a relative consensus that the gospel of Jesus Christ implied a doctrine of human "personhood in community" that must, of necessity, attend to the material well-being as well as the spiritual well-being of humanity, the social as well as the individual dimensions of life. This was called the "Social Gospel." Further, they believed that this entailed a recognition of the interdependence of human groups and interests in the economic order. Such a recognition, infused with the spirit of Jesus, could lead to a society that would overcome *laissez-faire* individualism, prevent political tyranny, and transform economic autocracy. Such a society would defeat the pathologies of capitalism and bring about a democratization of the economic order. This consensus held for subsequent years and was the basis for much activism in the churches, in labor unions, and in legal reform. But every one of the central terms in this consensus, together with the optimistic view they entailed, was to be subjected to intense debate and scrutiny from new, international voices.

In the United States the debates were prolonged and sometimes vicious, as R. M. Miller (chap. III) shows. Many who did not participate in the consensus attacked the ecumenically oriented churches that developed policies in these directions as being in league with the devil. If critics did not believe in the devil, they accused the figures I have mentioned of being "un-American." Some fundamentalists, in a prolonged debate with modernists, managed to connect the two critiques. Some liberals saw in the prospect of welfare capitalism an economic third way, which they endorsed without reserve. And some radicals saw in the labor movement of the 1930s the true secular church, which no longer had need of prayer, piety, or pastors. Within the United States, these debates were increasingly conducted with an eye to the international scene. The earlier struggles over slavery and the post–Civil War economic expansionism was an American struggle; but by the time of the Spanish-American War America had become a world power, and its debates could no longer be conducted in isolation, no matter how energetically many tried. Further, the impact of the missions movements of the nineteenth century had begun to internationalize the perspective of the churches and raise questions about the "Americanist" and rather exclusively Protestant focus. Soon the ideas of Marx, which had seemed to come to naught by the early failure of the Internationale, were to become a living, world-historical reality when Lenin carried them into practice in 1917 and began an earth-shaking experiment in "scientific socialism." Key questions were posed sharply and intently for several decades of Christian thought:

> What is the relationship of Christian personalism to economic
>   individualism beyond the boundaries of America?
> What is the relationship of Christian communitarianism to eco-
>   nomic collectivism in other cultures?

What, in fact, is the central character of capitalism and of socialism in their relationship to democracy?

What does the growing body of social scientific literature have
to teach us about the structures and functions of modern,
industrialized societies?

And what is the church to say and to do in the face of the new
upheavals of the age, especially as the newer modes of biblical criticism seemed to cast doubt on our capacities to know
the mind of Jesus?/6/

3. *The Reorientation of social science and its impact on Christian
sociology.* Among the decisive influences on Christian thought in the period between the Social Gospel and today, it is impossible to ignore the
thought of a nonreligious social scientist, one who claimed to be personally
"tone deaf" in religious matters. Max Weber had published his essay "The
Protestant Ethic and the Spirit of Capitalism," in German, in two volumes
of a scholarly journal in 1903–4. The essay was the subject of much critical
comment on the Continent, and Weber issued a new edition with responses
to criticisms within a few years. He also wrote three volumes on religion
and economics in comparative cultures, plus a massive systematic work,
Economy and Society, with extensive treatment of the social import of
religion. Soon his work was a matter of international debate. Weber's colleague, Ernst Troeltsch, adopted many aspects of Weber's thought and
included them in his massive *The Social Teaching of the Christian
Churches and Sects,* in 1911. After World War I, R. H. Tawney, the noted
British laborite scholar, gave his famous lectures, *Religion and the Rise of
Capitalism,* which took as the point of departure Weber's earlier essay.
This work, while it fundamentally distorted Weber's argument and offered
a "counter" argument under the guise of being a "supplementary" one,
opened the whole discussion of Weber's ideas to an English-speaking audi-
ence. Within a decade both Weber and Troeltsch were translated into
English and a significant shift in the thinking of Protestant scholars about
economic thought was under way (see Weber; Troeltsch; Tawney).

To put the matter briefly, no longer were Adam Smith or Karl Marx
taken by theologians and religious ethicists to be the chief "scientific"
voices in regard to the nature and character of capitalism. Both of these
held that economic structure, development, and process were not, and
ought not be, governed by religious consideration. To be sure, both business managers and political commissars (as well as numerous economists)
did follow Smith or Marx or their heirs, and the public political-
economic debates continue to be conducted very much in these terms—
even where the former has undergone extensive Keynesian modification

and the latter has been revised by post-Leninist developments. But the scholarly discussion of economic matters by leading social theorists like Kenneth Boulding, Robert MacIver, and Talcott Parsons tended to move in Weberian channels. Christian ethicists also worked in this general direction. The new generation of American clergy-ethicists led by Richard and Reinhold Niebuhr, John Bennett, Walter Muelder, James Luther Adams, Liston Pope, and Gibson Winter, all took major themes from Weber and Troeltsch with references to Tawney. They were paralleled in Europe by voices such as William Temple, Arend van Leeuwan, and Arthur Rich.

One must also point out in this connection that in the American seminaries an increased differentiation of the theological sciences cut off many biblical scholars and systematic theologians, not to mention religious educators, from Christian social ethics as a discipline. Thus, while Christian social ethicists, from the 1920s and 1930s through the 1960s at least, were developing more refined tools of social analysis on the basis of Weber-influenced perspectives, the impact of that development was severely limited among specialists in other fields. Further, their reliance on these ideas represented a move away from the dependence on the Bible that had characterized earlier generations of Christian social critics. Systematic theologians at this time were wrestling with the new proclamations of Karl Barth and Emil Brunner. Barth doubted the theological legitimacy of the social and cultural sciences as a resource in any sense for Christian ethics. Brunner doubted the historical accuracy of Weber's and Troeltsch's argument. In biblical studies, the influence of Rudolph Bultmann almost overwhelmed any effort to sustain dialogue between social ethics, as a field, and biblical studies. Only the "American school" of biblical criticism, led by Shirley Jackson Case, maintained such an interest until quite recently, and its influence was limited.

A survery of the categories used by leading teachers of ethics reveals that Weber, Troeltsch, and related figures continued to shape the development of Christian social ethics in decisive ways. The main point of this "school" of work is that modern economic developments cannot be understood simply on the basis of an analysis of material forces, inevitable processes of economic development, a drive for gain, the structure of classes, or the rational calculation of material interests. Nor can they be understood simply on the basis of religious or moral ideas. It is the elective affinity of material and ideal forces which, when routinized and institutionalized in an ethos, produces major shifts in societies and history. It is not possible to understand modern industrial society, in contrast to all the traditional societies in the world, without recognizing the hidden power of this essentially religious orientation. Weber's message was, in brief, that religion has been, and is likely to be again, historically decisive for economics and associated political ordering. This was a sharp break from Smith and Marx, both of whom removed religion from the realm of economic causation and claimed an autonomy from religion for economic rationality. In appropriating Weberian perspectives Christian social critics entered a new realm in understanding the relation between religion and society.

Between the Christian authors and the Weberian school of thought, of course, one great gulf remained. Weber, Troeltsch, and Tawney offered descriptive and historical analyses of socioeconomic matters. The Christian ethicists were specifically interested in a normative, future-oriented analysis. The specific responsibility of theologically informed social ethicists, working with church agencies and leadership, is to offer guidance about how the people of God *ought* to respond to socioeconomic developments in the present and coming days. Such a response, of course, requires close familiarity with how the structures, processes, and values of an ethos actually work, but the primary focus must be to identify and activate those fundamental structures, processes, and values that can move the ethos toward actualization of the laws of God, the kingdom of God, and the love of God.

Two Representative Figures

In order to show how the themes identified here influenced American ethics after World War II, I turn to two key essays by leading American church ethicists. I choose John C. Bennett and Walter G. Muelder for several reasons. Bennett represents in some ways the tradition from Walter Rauschenbusch, modified and modulated by the influences of Reinhold Niebuhr and of more recent "liberation theology." This can be seen in his books *Christian Realism* (1952) and *The Radical Imperative* (1975). Muelder's "Liberal Personalism" allies him in some ways with the traditions that also influenced Shailer Mathews, although Muelder's thought is also modified by a close association with Christian pacifism and the impact of the movements against racism, as led by Martin Luther King, Jr. These motifs can be seen in *Religion and Economic Responsibility* (1953) and *Toward a Discipline of Social Ethics* (1972), edited by P. Deats.

Both Bennett and Muelder were involved with the ecumenical movement; both taught at leading theological seminaries and trained generations of church leaders and scholars; both are still living and writing on ethics and economic life; both were and are alert to third world concerns and to Roman Catholic developments; and both find their roots in Christian sociology, including the influences of Weber. Bennett is closer to Tawney, and Muelder is more deeply indebted to Troeltsch.

John Bennett wrote "A Theological Conception of Goals for Economic Life" (Bennett, 1949) for the Amsterdam conference of the World Council of Churches in 1948. He begins his analysis by referring to the earlier Oxford conference, which had given considerable attention to economic and socioeconomic matters (see World Council of Churches, 1939), and by acknowledging that while Protestant thinking must draw out the implications of the biblical faith for economic life, "this must be done in an exploratory way in the face of new problems . . . which were quite unknown to biblical writers. . . ." He acknowledges that there are aspects of economic life that are beyond the scope of the church's concern as church; and he acknowledges that aspects of Protestant thought both gave rise to modern economic systems and turned it in directions that gave it a "rationalistic" character beyond the control of the church. Bennett argues for the partial, technical autonomy of economics, but against the moral autonomy of the economic order (1949:38). "Most observers, whether they are Christians, liberal secularists, or theoretical Marxists, would agree that the separation of economic life from ethical criticism did lead to vast exploitation and misery; that it did tend to dehumanize culture; that it did result in an intolerable inner conflict in the motives of men."

He turns then to the exploration of doctrines that illumine the Christian approach to the economic order. What is theologically fascinating about his essay is that he seldom focuses on Jesus. Instead, he focuses the organization of his remarks around Christological motifs: God, Humanity, and Salvation. The earlier American emphasis on the "principles and teachings of Jesus" has been modulated by the ecumenical accent on Christology to become thematized around these doctrinal issues.

Christians, says Bennett, hold that God is transcendent. Idolatry is a chief temptation. Thus, the greatest temptation in the world today is the idolatry of a social system, "whether it be Soviet communism or . . . [the] American idolatry [which] is a common private tendency rather than an official creed" (1949:39). Christians also hold that God created the world. Thus, concern for material things is not anti-Christian. But Christians are to utilize the resources of the earth "in the light of God's purpose." Private property, thus, is not and cannot be absolute (1949:40).

Christians also have developed extensive doctrines concerning human nature which bear on economic life.

> The first is the conviction that man is made in God's image, responsible to God, with unique dignity and possibilities derived from this relation to God. The second conviction is that man universally and persistently tends to be sinful. . . . [This] means that tendencies

toward pride and self centeredness are present on every level of
human life. . . . and the social consequences . . . are to be found in
all varieties of injustice. (1949:42)

Sin leads humans to individual and group self-interest, to viewing
the person in only economic terms, or to claiming a class-based self-
righteousness. It also leads to the use of power without responsibility, to the
oversimplification of the problem of "incentive," and to a yearning for
panaceas or utopias. Christians know that the only viable doctrine of
humanity is "the person in relation to the community." Thus, Christian
faith is "incompatible with an atomistic individualism . . . [and] is equally
incompatible with any collectivism which rides roughshod over the consciences or the welfare of the members of society . . ." (1949:43).

Christians speak of God and humanity in the context of salvation. The
goal, for Christians, is eschatological. "All our experiences of salvation in
the course of our lives in this world are regarded by Christians as intima-
tions of a fulfillment by which God will establish his Kingdom" (1949:44).
The implications of the vision of eschatological salvation imply that some
kinds of social organization and some kinds of economic welfare at least
remove barriers to justification, sanctification, and ultimate salvation. It is a
mistake to hold that economic programs bring these, but such concrete
considerations as housing conditions in modern cities, great contrasts of
wealth and poverty, unemployment, and commercial materialism, which
produces vulgarity in popular taste and corruption of community and
character, can be modified by humane programs of political economy
(1949:45–46).

On bases such as these, the Christian ethic induces a love that
"means a radical caring for the welfare and dignity of the neighbor," a
love that becomes the ultimate touchstone of lesser values particularly
proper to economic life, such as order, justice, freedom, and efficiency.
Bennett spends the remainder of his essay setting forth the implications
of "love-tested" order, justice, freedom, and efficiency in an economy
that must be founded on "persons in community."

Out of the conference to which Bennett gave this paper, the theme
of "The Responsible Society" became a predominant one. Walter G.
Muelder was one of the people responsible for bringing that concept into
common usage in Christian ethics soon thereafter. In his summary reflections on the idea and its importance he draws freely on the ecumenical
conferences referred to above. Muelder sees this idea as the modern
articulation of motifs from a deeper history, such as Augustine's City of
God, the Holy Commonwealth of the Puritans, and the Kingdom of God
of the Social Gospel leaders. The emergence of this theme in its new
form is shaped by a particular context:

> The sense of tension between the "Communist" and "non-Communist" parts of the world, the desire of some . . . to develop a "third force" politically and economically, and the awareness on the part of Protestant and Orthodox leaders that Christians needed to develop a standard which would be relevant to the needs of their members in all countries. . . . It would readily make contact with the sober constructive work of secular agencies such as the U.N. Commission on Human Rights. Moreover, it was essential that the rights and duties of Asians and Africans in the world situation would be as clearly expressed as those of the Europeans and Americans. (7–8)

In this context, a number of themes were articulated. The most comprehensive and ultimately the most basic was the theological one. He quotes the Amsterdam Assembly.

> [Each human] . . . is created and called to be a free being, responsible to God and his neighbor. Any tendencies in State and society depriving [a man or woman] . . . of the possibility of acting responsibly are a denial of God's intention. . . . A responsible society is one where freedom is the freedom [to] . . . acknowledge responsibility to justice and public order, and where those who hold political authority or economic power are responsible for its exercise to God and the people whose welfare is affected by it. (World Council of Churches, Amsterdam Assembly, 192)

Muelder sees an interactive and dialectical relationship between freedom, justice, and equality, between person and community, between just order and revolutionary change. He is careful also to recognize the ways in which the interaction of these values will render different combinations under specific historical conditions. He documents how subsequent work on the idea of the responsible society underwent modification in Bangkok (1949) and in Lucknow (1952). Increasingly the idea of the responsible society was spelled out in terms of Asian and African urgencies and were only subsequently to be incorporated into, and to broaden, the Western frame of reference (see further Margul).

In brief, whether we turn to John Bennett's modified "Christian Realism" or Walter Muelder's "Christian Personalism," we find major representative voices echoing and recasting the themes of Christian ethics and economic life that had been engendered more than a century ago and modified by diverse but convergent ecumenical themes and a shrinking world. In these voices, more forcefully, we find sustained elaboration of themes that had been present for some time: Persons live and work in community under God, whom Christians know in Jesus Christ. Therefore they must seek economic justice, guided by love, in a changing world. Economics is not morally independent of these facts. Nor can the church or theology supply a detailed guidance system that removes economic actors from the responsibilities of concrete decision makers in communion with their neighbors and with full awareness of the changing structural realities of public institutions. Some things can be ruled out: individualistic, commercial capitalism and collectivistic, politicized communism, the exploitation of workers, and the destruction of the environment. Racial and ethnic and class discrimination is wrong. On these fronts, the churches can say a clear No. But it is not clear what the church should say positively, in detail.

Conclusion

In recent years very little fresh thinking on these questions has been done by American church and ecumenical bodies. They tend to draw upon the reservoir of thought built up over the elongated century treated in this paper without replenishing the reserve. The exceptions to this broad judgment are the recent works on economics in social and political contexts by such scholars as Albert Rasmussen (1965), Bruce Morgan (1963), Victor Obenhaus (1965), Reginald Fuller (1966), Richard Taylor (1973), and J. Philip Wogaman (1977). Other new voices are also entering the discussion, and new questions are being raised. But still the lines of thought and development identified in this paper remain to influence the present debate. I have already, in the first section above, offered my conclusions about this development in its relation to the present and future; broadly, I argued there that we need to know about this past in order to avoid at least the more obvious pitfalls already encountered and to be able to build constructively on the best from this developing tradition of Christian thought and praxis. We are related to this tradition institutionally as well as intellectually, and as I believe this paper has revealed, the questions of today are not, after all, such different ones from those faced over the elongated century treated here./7/

In conclusion, then, let us review several of the most outstanding features of this lengthy development.

1. The foundation of Christian social criticism over this period is in biblical themes, and the teachings of Jesus in the New Testament takes the central place. While such ideas as justice and community are prominent in the Old Testament, they were incorporated into American Christian social criticism not so much directly as through reflection on Jesus' preaching, the life of the early Christians, and the idea of the kingdom of God. Nor was the biblical element equally prominent at every stage in the development treated here; yet it has consistently provided a core, a foundation to which Christian social criticism has returned. If it was unabashedly present in the argument over slavery and in the writings of persons like Shailer Mathews and Walter Rauschenbusch, it is nonetheless a feature of the writings of

contemporary scholars like John C. Bennett and Walter G. Muelder, of the contemporary ecumenical movement as well as the earlier Sunday school and missionary movements. But the use of the Bible for Christian social criticism has clearly shifted, even so. Despite the origins of such criticism in nineteenth-century revivalism, the brunt of present-day Christian economic, social, and political writing comes from within the least revivalistic sectors of the American church. Similarly, there has been a shift away from proof-texting as a means of applying biblical insights to social issues toward the use of broad biblical themes such as justice, love, and the kingdom of God. But it would be an error to judge present Christian social criticism the less biblical for this; it represents rather a different way of appropriating the message of the Bible for life in the world.

2. Christian social criticism in the period treated has consistently argued for a conception of Christian life as social rather than as purely individual, and accordingly it has regularly sought to focus on those aspects of corporate life most needing to be brought into conformity with the biblical vision of community. While this paper has concentrated on the economic critiques leveled by Christian authors and institutions, other aspects of social living were addressed as well, and even where the economic questions were central, they were dealt with in ways that often implied or envisioned the broader political or social transformation of society. The economic criticism treated here was, in this sense, always implicitly also a political criticism.

3. Alongside their dependence on the Bible for authority and their interest in contemporaneous problems of social inequity, Christian social critics have placed a concern to know existing and new social theory. The early Christian sociologists were different from earlier Christian social critics because of their use of social-scientific knowledge and perspectives; this concern continues right into the present in Christian social ethics. While this has undoubtedly been a source of stress at times in how to continue to utilize the more specifically biblical aspects of Christian social criticism, it has equally undoubtedly strengthened this criticism by keeping it tuned to contemporaneous developments in the understanding of how society works.

4. This tradition of Christian thought and praxis has been, implicitly from the beginning and explicitly from the missionary movement onward, ecumenical in nature. Despite the denominational character of American Christianity, it has from the first reached across denominational lines to involve a broad spectrum of socially concerned Christians. In the twentieth century this ecumenicity has developed further into a social critique of an international nature, and now the American tradition is receiving input from the Christian social critics of the Third

World, even as earlier the missionary movement helped to instill religiously based social concern in the missionary lands.

We have no chart of the future of American Christian social criticism. But if the development of a tradition of criticism over the elongated century treated in this paper can provide a guide for our expectations, then the development to come in Christian critiques of society must incorporate and utilize the themes identified here.

NOTES

/1/   It is true, of course, that a generation later John Maynard Keynes brought to the forefront of the debate a series of concepts and theories that were perceived as revolutionary by professional economists. Reintroducing some motifs from the mercantilists, who were thoroughgoing statists, Keynes called for a kind of governmental interventionism in economic life that had been viewed by many previously trained specialists as unscientific, counterproductive, and irrational and by Marxists as patchwork concessions to prevent capitalist collapse. Younger economists of the time spoke of the epochal transformations of consciousness that adoption of these ideas had in the profession. As is well known, the newer theories of Keynes became central to economists advising political authorities for at least a quarter of a century. It is not clear, however, that the Keynesian notions altered any of the already existing definitions of humans as economic agents, the nature of economic rationality, the purposes of the political economy, or the conception of the social order generally. They did offer a new array of technical constructs by which specialists could interpret practices already in place, constructs that could be used to guide public policy. However, by the 1960s sharp criticisms of Keynes's views increased from quarters that seem to the noneconomist to be refurbished versions of pre-Keynesian perspectives. From the standpoint of theology, ethics, and general social theory, therefore, even the Keynesian theories might well be seen as variations on more continuous themes, or, at most, as an interlude.

/2/   This is my chief criticism of such otherwise competent authors as Daniel Maguire. See Maguire, 1980.

/3/   The influence of Henry George was important in these areas. On George, see further the essay by Louis Weeks in this volume.

/4/   A further word needs to be said about this relationship with Calvinism. Calvinism had shaped the main contours of American religion in all its previous history (see P. Miller; Baltzell; on the Calvinistic roots of American attitudes toward politics, see further the essay by Mark Valeri and John Wilson in this volume). But in the nineteenth century, Calvinism split into three distinct streams. One stream, as Anne Douglas (1978) has artfully demonstrated, was "feminized"—an unfortunate choice of terms. Thus, one branch became almost totally preoccupied with the cultivation of the "gentler virtues" and the manicuring of the inner religious sensibilities. It lost its concern for public matters. A second branch became the bastion of antiscientific fideism, the forerunner of rationalistic and literalistic fundamentalism, an invention of nineteenth-century Protestantism that turned parts of American Christianity toward a "koranized" biblicism, a dominant feature of the "Bible Belt" ever since (see Marsden). The third branch became the advocate of a new economic and social ethic. This could be called the "Puritan evangelical" branch; it was connected with those denominations that became the core of the ecumenical Protestant movement in the twentieth century, and it claimed to be the true heir of the genuinely Catholic church, the Reformation, and the Puritan traditions. It is representatives of this stream of American Christianity whom Dombrowski has in mind when he writes that those who had a manifest interest in social and economic questions "had a correlative existence with Calvinism. It showed its greatest strength in . . . [those places] where Calvinism was most deeply entrenched." Thus, to some extent, the "this worldly" emphasis of Calvinism produced a social Christianity opposed to the "other worldliness" of Lutheranism and the "next-worldliness" of Catholicism (in this period). "Withdrawal from the world . . . was rejected in favor of participation in the world with a view to transforming it. . . . In some respects this was a reaffirmation of the Puritan ideal of a theocracy" (15).

/5/ Rauschenbusch sees verses 16–18 as later insertions.

/6/ Space limitations and the scope of the present volume prevent further discussion of the social ethics of the international ecumenical movement, though it is through dialogues shaped within this movement that some of the most creative and sustained efforts to respond to these questions can be found. These dialogues began with the "Universal Christian Conference on Life and Work" held in Stockholm in 1925, continued in a conference on "Christianity and Industrialism" in Jerusalem in 1928 and in subsequent meetings held in London, Basel, Geneva, and Regensburg. The greatest of the pre–World War II ecumenical conferences was held at Oxford in 1937; its proceedings fill eight volumes (World Council of Churches, 1939). This conference, which drew concerted work from some of the greatest theological minds of the day, gave articulation in the midst of the pending struggle against fascism to most of the themes treated in the present paper. It is on the basis of the work done in this conference and later reflection on it that we should regard the writings of such American social critics as John C. Bennett and Walter G. Muelder, treated below. (See further Bock; Derr: 20–33; and World Council of Churches, 1954.)

/7/ See, for example, Faramelli; Ferkiss; Kirby; Powers. Many of the themes treated in this paper are present in the emergent field of business ethics; see Jones, 1977; *New Catholic World*; Novak, 1979; Maguire; Benne. Other use of these themes is found in liberation theology (see Ruether; Gutierrez) and in the ecological movement (see O'Brien and Shannon; Sider). On the contemporary use of the Bible in ethics, see Birch and L. L. Rasmussen; Mott.

WORKS CONSULTED

Atwater, L.
1872   "The Labor Question." *Presbyterian Quarterly and Princeton Review* (fall): 491–92.

Baltzell, E. Digby
1979   *Puritan Boston and Quaker Philadelphia.* New York: Free Press.

Bascom, J.
1868   "Labor and Capital." *Bibliotheca Sacra* 25:98.

Benne, R.
1981   *The Ethic of Democratic Capitalism*. Philadelphia: Fortress.

Bennett, John
1949   "A Theological Conception of Goals for Economic Life." In
                Goals of Economic Life. Edited by A. Dudley Ward. New
                York: Harper & Brothers.

Birch, Bruce C., and Larry L. Rasmussen
1976   *Bible and Ethics in the Christian Life*. Minneapolis: Augs-
                burg.

Bliss, W. D. P., ed.
1908   *Encyclopedia of Social Reform*. New York: Funk and Wag-
                nalls.

Boardman, G. H.
1866   "Political Science and Christian Ministry." *Bibliotheca Sacra*
                23:98.

Bock, Paul
1974   *In Search of a Responsible World Society*. Philadelphia: West-
                minster.

Byron, William
1975   *Toward Stewardship*. New York: Paulist.

Carey, C.
1858, 1859,   *The Principles of Social Science*. 3 vols. Philadelphia: J. B.
1860   Lippincott.

Colwell, Stephen
1851   *New Themes for the Protestant Clergy*. Philadelphia.

Davis, John P.
1961   *Corporations*. New York: Capricorn Books.

Derr, Thomas S.
1982   "The Economic Thought of the World Council of Churches."
                This World 1:20–33.

Dombrowski, James
1966   *The Early Days of Christian Socialism in America*. New York:
                Octagon Books.

Douglas, Anne
1978   *The Feminization of American Culture*. New York: Avon
                Press.

Dunn, Edmund J.
1980   *Missionary Theology: Foundations in Development*. Lanham,
                MD: University Press of America.

Faramelli, Norman
1971   *Technethics*. New York: Friendship Press.

Ferkiss, Victor C.
1969   *Technological Man*. New York: Braziller

Fuller, R. H., with B. K. Rice
1966   *Christianity and the Affluent Society*. Grand Rapids, MI:
                Eerdmans.

Gilder, George
  1980   *Wealth and Poverty*. New York: Basic Books.

Gladden, Washington
  1908   *The Church and Modern Life*. Boston: Houghton, Mifflin.

Gutierrez, Gustavo
  1973   *A Theology of Liberation*. Maryknoll, NY: Orbis Books.

Harnack, A., and W. Herrmann.
  1907   *Essays on the Social Gospel*. Translated from the 1892 edition.
                  New York: Crown.

Harrington, Michael
  1973   *Fragments of the Century*. New York: Touchstone Press.

Hopkins, Charles Howard
  1940   *The Rise of the Social Gospel in American Protestantism:
                  1865–1915*. Yale University Press.

Jones, Donald G.
  1977   *A Bibliography of Business Ethics: 1971–75*. Charlottesville,
                  VA: University of Virginia Press.
  1981   *A Bibliography of Business Ethics: 1975–80*. Charlottesville,
                  VA: University of Virginia Press.

Kirby, D. J.
  1980   *Prophecy vs. Profits*. Maryknoll, NY: Orbis Books.

Maguire, Daniel
  1980   *A New American Justice*. Garden City, NY: Doubleday.

Manno, Bruce, and M. E. Jegen, eds.
  1978   *The Earth is the Lord's*. New York: Paulist.

Margul, H. J.
  1962   *Hope in Action*. Philadelphia: Muhlenberg.

Marsden, Geroge M.
  1980   *Fundamentalism and American Culture*. New York: Oxford
                  University Press.

Mathews, S.
  1897   *The Social Teaching of Jesus*. New York: Macmillan.
  1936   *New Faith for Old*. New York: Macmillan.

Miller, Perry
  1939   *The Puritan Mind*. 2 vols. New York: Macmillan.

Miller, R. M.
  1958   *American Protestantism and Social Issues: 1919–1939*. Chapel
                  Hill, NC: University of North Carolina Press.

Morgan, Bruce
  1963   *Christians, The Church and Property*. Philadelphia: Westmin-
                  ster.

Mott, Stephen C.
  1982   *Biblical Ethics and the Crisis of Society*. New York: Oxford
                  University Press.

Muelder, Walter G.
    1955   *The Idea of the Responsible Society.* Boston: Boston University
                    Press.

New Catholic World
    1980   Special Issue on Business Ethics. Vol. 223, No. 1338
                    (November–December).

Niebuhr, H. R.
    1937   *The Kingdom of God in America.* New York: Harper and
                    Brothers.

Novak, Michael
    1979   *The American Vision.* Washington, DC: American Enterprise
                    Institute.

Novak, Michael, ed.
    1980   *Democracy and Mediating Structures: A Theological Inquiry.*
                    Washington, DC: American Enterprise Institute.

Obenhaus, Victor
    1965   *Ethics for an Industrial Age.* New York: Harper & Row.

O'Brien, D. J., and T. A. Shannon, eds.
    1977   *Renewing the Earth.* Garden City, NY: Doubleday.

Peabody, F. G.
    1912   *The Approach to the Social Question.* New York: Macmillan.

Powers, C. W.
    1971   *Social Responsibility and Investments.* Nashville, TN: Abing-
                    don.

Rasmussen, Albert T.
    1965   *Christian Responsibility in Economic Life.* Philadelphia:
                    Westminster.

Rauschenbusch, Walter
    1907   *Christianity and the Social Crisis.* New York: Macmillan.
    1912   *Christianizing the Social Order.* New York: Macmillan.

Rifkin, Jeremy
    1978   *The Emerging Order.* New York: Viking Press.

Ruether, Rosemary
    1972   *Liberation Theology.* New York: Paulist.

Ruskin, J.
    1866   *Unto This Last.* New York: Wiley.

Schlesinger, Arthur
    1964   *Paths to the Present.* Rev. ed. Boston: Houghton Mifflin.

Schumacher, E. F.
    1973   *Small Is Beautiful.* New York: Harper & Row.

Seely, J. R.
    1866   *Ecce Homo.* London: Macmillan.

Sider, Ronald J., ed.
    1981   *Evangelicals and Development.* Philadelphia: Westminster.

Smith, T.
    1957   *Revivalism and Social Reform*. New York: Harper & Row.

Stelzle, Charles
    1903   *The Workingman and Social Problems*. Chicago: Revell.

Strong, Josiah, ed.
    1910   *Studies in the Gospel of the Kingdom*. New York: American
                    Institute of Social Service.

Sutton, F. X., S. E. Harris, et al.
    1956   *The American Business Creed*. New York: Schocken Books.

Tawney, R. H.
    1926   *Religion and the Rise of Capitalism*. New York: Harcourt,
                    Brace and World.

Taylor, Richard K.
    1973   *Economics and the Gospel*. Philadelphia: United Church
                    Press.

Troeltsch, E.
    1906   *The Social Teaching of the Christian Churches*. New York:
                    Harper and Brothers.

Ward, A. Dudley
    1961   *The Social Creed*. Nashville: Abingdon.

Ward, A. Dudley, ed.
    1949   *Goals of Economic Life*. New York: Harper and Brothers.

Webber, Robert
    1981   *The Moral Majority; Right or Wrong?* Westchester, IL: Cor-
                    nerstone Books.

Weber, M.
    1931   *The Protestant Ethic and the Spirit of Capitalism*. Translated
                    by T. Parsons. New York: Scribner.

Wogaman, J. Philip
    1977   *The Great Economics Debate*. Philadelphia: Westminster.

World Council of Churches
    1939   *The Oxford Conference Books*. 8 vols. Chicago: Willett Clark.
    1954   *Ecumenical Documents on Church and Society*. Geneva:
                    WCC Press.

World Council of Churches, Amsterdam Assembly
    1949   *The Church and the Disorder of Society*. Geneva: WCC Press.

VI

The Christian Element
in Christian Realism

Dennis P. McCann

At the dawn of the thermonuclear age, Reinhold Niebuhr, the foremost apostle of the approach to politics that has become known as Christian realism, advocated a "solemn covenant" renouncing the first use of the H-Bomb. His argument for this covenant appeals ultimately to the Bible for support:

> We would be saying by such a policy that even a nation can reach the point where it can purchase its life too dearly. If we had to use this kind of destruction in order to save our lives, would we find life worth living? Even nations can reach a point where the words of our Lord, "Fear not them which are able to kill the body but rather fear them that are able to destroy both soul and body in hell," become relevant. (1950:237)

Biblical allusions like this are not rare in Niebuhr's political writings. While it would be tedious to collect all the instances that resemble this one, it is helpful to concentrate on one cluster of examples in order to see the significance of Niebuhr's way of searching the scriptures for political insight. The examples chosen from *The Irony of American History* (1952a) constitute a biblical rhetoric of irony that may hold the key to understanding what Christian realism was meant to be.

Quite often Niebuhr's biblical rhetoric either has been misunderstood or has had its significance minimized. Those who claim him as the "spiritual father" of the American school of political realism, for example, have tended to dismiss the rhetoric as a kind of "homiletic charisma" that allowed him to be "the model of a successful publicist" (Fox: 245). On the other hand, the so-called atheists for Niebuhr have staked their claim on the rumor that there is "no logical connection"—merely a "personal" one—between Niebuhr's rhetoric and his politics (Hook). Contrary to both of these, I contend in this essay that Niebuhr's biblical rhetoric is what makes Christian realism distinctively Christian.

Critics and admirers who ignore his rhetoric often tend to blur the differences between Niebuhr's views and those of his "spiritual" children on various political issues as well. To his credit, Sidney Hook does not fall into this trap. "But these differences," he explains (1956), "are hard to assess because Niebuhr uses the language of religion to suggest the complexities and ironies and irrationalities of human behavior that escape the simple pieties of religious faith and popular science alike. To hold him to rigorous analytic discourse would be like imposing a proper logical syntax upon a poem." What seems in order, then, is a rhetorical analysis of Niebuhr's Christian realism, one which will highlight the poetic "syntax" that logically connects his use of scripture and his distinctive approach to politics./1/

In what follows, I will try to reconstruct Niebuhr's biblical rhetoric and show how it shapes his approach to one specific area of political theory and practice, the question of "national interest" in American foreign policy. I will then argue its significance by contrasting Niebuhr's perspective with Hans Morgenthau's, whose work on "national interest" may be taken as representative of the American school of political realism. This exercise should help clarify not only what is distinctively Christian about Christian realism, but also how and why the Bible continues to influence American political life and thought.

Niebuhr's Biblical Rhetoric: An Overview

Like Rudolf Bultmann and Paul Tillich, Reinhold Niebuhr reopened the scriptures by way of a new insight into the significance of myth. At some point between the publication of *Moral Man and Immoral Society* (1932) and *Reflections on the End of an Era* (1934), he took up the category of "mythology" as a basis for interpreting the ideological dimensions of the struggle for social justice. First evident in his analysis of the conflict between "bourgeois religion" and "proletarian religion," this category allowed him within the space of a few years to reconstruct the cognitive map of "prophetic Christianity." The result was his first major theological work, *An Interpretation of Christian Ethics* (1935)./2/

It may seem strange to characterize what happened as a reopening of scripture. Niebuhr's vocation as a Protestant pastor and his reputation as a Christian preacher would seem to count against it. Nevertheless, a review of his early works, from *Does Civilization Need Religion?* (1927) up to and including *Moral Man and Immoral Society* (1932), finds him speaking in an abstract idiom concerning the "resources" of "a vital religious idealism," the role of "religious passion," and the power of "illusions." Like many liberal Protestants he saw religion contributing "the concept of personality" and argued for "the support of both metaphysics and ethics" to work out the relevance of this contribution (1927:6–7). There is also little by way of explicit reference to scripture in these early works. What this suggests is that prior to his discovery of the meaning of myth, Niebuhr was an emotivist in his understanding of religion in general and, by implication, of biblical religion in particular./3/ In other words, he was interested in how a "vital religious idealism"—be it Marxist or Christian—might inspire people to commit themselves to the struggle for social justice. The cognitive dimension of religion, apparently, was to emerge in a synthesis of this "idealism" and the "astute intelligence . . . needed to guide moral purpose in a complex situation" (1927:140). Niebuhr's first agenda for theology, in short, pointed toward a mixed discourse consisting of liberal Protestantism's *Religionswissenschaft* and critical social theory. It did not envision any substantive role for a biblical rhetoric./4/

Fortunately, Niebuhr's own religious and intellectual habits—as well as his political experience—made it impossible for him to rest content with this agenda. Even its first fruits, "the frank dualism in morals" proposed in *Moral Man and Immoral Society*, was abandoned soon after the ink had dried, because Niebuhr discovered that any neat distinction between the emotive and cognitive elements in his synthesis could not stand up to the realities of both religious faith and politics./5/ With ideological conflict at a fever pitch during the mid-1930s, he began to rediscover Christianity's power for dispelling "illusions about the collective behavior of mankind in general in any age or under any social system" (1933:180). The category of mythology allowed him to explore the theoretical meaning of this fundamental insight. The result was a second agenda for theology, one that seeks "to combine political radicalism with a more classical and historical interpretation of religion" (1934:ix–x). While this formulation is still transitional, its new emphasis on "classical" religion meant that Niebuhr increasingly would turn to the Bible for substantive insight into the nature of "prophetic Christianity."

When approached from the angle afforded by "the mythical method" of interpretation (1935:51), scripture thus yields a cluster of myths, Creation, Fall, and Atonement, which disclose a paradoxical truth about "the dimension of depth in life" (1935:3) and dispel the illusions generated by competing ideologies. *An Interpretation of Christian Ethics*, in short, explores the irreducible "tensions" between "infinity" and "finitude" (1935:40), between the Eternal and the temporal, between "spirit" and "nature" in human existence (1935:44), in such a way that "the absolute and transcendent ethic of Jesus" may be related to the realities of moral conflict—both public and private—as an "impossible possibility" (see McCann, 1980). Among other things, this new method allowed Niebuhr to break the tyranny of abstract theological concepts in order to speak once more in a biblical idiom about the drama of sin and grace in human affairs.

In announcing this return to the Bible Niebuhr, of course, wished to remain as distant from fundamentalism as he had come to be from liberalism. His use of scripture thus presupposes a distinction between "permanent myth" and "primitive myth" (1937a:16) designed to insure that its meaning be taken "seriously but not literally" (1943:50). Only the Bible's "permanent" insights into the "dimension of depth" are retrievable. Similarly, the cognitive claims implicit in these insights are to be expressed and assessed in forms of discourse appropriate to their paradoxical nature. In contrast to Kierkegaard on this topic, Niebuhr favored aesthetic strategies to convey the religious meaning of permanent myth. Just as the theologian is like a portrait artist who "falsifies some of the physical details in order to arrive at a symbolic expression of the total character of his subject" (1937a:27), so the Bible's permanent insights can only be expressed in forms of indirect communication, "which contain a certain degree of provisional and superficial deception" (1937b:3). Theological discourse faithful to scripture, in short, will be more akin to poetry than to science or philosophy./6/

The "mythical method," nevertheless, does not amount to a retreat into obscurantism. The insights generated by seeking to understand the Christian cycle of myths must be interpreted. Two distinct strategies eventually emerge from Niebuhr's attempts to do this, both of which make an appeal to common human experience for existential verification./7/ The first strategy moves away from a first-order encounter with biblical myths toward a new set of second-order theological concepts. This is the trajectory that begins with *An Interpretation of Christian Ethics* (1935) and culminates in Niebuhr's magnum opus, *The Nature and Destiny of Man* (1941, 1943). Characteristic of this trend is his attempt to formulate conceptual systems—what elsewhere I have diagnosed as "theological anthropology" and "theology of history" (McCann, 1981)—which make their paradoxical claims through interdisciplinary dialogue with certain theories in psychology and historical sociology. Niebuhr's second strategy continues to explore certain aesthetic approaches in order to sustain and renew the first-order encounter with biblical myths in a religious rhetoric operating at the level of "second naiveté."/8/ This trajectory also begins with *An Interpretation of Christian Ethics*, but from there it proceeds through the sermonic essays of *Beyond Tragedy* (1937b) and *Discerning the Signs of the Times* (1946), culminating in *The Irony of American History* (1952a). Since this trend eschews conceptual systems in favor of an increasingly sophisticated rhetorical use of scripture, let us take a closer look at its fullest expression in *The Irony of American History*./9/

A Biblical Rhetoric of Irony

Niebuhr's discovery of a biblical rhetoric of irony came at a time when it was not at all clear that America could avoid nuclear Armageddon. Once more searching the scriptures for some clue to our destiny, he discerned a derisive laughter aimed at the frustration of America's aspirations for the postwar world:

> Over these exertions we discern by faith the ironical laughter of the divine source and end of all things. "He that sitteth in the heavens shall laugh" (Psalm 2, 4). He laughs because "the people imagine a vain thing." The scripture assures us that God's laughter is derisive, having the sting of judgment upon our vanities in it. But if the laughter is truly ironic it must symbolize mercy as well as judgment. For whenever judgment defines the limits of human striving it creates the possibility of an humble acceptance of those limits. Within that humility mercy and peace find a lodging place. (1952a:63–64)

The "framework of irony" derived from this discernment must not be misunderstood. To dismiss it as merely a clever device for organizing his lectures fails to do it justice, for so many of his judgments regarding the substantive meaning of American history depend on it. To criticize it as evidence of a subtle betrayal of "prophetic Christianity" is also a serious mistake. For Niebuhr uses this framework to link Christian realism formally as well as substantively to the biblical demand for *metanoia*, "repentance." In other words, it allows him to move beyond the negative description of Christianity as "a religion that transcends tragedy" (1937b:155) to a positive insight into the nature of that transcendence. This shift is worked out with reference to the rhetorical strategies of "pathos," "tragedy," and "irony." Pathos, he claims, arises in "fortuitous" circumstances, for example, in natural disasters. It "elicits pity, but neither deserves admiration nor warrants contrition." Tragedy, on the other hand, is a reflection of "necessity," for example, when "men or nations [are forced] to do evil in a good cause." It "elicits admiration as well as pity because it combines nobility with guilt." In contrast to both, irony arises from circumstances that at first may appear fortuitous or necessary but actually turn out to be neither. For irony involves the recognition and acceptance of "responsibility":

> While a pathetic or a tragic situation is not dissolved when a person becomes conscious of his involvement in it, an ironic situation must dissolve, if men or nations are made aware of their complicity in it. Such awareness involves some realization of the hidden vanity or pretension by which comedy is turned into irony. This realization must either lead to an abatement of the pretension, which means contrition; or it leads to a desperate accentuation of the vanities to the point where irony turns into pure evil. (1952a:viii)

Far from softening the biblical demand for *metanoia*, the rhetoric of irony actually brings it to a climax.

The Irony of American History thus proposes a new pattern of historical interpretation, so that the unprecedented crisis of the Cold War can be dealt with responsibly. While there are elements of a "tragic dilemma" evident in the nuclear balance of terror, what Niebuhr seeks to illuminate is the possibility for peaceful change based on the aesthetic distance opened up by biblical irony. He begins with the standard "religious version of our national destiny": the myth of "our nationhood as God's effort to make a new beginning in the history of mankind" (1952a:4). Yet instead of repudiating altogether the nation's rhetorical identification with biblical Israel, Niebuhr follows out the "syntax" of biblical history as it culminates in prophetic criticism./10/ To be Israel is to stand under judgment and in need of repentance. To be chosen by Providence, in short, is to be called to deeper levels of ironic self-awareness:

> Our . . . concern must be the double character of our ironic experience. Contemporary history not merely offers ironic refutation of some of our early hopes and present illusions about ourselves; but the experience which furnishes the refutation is occasioned by conflict with a foe who has transmuted ideals and hopes, which we most deeply cherish, into cruel realities which we most fervently abhor. (1952a:11)

Rather than rehearsing Niebuhr's attempt to show how this "double irony" emerges from the vicissitudes of American history, we should concentrate here on how it works rhetorically. The first level, "the refutation of early hopes . . . and present illusions," proceeds generally within the framework of biblical prophetism. On the one hand, Isaiah's warning to Babylon, "Thou saidst, I shall be a lady forever . . . therefore . . . these two things shall come to thee in a moment in one day, the loss of children and widowhood" (Isa 47:7, 9), illustrates a providential judgment on the pretensions of powerful nations; while on the other hand Luke's parable of the publican and the Pharisee shows that Israel's "pretensions of virtue are as offensive to God as the pretensions of power." Niebuhr interprets these passages to suggest that American history involves "ironic perils which compound the experiences of Babylon and Israel" (1952a:159–60). The second level of irony, our "conflict with a foe" who transforms illusions into "cruel realities," goes beyond prophetism in requiring a substantively Christological perspective. In order to achieve this, Niebuhr situates Miguel de Cervantes's Christian parable of *Don Quixote* in relation to the apocalyptic struggle between Christ and Antichrist. His warrant for making this move rests on the dialectic of wisdom and folly outlined by Paul in 1 Corinthians, compounded by a Christological "transvaluation of values": "The Christian faith is centered in a person who was as 'the stone which the builder rejected' and who became the 'head and corner'" (1952a:161). How this allows Niebuhr to enlist the aid of Don Quixote in discerning the double irony of the Cold War deserves exploration.

Briefly stated, for Niebuhr Quixote's foolishness exhibits the wisdom of irony. For Cervantes not only allows us to laugh at Quixote's own illusions but also calls us to reconize "the bogus character of knighthood itself." Quixote thus plays the role of a "Christ-like" fool ironizing the culture of medieval knighthood. By contrast, our own culture is ironized by a "demonic Quixote" who "changes only partly dangerous sentimentalities and inconsistencies in the bourgeois ethos into consistent and totally harmful ones" (1952a:15). "Communism," for Niebuhr, "is thus a fierce and unscrupulous Don Quixote on a fiery horse, determined to destroy every knight and lady of civilization; and confident that this slaughter will purge the world of evil" (1952a:15). In both cases, the possibility of double irony depends on the simultaneous presence of illusion and the pretense of being illusion-free; but in the latter the discrepancy between these is suppressed by the realities of power, thus giving to both "a satanic dimension," whereas in the former the lack of power renders the discrepancy vulnerable first to laughter, and perhaps ultimately to repentance.

Ironizing the National Interest

Niebuhr's effort to employ the concept of irony provides convincing evidence of his increasingly sophisticated rhetorical use of scripture. In order to go a step further and illustrate its impact on his approach to questions of political theory, we now turn to the idea of "the national interest." Given the complexities of Niebuhr's biblical rhetoric, the subtleties involved in his position here will come as no surprise. *The Irony of American History* (1952a:147) addresses this question in a context provided by George F. Kennan's *American Diplomacy, 1900–1950* (1951). In principle Niebuhr accepts Kennan's analysis of the "weaknesses" of "a too simple 'legalistic–moralistic' approach" to foreign policy and interprets these as "the perils to which all human idealism is subject and which our great power and our technocratic culture have aggravated" (1952a:148). Yet he criticizes Kennan's alternative, namely, "a return to the policy of making the 'national interest' the touchstone of our diplomacy," insisting that "egotism is not the proper cure for an abstract and pretentious idealism." Since in his view "a preoccupation with our own interests must lead to an illegitimate indifference toward the interests of others," the alternative is not egotism but a "concern for both the self and the other in which the self, whether individual or collective, preserves a 'decent respect for the opinions of mankind,' derived from a modest awareness of the limits of its own knowledge and power." What this amounts to is not a repudiation of national interest, but an attempt to limit its overriding authority in light of the framework of irony.

The question of national interest, in short, is just one dimension of the general problem of knowledge, power, and justice. Since the moral norm of justice remains ultimately religious—and, more particularly, biblical—in Niebuhr's ethic, his criticism of national interest predictably is also religious. This perspective may be derived from the conceptual systems of his "theological anthropology" and "theology of history" (see McCann, 1981). Here, though, we need to focus on how this perspective also emerges from Niebuhr's rhetorical use of scripture.

Within the framework of irony Niebuhr evaluates three strategies for bringing "power into the service of justice": (1) principles of distributive justice seeking a balance of power, (2) principles of "social and political review" that submit international relations to "the scrutiny of world public opinion," and (3) principles for "disciplining the exercise of power" through "an inner religious and moral check" (1952a:135–38). The biblical rhetoric of irony may be explicit only in the latter, but it is implicit in Niebuhr's assessment of the other two strategies. He concedes, first, that the balance-of-power principle will not provide permanent security in the absence of world government, and second, that the United Nations—if it does not pretend to be such a government—may play a constructive role as the forum of world public opinion. Even as he hopes that this forum will prevent "the fragmentary wisdom of any nation . . . from achieving bogus omniscience . . . ," he also knows that it cannot perform this role unless some "approximate equilibria of power" allow the weak to challenge the "inevitable biases" of the powerful. In other words, the first two strategies depend upon each other for their success. Yet the present situation, Niebuhr judged, offers little prospect that either will actually govern the conduct of international relations. Hence, Niebuhr turns to the third strategy, "the inner religious and moral check." By this he means that abuses of power are to be restrained by "the cultivation of a sense of justice" (1952a:138). It is precisely at this point, however, that Niebuhr's sense of justice presupposes a biblical rhetoric of irony.

The need for irony results from his assessment of the inadequacy of standard notions of justice as fairness. While "the inclination 'to give each man his due'" is necessary, it nevertheless is not sufficient inasmuch as "too confident a sense of justice always leads to injustice" (1952a:138). The difficulty lies not in the virtuous inclination as such but in our "inevitable" inability to see the true dimensions of the situation in which it is exercised: "Insofar as men and nations are 'judges in their own case' they are bound to betray the human weakness of having a livelier sense of their own interest than of the competing interest. That is why 'just' men and nations may easily become involved in ironic refutations of their moral pretensions" (1952a:138–39). Such blindness, in Niebuhr's opinion, can be overcome only through "religious humility." "This includes the charitable realization that the vanities of the other group or person, from which we suffer, are not different in kind, though possibly in degree, from similar vanities in our own life. It also includes a religious sense of the mystery and greatness of the other life, which we violate if we seek to comprehend it too simply from our standpoint" (1952a:139). His claim, in short, is that the framework of irony provides the religious perspective necessary to restrain "a too confident sense of justice" with a self-discipline born of "repentance."

The general argument can now be related to his specific criticism of national interest. In reading Kennan's proposal as a defense of national egotism, Niebuhr underscores the need for the "religious humility" that biblical irony should foster./11/ Realistic calculations of national interest may be less dangerous in foreign policy than the idealistic "pursuit of unlimited rather than limited ends," but they fail to escape the "peril of moral and spiritual complacency" (1952a:149). If the defense of national interest becomes the ultimate criterion of foreign policy, inevitably it will generate "pretensions" that tend not only to ignore the interests of others but also to obscure the true interests of the nation itself. Such pretensions, in turn, not only will inspire moral protest but also will be subject to "ironic refutations" as the narrowly realistic calculations based on them yield yet another round of incalculable consequences. This point, Niebuhr insists, can be grasped only in the perspective of biblical faith:

> The God before whom "the nations are as a drop in the bucket and are counted as small dust in the balances" is known by faith and not by reason. The realm of mystery and meaning which encloses and finally makes sense out of the baffling configurations of history is not identical with any scheme of rational intelligibility. The faith which appropriates the meaning in the mystery inevitably involves an experience of repentance for the false meanings which the pride of nations and cultures introduces into the pattern. Such repentance is the true source of charity; and we are more desperately in need of genuine charity than of more technocratic skills. (1952a:150)

National interest, in other words, may be a necessary criterion for Christian realism in foreign policy, but it cannot serve as an ultimate norm.

Niebuhr's use of the framework of irony for interpreting the context of foreign policy decisions is a biblically inspired rhetorical strategy designed to bring this religious insight to bear on these decisions./12/

Niebuhr and Morgenthau on the National Interest

The political significance of Niebuhr's biblical rhetoric can be identified by comparing his approach to the question of the national interest with that of other American political realists. Although his brief criticism of Kennan's *American Diplomacy: 1900–1950* is suggestive, the comparison is better drawn systematically by means of the writings of Hans Morgenthau. For at the same time that Niebuhr was defending his view of *The Irony of American History*, Morgenthau was writing without irony *In Defense of the National Interest*. Like Kennan and Niebuhr, Morgenthau vigorously criticized idealism in foreign policy. What Kennan and Niebuhr had identified as the "legalistic–moralistic approach," Morgenthau broke down into "The Four Intellectual Errors of American Postwar Policy": utopianism, legalism, sentimentalism, and neo-isolationism (1951:91–138). Despite their consensus regarding these perils, Morgenthau differed from Kennan—and both of them differed from Niebuhr—in how they construct the alternative.

Kennan's appeal to national interests seems based on skepticism. It is not only wrong to assume "that state behavior is a fit subject for moral judgment," it is also disastrous in terms of its historical consequences (Kennan: 100). Moreover, in international relations we must "have the modesty to admit that our own national interest is all that we are really capable of knowing and understanding . . ." (Kennan: 103). Morgenthau's defense, in contrast, is both less skeptical and more elaborate. Indeed, he emphasizes "the moral dignity of national interest," arguing for a "set of moral principles derived from political reality" (Morgenthau, 1951:33). Invoking the authority of Hobbes, he asserts that "universal moral principles, such as justice and equality, are capable of guiding political action only to the extent that they have been given concrete content and have been related to political situations by society" (1951:34). His emphasis on concreteness means two things: (1) Since no moral consensus exists beyond the national community, "the appeal to moral principles in the international sphere has no concrete meaning" (1951:35). (2) As a result, the defense of national interest becomes the highest "moral duty," inasmuch as "the attainment of a modicum of order and the realization of a minimum of moral values are predicated upon the existence of national communities capable of preserving order and realizing moral values within the limits of their power" (1951:38). In short, the defense of national interest requires not the sacrifice of moral principles but a careful reckoning of the only ones morally appropriate in international relations.

Nor are these principles strictly equated with self-interested "considerations of material power." In answer to critics who tried to picture him as advocating a ruthless utilitarianism, Morgenthau asserts that there are some subtle "ethical limitations" on the conduct of statesmen and diplomats: "They refuse to consider certain ends and to use certain means, either altogether or under certain conditions, not because in the light of expediency they appear impractical or unwise, but because certain moral rules interpose an absolute barrier" (1952:984). While he observes in a manner reminiscent of Thucydides that "their restraining function is most obvious and most effective in affirming the sacredness of human life in times of peace," it is clear that these unspecified moral rules for him constitute some sort of deontological limit to the theory and practice of power politics./13/ Nevertheless, lest his recognition of such "ethical limitations" tempt him to idealism, Morgenthau once more emphasizes the basic differences between public and private morality, the different approaches to "universal moral principles" required of individuals as opposed to states. In this way he hopes to sail his political ethic between "the Scylla of national suicide, the threat of which is ever present in the emphasis on moral principles to the neglect of the national interest . . . [and] the Charybdis of the crusading spirit which is the great destroyer of morality among the nations" (1949:211).

Morgenthau's use of the Niebuhrian metaphor of Scylla and Charybdis may evoke the question what, if anything, distinguishes their two perspectives. Before we take a final look at that issue, one further comparison between Kennan and Morgenthau is necessary as a preliminary, and it too is a subtle one. If they exhibit different levels of skepticism regarding the relevance of moral principles, similar differences are evident in the way they actually use the concept of national interest in their assessment of the Cold War. Kennan seems more the historicist and Morgenthau more the political scientist. Kennan's basic message seems to be flexibility in negotiations, on the premise that any more concrete proposal would be intellectually presumptuous. Morgenthau, in contrast, makes proposals based on calculations not only of the national interest of the United States but that of the Soviet Union as well (1951:159–220). These calculations, for the most part, involve analyses of the shifting balance of strategic power. The point here is that Morgenthau seems to know more than Kennan does, in the sense that the national interest functions for him not only as the ultimate principle at stake in foreign policy decisions but also as a scientific paradigm, the elements of which are measurable and therefore capable of generating a calculus of power for rational policy-making.

Given Morgenthau's pretension of political "science," it is not surprising that his rhetorical strategy consists of exposing the "errors" of his opponents and condemning their moral "failure of will." Indeed, in a manner that would hardly surprise Niebuhr, this claim to science ultimately is expressed religiously./14/ Morgenthau concludes his defense of national interest with a sermon reminiscent of Deuteronomy. Since "this is a tale of a noble people ignobly led," Morgenthau addresses his "indictment and . . . prophecy" (1951:239) to both the administration and the American people. But unlike the Hebrew prophets, who had a similar message and a similar audience in ancient Israel, he demands faith in "but one guiding star, one standard for thought, one rule for action: THE NATIONAL INTEREST" (1951:242; emphasis his own). This peroration, an unwitting parody—perhaps—of the "Shema Yisrael" (Deut 6:4), if meant seriously, can only be regarded as idolatrous from the perspective of Christian realism.

Morgenthau's attempt at biblical rhetoric, however, should not mislead us into seeing the differences between his approach to national interest and Niebuhr's simply in terms of the differences typical of idolaters and believers. For Morgenthau, like Niebuhr, does invoke biblical providence at least once in condemning "the blasphemous conviction that God is always on one's side and that what one wills oneself cannot fail to be willed by God also" (1967:10). Such a "lighthearted equation," he writes, is not only "politically pernicious" but also "morally indefensible, for it is the very sin of pride against which the Greek tragedians and the Biblical prophets have warned rulers and ruled" (1967:10)./15/ How can this be reconciled with the invocation of the national interests cited above, which may be read as the sum and substance of Morgenthau's "theology"? As lean as the evidence is, there is enough here to allow a more subtle interpretation of Morgenthau's differences from Niebuhr than we have thus far offered.

The reference to Greek tragedy and biblical prophecy provides the first clue. For Morgenthau, the lesson in both traditions apparently is the same: the condemnation of the sin of pride. Greek *hybris* (pride) and Hebrew *pasha'* (idolatry) for him apparently are equivalent, as are their consequences. Yet for Niebuhr, in contrast, Christianity is "beyond tragedy," precisely because while God does condemn sin, he also redeems it. History, in short, is a "conflict of grace and pride" (1943:127–212; see McCann, 1981:72–74) and not simply a judgment. Niebuhr's view of Greek tragedy highlights this difference:

> The hero of Greek tragedy suffers either because he defies God or because he is forced to violate some code of historical morality in the name of what seems to him a higher duty. He perishes because of his very strength. In the Promethean myth the hero is not a man at all but a demigod who defies Zeus for the sake of endowing mankind with all the arts. In this myth we come very close to the Christian conception of the inevitable guilt of pride which attaches to the highest human enterprise. Man becomes guilty of "hybris" and arouses the jealousy of God. But since God is conceived as only just and not loving he is something less than just. He is vindictive. The Promethean tragedy, in other words, recognizes the perennial self-destruction of man by his overreaching himself. But it sees no solution to the problem. Aeschylos, indeed, suggests again and again that men must observe the law of measure, thus introducing the solution of prudence, which became the very foundation of Aristotelian ethics. But the heroes of Aeschylos are tragically noble precisely because they disregard the author's pious advice. (1937b:160-61; cf. 165-66)

Yet this is precisely the kind of prudence upon which Morgenthau bases his political ethic (1952:986). The difference between this and Niebuhr's religious ethic may thus be understood as the difference between one theology rooted in Greek myth and another in the Hebraic mythical framework of the Bible. Greek *hybris* ultimately is not to be equated with the idolatry denounced by the Hebrew prophets, and thus the two forms of political realism, apparently so similar, diverge in subtle but significant ways.

But this is only the initial clue. Pursuing it further, we find that just as their views of the human predicament diverge systematically, so do the metaphors Niebuhr and Morgenthau use to depict God's relationship to it. Morgenthau's "Providence" is an abstraction, the negative limit to human aspiration and achievement—in short, the divine "Nemesis" of Greek tragedy. His brief remarks suggest that any identification with the will of God is "blasphemous," that under no circumstances can any nation claim legitimately to be God's chosen people. History, being thus exorcised of any claim to religious significance, is handed over to "Aristotelian prudence," now systematized as "political science." In contrast, the Providence discerned by the Hebrew prophets and apostles and assumed by Niebuhr is manifest in and through history. God is present not as an abstract Nemesis but as a personal Lord who enters into covenants with the nations. It is therefore not always blasphemous to identify or be identified with the will of God, although sins of pride and idolatry do occur within this identification. Apart from faith's discernment of God's active sovereignty there is, in short, no basis for transcending the national interest. If, following Hobbes, the national community is the ultimate source of morality, then Morgenthau quite logically regards the national interest as the highest moral duty and Providence as the symbol of its negative limit in political prudence. If, following the Bible, the national community is called into being by One

Who Is the ultimate source of morality, then Niebuhr quite logically must try to criticize national interest in the presence of a Providence who smiles ironically on all human aspiration and achievement.

The differences between Niebuhr's approach to national interest and Morgenthau's hinge on this theological point. Morgenthau does not entirely lack a notion of God and sin; but since his God is unobtrusive and his sin abstract, the theological dimension can be disposed of in a few short paragraphs as a negative precondition for political realism. Since Niebuhr, in contrast, confesses a living God and a sin defined as rebellion against God's will, the theological dimension can never be disposed of as merely preliminary but must continually be reenacted as a rhetorical "frame of meaning" for Christian realism (1958:44). Niebuhr's biblical rhetoric of irony is not just incidental to his approach to national interest. On the contrary, that rhetoric illumines the ultimate context in which appeals to national interest have any legitimacy at all./16/

The Christian Ingredient in Christian Realism

The difference between Niebuhr's Christian realism and other forms of American political realism should not be exaggerated. In words borrowed from Morgenthau, they lie not so much in "the practical judgments" as in "the philosophies and standards of thought" by which foreign policy decisions are assessed. The fundamental difference between the two is a difference in rhetorics. Does this also amount to a significant difference in substance?

If we accept that rhetoric is never merely a literary embellishment of concepts already given but rather can itself define and carry such concepts, then the difference between Morgenthau and Niebuhr is in fact a substantive one. The need for Niebuhr's biblical rhetoric of irony emerges precisely at the point where he and Morgenthau most agree, namely, in their common resolve to resist all forms of political idolatry. They are one in viewing their resistance as inspired by the legacy of the Hebrew prophets. But, while Morgenthau sees this legacy only in negative terms, Niebuhr recognizes something positive, an invitation to the renewal of faith in God's sovereignty in history. Given Niebuhr's keen awareness that idolatry, like all forms of sin, may be overcome "in principle but not in fact," it is not surprising that he should emphasize the "perils" implicit in this positive insight. Any attempt to render it in terms of a closed conceptual system would surely result in one more idolatrous theology. Understanding that, Morgenthau apparently chose silence. Niebuhr, however, understood better that such silence soon becomes vacuous, thus opening itself to "ironic refutations." His biblical rhetoric, in short, risks speech in a space where even silence is unsafe. To the extent that it can be resisted at all, idolatry is best exorcized through prophetic forms of speech. The authenticity of Christian realism, therefore, depends on its faithfulness to these forms in a biblical rhetoric of irony. It is biblical through and through, and in contrast to Kennan and Morgenthau it is an authentically Christian effort to cast realism at the center of American political life.

NOTES

/1/   A definitive analysis, which is not possible in the present context, would have to elaborate the following points: (1) A clarification of the theory of rhetoric: I understand rhetoric not as a form of literary embellishment, but as a form of substantive argument based not upon logic alone but also upon the traditions of some community of discourse. Rhetoric, therefore, is an art of persuasion, but not the kind of emotional manipulation allegedly practiced by the Sophists. While its appeal is always already emotional as well as cognitive, its claim in any given argument remains subject to discursive criticism and revision. This notion of rhetoric is consistent, I believe, with that proposed by Kenneth Burke, Wayne Booth, and Paul Ricoeur. (2) A clarification of the relationship between Niebuhr's biblical rhetoric and his theology based on the concepts of "biblical religion." In what follows, I outline two trajectories in Niebuhr's Christian realism, the one moving toward conceptual system, the other toward rhetorical argument. The question persists whether Niebuhr's rhetoric is directly related to scripture or indirectly filtered through the conceptual system of "biblical religion." In claiming that the one is not reducible to the other, I am minimizing the influence of the conceptual system upon the rhetoric. In other words, Niebuhr's reconstruction of "biblical religion" as mythology opens up the possibility of a rhetorical use of scripture without predetermining the content of that rhetoric. This thesis would have to be argued in detail to be persuasive, but one piece of evidence favors it already: the fact that "the framework of irony" was not discovered until some fifteen years or so after the adoption of the category of mythology. The "framework," in short, slowly emerges over the years from Niebuhr's habitual recourse to scripture, a habit that was reinforced, if not made possible, by his insight into the nature of biblical mythology.

/2/   The evidence for this interpretation of Niebuhr's early work is available in McCann, 1981:37–45.

/3/   Alasdair MacIntyre (1981:11) defines emotivism as "the doctrine that all evaluative judgments and more specifically all moral judgments are *nothing* but expressions of preference, expressions of attitude or feeling, insofar as they are moral or evaluative in character." In saying that Niebuhr was an emotivist in his understanding of religion, I am dramatizing the fact that he saw religion's contribution essentially as a profound feeling, specifically, the feeling of reverence for personality. This emotion, once identified, was to be construed theoretically with the help of metaphysics and ethics. The point is that this understanding of religion is different from one that makes cognitive claims for religious "emotions" as such. Niebuhr's use of the concept of personality is discussed at greater length in McCann, 1981:19–22.

/4/   This statement, of course, is a reconstruction of Niebuhr's intentions. He never was an "academic" theologian, and therefore one cannot expect to find sustained methodological reflection in his writings. Nevertheless, had he followed out the logic of his occasional remarks on method, something like the pattern I have described would be apparent, with the consequences I have suggested. See McCann, 1981:25–41.

/5/   This view of Niebuhr's "frank dualism in morals" is somewhat at odds with that outlined by David Little (125–57). Little apparently takes *Moral Man and Immoral Society* as Niebuhr's definitive statement on the "two moralities." Thus, he sees Niebuhr as postulating a dichotomy and then, somewhat inconsistently, compromising it: "It is never quite clear how this second position gets on with the one we have just summarized" (128). The lack of clarity can be dispelled if *Moral Man and Immoral Society* is read as representing merely a stage in the development of Niebuhr's thought. Its dualism, which Niebuhr inherited from Max Weber, becomes the point of departure for his attempt to define a truly "independent Christian ethic." Niebuhr's intention and his fundamental argument, as outlined in *An Interpretation of Christian Ethics*, are clear. Theologians legitimately may still dispute the merits of Niebuhr's way of overcoming this moral dualism.

/6/   Niebuhr's meditation on the art of portraiture suggests both the possibilities of and the limits to his understanding of theological discourse as a form of biblical rhetoric. The possibilities emerge from the thesis that he actually argues, namely, that theology is more like poetry than it is like science. This opens the way for taking rhetoric seriously as a form of argument. The limits are implicit in his actual remarks on the portrait artist. He implies that the truth of the portrait is independent of the act of portraiture, since the artist deliberately falsifies some of the details for an overall symbolic effect. This notion is dangerously close to the outmoded theory of rhetoric as a form of literary embellishment. A more insightful view of the artistic process of portraiture and its relationship to truth is given in Gibson Winter's *Liberating Creation: Foundations of Religious Social Ethics* (1981). Winter's discussion is genuinely dialectical, because it also notes how the one portrayed comes to embody the truth as symbolized in the portrait. This implies that truth emerges from the artistic process as a whole and cannot be grasped independent of it. A similar claim may be made for biblical rhetoric. The truth of "biblical religion" cannot be grasped independent of the process by which it is reenacted rhetorically. This clarification, I believe, is consistent with Niebuhr's overall intention. The inexhaustibility of the theologian's attempt to reenact "the truth in myths" is emphasized by Niebuhr. It is the point at issue in his differences with Bultmann's method of "demythologization" (1955:171–72) and with Tillich's attempt to translate biblical myth into an "ontology" (1952b:216–27).

/7/   This term, taken from Paul Ricoeur's *The Symbolism of Evil* (1969), emphasizes the fact that truth disclosed in myth can be validated by attempting to live it as a way of life. It also implies that the claims of myth are open to reflection in practical discourse, and are not simply the expresison of an emotional preference.

/8/   This term, also taken from Ricoeur's *Symbolism of Evil* (1969), refers to the level of reflective awareness characteristic of those who attempt an "existential verification" of myth. Their's is a "naiveté" insofar as they continue to participate in the world disclosed by myth; but it is "second naiveté" insofar as they are wrestling with the various critiques of myth (historical, social-psychological, and philosophical) and thus have abandoned their "first naiveté" or literal-minded faith in myth. This is precisely what Niebuhr had in mind when he said that "biblical symbols" must be taken "seriously but not literally" (1943:50).

/9/ This interpretation of the rhetorical trajectory in Niebuhr's work does not contradict what was said about the conceptual trajectory in McCann, 1981. On the contrary, it is complementary insofar as it helps clarify the discussion there regarding the inadequacies of Niebuhr's "theology of history." The point made there was formulated negatively. Niebuhr's theology of history is conceptually inadequate because it is but a metaphorical extension of his theological anthropology. A recognition of the rhetorical trajectory in Niebuhr's work allows for a more positive interpretation: The theology of history cannot be reduced to a rigorous conceptual system because it includes a continual reenactment of the biblical rhetoric of irony. Niebuhr gives indirect testimony to this point in his methodological criticisms of Bultmann (1955) and Tillich (1952b).

/10/ Niebuhr's strategy is misunderstood by those who, like Richard Fox, see his refusal to repudiate America's rhetorical identification with biblical Israel as undermining "the basis of 'prophetic Christianity'" (Fox: 262). It is not surprising that Fox's misunderstanding is rooted in his failure to appreciate Niebuhr's biblical rhetoric as anything more than a "potent coupling of Augustinian insight and homiletic charisma" (1976:245). This formulation presupposes that the truth in myth is independent of myth and safely detachable from it. Niebuhr knew that this was impossible. Instead, he invites participation in myth as a precondition for discovering the truth within it. Hence America's role in the postwar world is accepted as the will of God, thus establishing the link with biblical Israel, but the history of Israel then is scrutinized for clues to the specific meaning of that will. God's judgments on Israel thus are transferred to America. Far from undermining "prophetic Christianity" Niebuhr's biblical rhetoric seems to be a promising way to carry it forward as an interpretation of American history.

/11/ Niebuhr's critique of Kennan's political realism should be kept in mind when one evaluates the current controversy among Niebuhr's students over human rights in American foreign policy. The analysis here is congruent with Ronald H. Stone's attempt to distinguish Niebuhr's position from that of Ernest W. Lefever and Michael Novak (unpublished paper, "Christian Realism and Human Rights," presented to the 1982 annual meeting of the Society of Christian Ethics).

/12/ The pattern derived here from *The Irony of American History* is readily discernible in Niebuhr's other works on this topic. In an essay, "America's Moral and Spiritual Resources," edited by Ernest W. Lefever for *The World Crisis and American Responsibility*, Niebuhr makes the same points about the inadequacy of political realism and places them in the context of a proper "frame of meaning" for interpreting the world crisis (1958:30–48). Here Niebuhr's differences from Kennan and Morgenthau are prominent.

/13/ The absence of irony in Morgenthau is evident from the examples he selects in order to define this deontological limit. Soviet foreign policy is criticized for its failure to recognize or to adhere to these moral principles, while the United States' Good Neighbor Policy in Latin America is praised as an example of how it is possible, once a nation's "minimum of vital interests" is secure, "to transfer those principles of political morality to the international scene and to deal with divergent interests there with the same methods of genuine compromise and conciliation which are a permanent element of its domestic political life" (1952:985). With the wisdom of hindsight, it is possible to regard this statement as illustrating precisely the point of Niebuhr's sensitivity to the "ironic refutations" that a self-sufficient realism inevitably evokes.

/14/   Niebuhr's criticisms of the religious pretensions of social science are available in two essays published in *Christian Realism and Political Problems*, "Faith and the Empirical Method in Modern Realism" (1953:1–14) and "Ideology and the Scientific Method" (1953:75–94). Kenneth W. Thompson, in his analysis of Niebuhr's position on national interest, acknowledges the importance of this line of criticism; he does not, however, call attention to the fact that Niebuhr's skepticism here distinguishes his position from Morgenthau's (Thompson: 167–88).

/15/   It is difficult to reconcile Morgenthau's austere theology with his attempt at biblical rhetoric. Morgenthau's demand for "faith" in "but one guiding star . . ." seems just as idolatrous as any overtly religious identification of the national interest with the will of God. This difficulty unwittingly illustrates Niebuhr's point that those who lack an appreciation for biblical irony most surely will be subject to "ironic refutations."

/16/   For a similar understanding of Niebuhr's realism, and particularly his differences from Morgenthau and Kennan, see Good.

WORKS CONSULTED

Fox, Richard W.
    1976   "Reinhold Niebuhr and the Emergence of the Liberal Realist
                            Faith, 1930–1945." *Review of Politics* 38 (No. 2, April):244–
                            65.

Good, Robert C.
    1960   "The National Interest and Political Realism: Niebuhr's
                            'Debate' with Morgenthau and Kennan." *Journal of Poli-
                            tics* 22 (November): 597–619.

Hampshire, Stuart, ed.
    1978   *Public and Private Morality*. Cambridge: Cambridge Univer-
                            sity Press.

Hook, Sidney
    1956   "Prophet of Man's Glory and Tragedy." *New York Times Book
                            Review* (January 29, 1956): 6–7 and 22.

Kennan, George F.
    1951   *American Diplomacy: 1900–1950*. Chicago: University of Chi-
                            cago Press.

Little, David
    1978   "Duties of Station vs. Duties of Conscience: Are There Two
                            Moralities?" In *Private and Public Ethics*. Edited by
                            Donald G. Jones. New York: Edwin Mellen Press.

MacIntyre, Alasdair
    1981   *After Virtue: A Study in Moral Theory*. Notre Dame, IN:
                            University of Notre Dame Press.

McCann, Dennis P.
1980   "Hermeneutics and Ethics: The Example of Reinhold Nie-
            buhr." *Journal of Religious Ethics* 8/1 (Spring): 27–53.
1981   *Christian Realism and Liberation Theology: Practical Theolo-
            gies in Creative Conflict.* Maryknoll, NY: Orbis Books.

Morgenthau, Hans J.
1949   "The Primacy of National Interest." *American Scholar* 18
            (Spring): 207–12.
1951   *In Defense of the National Interest.* New York: Alfred A.
            Knopf.
1952   "Another 'Great Debate': The National Interest of the United
            States." *American Political Science Review* 46/4 (December):
            961–88.
1967   *Politics among the Nations: The Struggle for Power and
            Peace.* 4th ed. New York: Alfred A. Knopf.

Niebuhr, Reinhold
1927   *Does Civilization Need Religion?* New York: Macmillan.
1932   *Moral Man and Immoral Society.* New York: Scribner.
1933   "Optimism and Utopianism." *The World Tomorrow* 16/8
            (February 22, 1933): 179–80.
1934   *Reflections on the End of an Era.* New York: Scribner.
1935   *An Interpretation of Christian Ethics.* Reprint. New York:
            Seabury, 1979.
1937a   "The Truth in Myths." In *Faith and Politics.* Edited by
            Ronald H. Stone. New York: George Braziller, 1968.
1937b   *Beyond Tragedy: Essays on the Christian Interpretation of
            History.* New York: Scribner.
1941   *The Nature and Destiny of Man,* Vol. 1. New York: Scribner.
1943   *The Nature and Destiny of Man,* Vol. 2. New York: Scribner.
1946   *Discerning the Signs of the Times.* New York: Scribner.
1950   "The Hydrogen Bomb." Pp. 235–37 in *Love and Justice:
            Selections from the Shorter Writings of Reinhold Niebuhr.*
            Edited by D. B. Robertson. Cleveland: World/Meridian Books,
            1967.
1952a   *The Irony of American History.* New York: Scribner.
1952b   "Biblical Thought and Ontological Speculation in Tillich's The-
            ology." Pp. 216–27 in *The Theology of Paul Tillich.* Edited by
            Charles W. Kegley and Robert W. Bretall. New York: Macmil-
            lan, 1952.
1953   *Christian Realism and Political Problems.* New York: Scrib-
            ner.
1955   "The Heresy Trials." *Christianity and Crisis* 15/22 (December
            26, 1955): 171–72.
1958   "America's Moral and Spiritual Resources." Pp. 30–48 in *The
            World Crisis and American Responsibility.* Edited by
            Ernest W. Lefever. Westport, CT: Greenwood Press.

Ricoeur, Paul
1969   *The Symbolism of Evil.* Boston: Beacon Press.

Thompson, Kenneth W.
    1955   "Beyond National Interest: A Critical Evaluation of Reinhold
                         Niebuhr's Theory of International Politics." *Review of Poli-
                         tics* 17 (April):167–88.

Winter, Gibson
    1981   *Liberating Creation: Foundations of Religious Social Ethics.*
                         New York: Crossroad.

VII

The *Polis* in America as *Imago Dei*: Neither Secular nor "Born Again"

James E. Sellers

The oldest formula for community in America is in deep trouble. I have in mind the venerable claim that if community in America is to have true political substance—that is, any standing beyond the private and the familial—it must be based on two moral components. These are the integrity of the secular and the relevance of the religious. The two components in interplay—now as consensus, perhaps more often as tension—provide a unique basis for life together in the larger context, for the *polis*.

The historic doctrine of separation of church and state is but an example, and a negative one, of this formula. The implications of the formula go beyond—so long as the two components work as a true dialectic, which means that neither can fare well without the good health of the other. Under such conditions, each component checks, reinforces, compensates; together, they provide the very constitution of the possibilities for a community larger than the local, racial, and mean.

The trouble stems from what has befallen the dialectic. The two components, in our time, may be coming apart. What was a dialectic may be turning into a dualism, a confrontation of dubious, even exhausted, options. What was once a saving touch of grace in the appeal beyond the here and now to "religious" yearnings may be turning into little more than an ill-tempered rush to narrow religiosity. What was once a bracing aperture to the honest, sometimes breathtaking fresh air of the secular today shows the overtones of a cave-in to the normless and the aimless.

Both the secular and the religious pediments of American community, I believe, ultimately stem from biblical symbols, especially those dealing with the idea of the neighbor. When these foundations seem to fail, what may be needed is a new biblical basis for the intrepretation of political community in America, a new conception of religious meaning in the public, political arena. I propose, in what follows, an attempt at recovery by way of reviving an old biblical idea in a new setting. The new setting is the pluralistic American experience, deeply in need of new ethical guidelines—religious yet nonsectarian, public and open to all yet pledged to historic ethical values.

The old idea is the biblical teaching of humankind as created in the image of God—a symbol neither "secular" nor "born again" but dedicated to the spiritual renewal of the *polis*, the realm of our common life. Let us pursue, then, the idea of humankind—exemplified in America's kind—as constituted in the image of God. In this pursuit we may hope to recover the vision of human wholeness, rising beyond the divided self and the fragmented allegiance of persons to this preliminary loyalty or to that, to the raising of a *polis*.

The Biblical Question of the Neighbor

Any attempt to discern biblical themes in the formation of community—political or social, larger in any event than the familial—must deal first with a prior problem, the question of who is the neighbor. If progress can be made on that problem, then the question of community, even so vexed a question as the constitution of "political" community, can be more confidently addressed.

Both the Hebrew Bible and the New Testament hold out love of neighbor, a benefit or epiphenomenon of God's love, as the basis for community. Moreover, there is not a split between the two Testaments on the subject, as is commonly supposed. Both Judaic and Christian thought cast up contrasting biblical approaches to the question of the neighbor and, derivatively, to the larger problem of community.

Ernst Simon, after pondering biblical and rabbinical meanings of the Hebrew *rēʻâ* (neighbor), moves from the orthodox Jewish view that *"reʻa* is not any neighbor at all but only a fellow Jew" (Fox: 35) to the assertion, which troubles him in the process of adopting it, that "our neighbor is every man. . . ." He justifes this revisionism by arguing that halakah, the unwritten law, "cannot satisfy all our needs."

In a spirited dissent, Harold Fisch argues that not only can we not love our enemies, but that the operative mandate in the Torah—"You shall love your neighbor as yourself" (Lev 19:18)—refers specifically to the Jewish people. "To attempt to widen the concept into a general, and undifferentiated love of mankind after the manner of some impractical ethical humanism is to blur, and ultimately to render meaningless, the particularistic side of Judaism" (Fox: 59).

The same tension prevails in Christianity: there are two camps, which I will call for the moment the "wideners" and the "narrowers." Men and women are enabled to engage in larger community (beyond the family level, chiefly the political and social levels), goes the "widener" argument, because we are all children of God. This claim rests on the biblical teaching on the "image of God" (Gen 1:26), a powerful idea that I will reinterpret later on for American political community. On the basis of this idea the "wideners" say that our capacity to enter into a social or political contract is an intramundane reflection of God's own creativity, even of his covenant making with his creatures. When we are most human, in intercourse with each other (sexual, existential, and political), we most truly reflect God's own being. We are thus chosen for community by birth rather than rebirth, as creatures of God, and we come equipped with the aptitude for fellowship- and *polis*-making by reenacting in our own lives the fellowship offered us by God.

"Love's outreach is many-sided and wide-aimed," argues Joseph Fletcher (107), one of the most eloquent recent representatives of this view. "It is pluralist, not monist; multilateral, not unilateral." Christian ethics radically obligates Christians to love not only acquaintances but also strangers, and beyond that "even the enemy-neighbor." Christians are not asked to abandon their ethical judgments, but they are asked that, with respect to all of these neighbors, "however we rate them, and whether we like them or not, they . . . are to be loved"—as neighbors.

A second view of community, that of orthodox, evangelical Christianity, is more pessimistic in its premises. In this version, human fellowship-making capacities were destroyed, or nearly so, in the Fall, and thus the restoration of community is dependent on spiritual rebirth—or, in the phrase popular of late, becoming "born again." A direct connection is made here between the possibility of community and the reality of salvation. If we couple that claim with a fairly restricted view of those who are reborn—either the Reformed doctrine of election, which limits the number by God's prior, somewhat penurious decision, or the Arminian doctrine of sanctification, which limits the number by the arduous, pleasureless nature of born-againness—we can see why it is reasonable to speak of this view as a "narrower" vision of community.

"It is not to be supposed," says Jonathan Edwards, prince of neo-Puritan thinkers, "that all that are now moved and awakened will ever be savingly converted." Who knows but that God "is now gathering in his elect?" In that case, the scope of community—I suppose we must qualify it and say "spiritual" community—may turn out to be somewhat limited. Edwards hopes not, but the truth must be faced: those who aren't in are out. "Your neighbors, your relations, acquaintances, or companions that are converted, will that day appear against you. They will not only be taken while you are left. . . . They will rise up as witnesses and will declare what a precious opportunity you had, and did not improve . . ." (1959: 104–5).

This is eighteenth-century neo-Reformed American thinking, but it is echoed in our own day: conservative religion is growing, and there may well be valid reasons for it. People may need in any age in history to be identified with well-defined spiritual and moral values, to be given a spiritual anchor in a troubled sea of social ferment (Jung: 95; cf. Kelley).

The tragedy is that, in our day, these two visions of community—the alternative bases of human consociation—have little contact, seem to have little in common, and are growing farther and farther apart. The tension becomes so great that no kind of accommodation seems any longer possible. Indeed, the tendency is for the two camps to tend, each in its own way, toward a *reductio ad absurdum*. With the "narrowers," the inclination toward particularity, sacrificing larger ethical concerns, is well ingrained. According to J. H. Houlden, this tendency may well go back to the New Testament. Houlden is especially critical, in this respect, of the Johannine literature. Of the first letter of John, he suggests, the idea of love *beyond the group* (and thus of political community, we could add) is virtually ruled out: "Love seems almost like a huddling together for warmth and safety in the face of the world. . . . there can be no obligation here any more than in the Gospel [of John] to love beyond the bounds of the brotherhood" (39). The authors of both Gospel and Letter, Houlden says, "write as members of a small enclosed christian group, confident of salvation, sure that the world is reaching its end, convinced indeed that the God who created all things has acted to save but unable to feel that his action works effectively outside the brotherhood of Christ's people" (41).

Perhaps there was justification for such "huddling" in the Roman world: perhaps there was good reason for spiritual elitism among the Puritans. But it is not clear that this same zealous drawing of lines is the right response to diverse, pluralistic America today—especially when Christians are no longer a pressed, harried minority, and since they may not claim elitism morally in a world in which a Muslim and a Jew (Sadat and Begin) have won the Nobel Peace Prize.

If the narrowers risk the loss of larger ethical and political concern, the wideners tend, just as dangerously, toward a loss of religious substance. This problem—the yielding of the spiritual to the secular—has plagued American Christianity from its earliest days. Joseph Haroutunian, in *Piety Versus Moralism*, chronicles "the passing of the New England Theology," and tells how the modified Calvinism of what was once Puritan New England, far from being invigorated by the new currents of liberty, individualism, and the right to happiness, gave up the God of their fathers and settled for respectability.

"Really bad ideas," he says, "such as original sin . . . were quietly set aside. . . . Divine grace became moral, resistible, insufficient. . . . Such Calvinism was really not very objectionable, but it also was not Calvinism. It was the faith of the fathers ruined by the faith of their children" (281).

This trend continues to the point that Protestantism, at least, not to mention some strands of Judaism and Roman Catholicism, "runs the risk of becoming a cultural religion, engendering very little in the way of identity or belonging" (Jung: 102). Joseph Fletcher surely did not intend to illustrate this loss of centeredness in his description of the centrifugal possibilities of Christian love in the "new morality," but his language is witness: "Love uses a shotgun," he writes, "not a rifle!" The idea of widening becomes a flood; love must be "omnified, taking everything into account and optimific, doing all that it can" (89).

What is wrong here is not the widening per se. It is the loss of centered religious substance, of religious identity. In today's public schools, for example, children cannot come up with "the rudest outline of what Christians or Jews believe"; they could not "recount accurately a single story from the Old or the New Testament." Yet they may very well be instructed in Hindu or Buddhist religion (Cameron: 44).

Nor is the problem "secularism" (or "secular humanism," in the current jibe-phrase of the religious right). Secular values, from the day of Franklin, Paine, and Jefferson, have been one of the pediments of political community in America. The inalienable rights of the Declaration of Independence, the Bill of Rights, even the crude, nose-thumbing vulgarity of the frontier, all of these profane values are a vital part of the American ethic—and the best friend the religious forces ever had: "Congress shall make no law respecting an establishment of religion. . . ."

The genius of the American system is not that it is secular, and certainly not that it is a "Christian nation." Its genius is that it has evolved as a partnership—read tension, if you like—between the secular and the religious. But the religious foundation, when it suicidally divides into its own opposed subcamps, the narrow and the widening, risks yielding its role, its effectiveness, in the partnership. One group from the religious side insists on what can only be called sectarian values that defy rather than support political community. Another faction seems bent on selling out its religious stock, as if there were a bear market, and joining the secularists. The result is the worst of worlds. If there is no longer a partnership—the secular as a going concern, the religious as a going concern—the distinctive values of the American experience are in jeopardy. The wideners, revolted by the strictures of the born-again, find it

all too easy to retreat entirely out of the camp of religion. The narrowers, ever retreating from the vision of equality, call for impossible
possibilities—"Christianizing" the country, reducing the scope of the
political to the family. The fact that lately these latter forces have color-
fully entered the political arena (the Moral Majority, pro-life proposi-
tions, proposals for book-banning legislation, and so on) in no way shows
them supportive of political community.

What we need in America today, in sum, is a new face for religious
meaning in the public, political arena. The old formula secular/
religious—the two in creative tension—that has worked for all these
years may now need to yield. We may have to look to a third, mediating
possibility, a religious possibility lodged between the two camps of
exhausted options, the capitulation to the worst of the secular, on the one
hand, and the theological one-sidedness of the "born-again" on the other.
What I advocate is the recovery of an old, biblical idea in a new setting.
The new setting is the pluralistic American experience. The old idea is
the biblical teaching of humankind as created in the image of God./1/

Imago Dei *as a Political Teaching*

Then God said, "Let us make man in our image." (Gen 1:26)

Although there are only a half dozen or so references, direct and indirect, in the entire Bible to the *imago dei* story, it has played a remarkable
role in the interpretation of religious anthropology—in rabbinical thought
and in both Roman Catholic and Protestant theology, from Irenaeus and
Augustine through the Reformers to Barth and Brunner./2/

From the literature I conclude that there are five major approaches
in Christian theology to the *imago dei* story:

1. The "image of God" may be defined as that personal human attribute that, abstracted from the self, is most nearly godlike. Reason and
will are the leading contenders, but the also-rans include soul, conscience, freedom, and moral sense. There are two problems with this
approach. One is that this way of thinking—abstracting an attribute
from the self—is an utterly un-Hebraic way of dealing with a Hebraic
story. Hebrew thought takes the self to be a unity. A second problem, for
our purposes, is that the *imago dei* is not even to be looked for in the
total self, "but in an active relation of man to his neighbour and to God"
(Cairns: 178). Thus, the concept of *community* rather than personal
anthropology may be a more appropriate locus for reflecting on the
image of God. Jacob Jervell points out that rabbinical thought, in dealing
with the story of the *imago dei*, thinks of Adam as *Kollektivpersönlich-
keit*—"Adam ist die Menschheit" (105). We are immediately reminded,

in the field of American religious studies, of Jonathan Edwards, who in his treatise *Original Sin* describes Adam as a "public person," including, ultimately, the whole of humanity (1974:187).

2. The *imago dei* may be defined purely by the New Testament or by Christology, saying *tout court* that Jesus Christ is *imago dei*. But this approach rashly dispenses with the presupposition of Christian faith, the Hebrew Bible. To be sure, Christians are to think of grace in Christ as rehabilitating the sin-scarred *imago dei*. Chistians must nonetheless simultaneously think about the subject by taking seriously the story in the Hebrew Bible. (For a close approach to this position, see Muckenhirn: 58–59.)

3. A dubious approach, related to the preceding idea, is that of the "relic school," classically the Protestant Reformers, who held that the Fall obliterated or nearly vitiated the image of God, leaving only a "relic" of it. Emil Brunner and Karl Barth spilled much ink debating this view in the early 1930s. Each went on, in subsequent writings, to a more ample, helpful statement (Brunner and Barth; Barth, 1958; Brunner). Neither thinker's views gained any large lasting audience in America. Still, the "relic" theory offers us a clue. The image of God may remain, but the Fall changes it. The transition from innocence to experience does not vitiate its substance, but it does make of it a very different thing. We are like God before the Fall, like him after the Fall—but being so becomes a tougher and less happy assignment. In any event, the Hebrew Bible "never suggests that the image of God was lost by the Fall" (Porteus: 682). To begin with it points us in a quite different direction from that taken in previous theology. Thus we must keep in mind for later the question of what effect the Fall may have had on the image of God in humankind.

4. A more promising approach is to ask the question: Compendiously speaking, what is God like? Augustine asked that question but got side-tracked on a variation of the second approach above, that is, to refer the question to Christian theology. The *imago dei* for Augustine is a reflection of the Trinity. In a recent effort, Gordon Kaufman, arguing from a broader perspective, maintains that since God is known to us—in both Testaments, we might add—by his creative acts in history, the signal thing about human existence, if it is like God, is its historicity. "Being intrinsically historical like God himself, man is capable of entering into community with him, responding to him creatively and freely" (Kaufman: 329). An advantage of this approach is that Kaufman has seen in the *imago dei* not something interior to personal being, but something transpersonal—the basis of community. Indeed, my only problem with his approach is that he does not draw out its implications.

5. A fifth approach is striking in the simplicity of its plan, even if it turns out to be protracted in its application. This is to ask the obvious question: What does the *imago dei* story itself say about humankind? Bonhoeffer (1959) and Barth (1958) ask this question and conclude that the image of God is human sexuality, our potential to enter into creative relationships. "The only thing that we are told about the creation of man," says Barth—apart from the fact that it was done by the Word in God's image—is that "God created them male and female." Barth goes on to say that man's constitution as a sexual being reflects his calling to fellowship: he has a creaturely version of an "I–Thou" nature (1958:199).

What is amiss here is that sexuality is decidedly not the "only thing" that we are told in this story about the creation of the human. It may be the first thing, but we are told at least two other things. We are told in addition that humans are constituted as God's chosen creative managers. "In its immediate setting," says J. Philip Hyatt, "the making of man in God's image probably meant that man was created to have dominion over the . . . other works of God's hands." Hyatt adds that Psalm 8—the one with the familiar line about man as nearly up to the angels—repeats the conferring-of-dominion theme (105–6).

One further thing is said about humans in the story. They are the crowning part of a creation that is good—not good in itself, and as for humans, not morally good in themselves—but good as blessed by God. In Psalm 8 humanity is said to be crowned with "glory and honor." The modern word for this attribute is *dignity*.

Barth and Brunner, indeed most of the so-called Continental theologians of their era, had little influence on American life at large, and only limited effect on American religious thought. One reason is the "verticality" of that theology, which, as we shall see, is largely inappropriate in the American world of reference. An exception, however, is the *imago dei* discussion—which, reinterpreted in the American context, may bear fruit not foreseeable under the auspices of European theology.

Of the foregoing approaches to the *imago dei*, the third, fourth, and fifth offer the best clues for an American reinterpretation of the political meaning of community. And if we seek the predominant themes of these approaches, three stand out. All are given in the story itself (if we include the Fall). All reflect what God is like. All point to humankind as constituted for community.

These three are:

1. Creativity. Humanity is creatively godlike in two ways. One way is the human capacity for relationships reflected in sexuality (Barth). The other is close to what Kaufman means by historicity, but I think we must stress the historical mandate to "have dominion" (Gen 1:26b), so that the

capacity for management becomes the second aspect of our human creativity./3/

2. A twofold dignity, the first part being the "worth" (which must not be confused with moral goodness) of whatever God creates, especially the worth of that being created and endowed with deputyship. This dignity is built in and inalienable, even in the face of sin. The second aspect of human dignity emerges from the story of the Fall, where one can see how the *imago dei* is changed. It, along with sin, is self-conferred. No one who has read Erik Erikson on the transition from childhood to adulthood can miss the suggestion that the *imago dei* is rounded out (admittedly at a stiff price) by that rebellion that we call the Fall. The Fall corresponds, in some respects, to primitive initiation rites; both Erikson and the New Testament expect that the rebellion, to be salvaged, must sooner or later be followed by reconciliation, the return from a "moratorium" in Erikson's word (236).

3. The "curse" of ethics. The *imago dei* story represents humanity as pre-ethical. But if we are asking the question how humankind is like God we have to see that the Fall, for better or worse, specifically brings in another godlike feature. "Behold," says God, "the man has become like one of us, knowing good and evil" (Gen 3:22). In a sense this new way of being like God is a curse, for who can really know good and evil except God? But it is a curse that humanity must live with. After the Fall, which means since humans have been human, ethics—reflection on moral choice—is part of the being of humanity.

Three Aspects of the Imago Dei

Political and Social Creativity

Bonhoeffer and Barth, as we have seen, interpreted the *imago dei* story in terms of our creation as "male and female." The image of God, for Barth, consisted of the constitution of humankind as "an I and a Thou in the co-existence of man and man, of male and female" (1958:199). Bonhoeffer, in his account, said that our sexuality "is nothing but the ultimate realization of our belonging to one another." This means that man "is the image of God not in spite of but just because of his bodiliness. For in his bodiliness he is related to the earth and to other bodies, he is there for others, he is dependent on others" (62, 46).

Perhaps because of the reluctance of commentators to review such deliverances of neo-orthodoxy in the American context, these interpretations have been read too narrowly, as only sanctifying personal and sexual relationships and family life. That is to miss the scope, in the American sense, of the *imago dei* for community. Let us resist the implication that "community" in America today means mostly "nuclear family" (small, with few extended kinships across cousinates or generations) and that "privatism" or even "personalism" is a sufficient scope for the true meaning of the *imago dei*, trapping it in effect at the personal and family level. Thus Barth and Bonhoeffer on the *imago dei* need American amplification. In this sense, Kaufman's interpretation of the *imago dei* is the sounder approach. The historical embraces the social and political and is not to be limited by the purely personal zones of existence or even applied in an exclusive way to them. According to Christopher Lasch, it is just this sense of the historical that is threatened today in American life—by "narcissism." Americans seem bent on turning their backs on their own tradition, "the sense of belonging to a succession of generations originating in the past and stretching into the future" (30).

Taken alone, then, the male–female aspect of the *imago dei* is insufficient. It may, especially in the American context, be interpreted privatistically, failing to remind us of our destinies to be social and political beings. There is an undying truth in the relationship aspect of the story—if we can make the transition from the personal to the *polis*. What helps us to do so is another aspect of the story, the conferral upon humanity of the responsibility of "having dominion."

Broader human relationships cannot be achieved by affection, love, existential openness to others. What is required, as John McDermott argues in a seminal essay, is "the management of experience for human ends." And this is just what the charter of Gen 1:26–31 provides for, in my judgment. But it took the American experience, McDermott suggests, for this aspect of our calling to become manifest. It is the American tradition, he says, "awkward in doctrinal unity and vague in goal," where the idea of "experience" has come into its own. This idea, in fact, has in a sense superseded the classical Euorpean reliance on "tradition." Located in a different environment, the New World was "forced to start from scratch" on many major human questions, "particularly the fundamental and pressing problem of generating a *polis*." The very novelty of the situation, in which tradition could not guide with a sure hand, but where experience could be wrestled with and thus become a teacher, gave a new vision of community (70, 79, 80). This epochal grappling with experience takes on the character of the religious, McDermott seems to say.

Giles Gunn, in a recent statement, speaks in a similar vein of the religious implications of the American struggle "in which its various peoples have had to work out their own salvation, whether in fear and trembling, in outrage and dismay, in wonder and hope, or in madness and despair." The symbols that have been tested in this ordeal have undergone a "sacralization" (81). If medieval Europe expressed its piety in cathedrals, America did so in a new medium: the management of experience as if the glory of God (whether God is named or not) were riding on the outcome.

But we must now ask a skeptical question. We have already noticed the American tendency toward privatism. Given that tendency, is not the capacity to manage experience for human ends denied rather than affirmed? That question may be more important than the query whether God is named or not in the doing.

Let us take an example. In John Cheever's *The Wapshot Scandal*, the Reverend Mr. Applegate is rector of an Episcopal church in a small New England town. He is under no illusions about what must have gone on in the minds of his parishioners when they came to the altar for the Eucharist.

"Shall I paint the stairs?" he imagines one of them saying. "Lord God of Hosts," another seemed to ask, "shall I sell the laying hens?" Still another could well have thought, "Shall I cut down the apple tree?" or "Shall I buy a new icebox?"

The rector resisted. "Drink this in remembrance that Christ's blood was shed for thee," he sternly admonished his faithful, before him on their knees. Yet what he got back from them, in his mind's eye was: "Shall I send Emmett to Harvard?" or "Shall I take a liver pill?" (8).

For years this passage bothered me—for the wrong reason, I now say. Cheever himself summed it up that "the chain of being was a chain of humble worries." In my neo-orthodox stage, it seemed worse than that. In the phrase of the day, these folk were wallowing in "meaninglessness." A people who took their religious charter seriously would not think such idle thoughts on their knees, *coram Deo*.

Now the passage bothers me for another reason. More accurately, it suggests a new modality of the Americanly religious but also what may be wrong with it. These parishioners are fulfilling, in their activist way, the image of God. They are managing experience. In a new form of deputyship, they are not saying novenas or contemplating the impassibility of God or dreaming of the rapture to come. Here is a new piety, a new conception of what it means to undertake sacred rites: "Shall I paint the stairs?" A small step indeed. But a step, perhaps, in the direction of serving God under the color of human agency: these stair-painters see themselves, in microcosm, as managing the creation that at its limit approaches action in the image of God.

But it will not quite do. The scope of management is too narrow. Painting the stairs as a constructive act of piety does not contract all the way down to Christopher Lasch's narcissism, but it does reflect the tight,

centripetal psychic style of much of American life. There may be, however, religious or even theological reasons for this failure to see stewardship as broad and political rather than as constricted and familial. The
failure may stem partly from our having invoked a dualism between the
secular and the piously huddled. These parishioners of Applegate are
working with the right medium but, much like the born-again, are devotees of "narrowing."

Could it be that what is left undone is a task of "proclamation"? To
speak anew of the image of God and its demands, between the secular
and the familial, might open the way to broader visions for the scope of
management. I do not mean "proclamation" here in the sense of television preaching, but rather a low-keyed way of putting the call upon
Americans to see themselves as living in a *polis*. This cannot be wrought
by evangelism, but it is nonetheless a theological task, for what I have in
mind is rethinking the idea of transcendence on a horizontal plane./4/
Such an idea is not as inappropriate as it might seem. "Transcendence"
itself literally means "climbing over" or "climbing across," giving us at
once an aperture for the horizontal, or the transcendent claim of the
Other.

Alfred Schutz (317) speaks of three forms of transcendence in inter-
personal affairs—none of them having to do with a divine vertical, all of
them having to do with Thoreau's question, "Could a greater miracle
take place than for us to look through each other's eyes for an instant?"
(Thoreau: 6). (1) Facing another, says Schutz, "I see things unseen by
him and he sees things unseen by me." This may be thought to hold
purely for face-to-face relationships. But Schutz adds: "The same holds
for our manipulatory spheres." Thus we are carried over into the realm
of experience-management. "In this sense, the world of another transcends mine" (316–17). (2) Though in the "we-relation," the vivid inter-
personal process of "growing older together," we are in some kind of
synchronism with our consociates, there is a second sense in which the
world of the other transcends my own. "We have in common only a
small section of our biographies." We give to the other only a part of our
personalities, all the more so as we invest our being in social roles. The
life of the other "cannot be congruent with mine" (317). Already the
inappropriateness of family life as a model for political community is
suggested, for in the latter I am challenged to live with others whose
lives are more out of reach. (3) Finally, then, Schutz argues, the we-
relation, the basis of sociality, though it originates in mutuality, still
"transcends the existence" of the consociates. Its meaning eludes the
meanings attached to everyday life—read, in our context, family, worka-
day life—and can be grasped ultimately "only by symbolization" (318).

The symbolization that is required, I suggest, is that of the *imago dei*. Confrontation as well as mutuality is part of a relationship. In Judeo-Christian theologies, God is both covenant-partner and caller-into-question of our management schemes. On the level of social existence, the human person, created in the image of God as deputy manager of the political cosmos, is challenged to build a *polis*, which means calling into question isolated, privatistic living.

"Shall I paint the stairs?" then as a vocation is called into question and set in a larger arena. Let us use the skills of stair-painting to build new cities with fewer ghettos and more parks. "Shall I send Emmett to Harvard?" is transcended by the vision of a decent education for everyone who wants it. Even the piddling question, "Shall I take a liver pill?" can be surpassed by the vision of medicine as a healing art. What is medical ethics, for example, but the transfer of this picayune question from the realm of the private to the realm of the *polis*?

A question remains. Is horizontal transcendence, even enlisted in the wider management of experience for human ends, truly "religious," as McDermott implies? For it to be "religious," do we not have to name the Creator as we go about this widening of relationships and of management of the creation? Even this, in the context of American community, may not be called for. Alexis de Tocqueville suggests that in a democracy, reflection upon the poetic (or the spiritual, as we might paraphrase) tends to focus less on what is external to humanity (namely, the vertically transcendent, the realm of "gods, demons, or angels") and more on the realm of human affairs. He traces the beginnings of this process to the "settlers of New England." With religious motives, they strove for wealth, morality, liberty (Tocqueville: 1, 33; 2, 88–91). We could go on and say that here the religious becomes merged with the mundane, that God-agency is expressed in righteous acts. It is always a danger to blur the distinction between the divine and the human. But what if the reality here is that we have a *change of media*—rather than an intentional blurring—from the vertical to the horizontal? If God makes humans his deputies, why may not God's demand that we manage the creation be heard in the confrontation from the Other?

Later in this essay we must attempt to rehabilitate the role of the God-namers and also the Christ-namers. We do need to make the connection between the work of creation management and the attribution of our authority for this work to the biblical God. But there is another sense in which the work of creation management, rightly done, speaks for itself./5/

Dignity and Depravity

Whereas creativity—the capacity for relationships and for community management—is wholly an original part of the *imago dei* (though distorted by the Fall), human dignity is a hybrid. At base it, too, is a gift from God, part of our createdness. Yet human dignity, on its own terms, requires at some point a declaration of self-affirmation. For better or worse this declaration takes the form of the Fall—rebellion against the Creator, which carries with it, as the price of self-actualization, a daunting penalty.

But this twofold conception of human dignity—taking the worth from God and running with it—is neither as unpalatable nor as impious as orthodoxy has fancied. The way is still left open for proclamation of the Lordship of God: the rebels, in their new status, are all the more the agents of God, for they now act out of, and after, gaining experience "outside the Garden." The way is still left open for an affirmation of human depravity, even "total depravity," in the sense that the community is a whole (not merely restricting such sinfulness to the self, as the Reformers had in mind) and that the price of actualization is charged against the whole.

The biblical testimony to the created dignity of humanity is clear. We have already, in preliminary remarks, observed that the human status as created for deputyship has a worth rooted in the divine origin— a worth that is implicit in the *imago dei* story and explicitly rendered in the commentary on this story in Psalm 8. This basis of human dignity is in no way attributable to human self-actualization; it is the primordial, innocent ("pre-mature") worth of a creature specially blessed for management—which can only presage loss of innocence.

Is this primordial dignity lost in the Fall or, as I have suggested, reaffirmed? The Reformers, as we have seen, hedged: it was almost lost. They put the weight of their comment, however, on the destructive acids of sinfulness. Among the ways that Luther characterizes natural man, lacking in grace, are the following: He suffers the "leprosy of sin" (the "leper" metaphor is often repeated); life is "corrupt"; human faculties are "utterly dead"; we are "disfigured" by sin, "dull, ignorant, and deaf." Adam has "lost everything," especially immortality. Now the heart is full of "distrust, fear, and shame." Original sin is "an inexhaustible evil." Sin goes with "perversion and stupidity." Our righteousness is "completely buried by sins" (1958:62, 64, 66–68, 165, 167, 172). Calvin (*Institutes* II. iii.2 and passim) is equally energetic and colorful, although more subtle.

For Luther, convinced of a destructive depravity in the Fall, the image of God was at first something "distinguished and excellent"

(1958:62). Even after the ravages of the Fall, when the image has been "almost completely lost," Luther conceded that "there is still a great difference between the human being and the rest of the animals" (1958:67). If Luther does not sound this affirmation with the exuberance of the author of Psalm 8—who also wrote after the Fall—he still demonstrates, in this concession, the difficulty of denying the basic dignity of God's chosen (but fallen) creature.

In any case, the Hebrew Bible asserts that the image remains operative after the Fall, and that God reaffirms his covenant with humanity, thereby reaffirming basic human dignity. In Genesis 9 we learn of a new blessing, after the flood, conferred upon "Noah and his sons" (Gen 9:1). Here the image of God teaching is repeated (9:66), and so is the franchise to "have dominion" (9:3). The difference is that in this later, more realistic affirmation, God moves to make arrangements for his beloved but errant deputies to live henceforth with some kind of protection against the worst in them: "Whoever sheds the blood of man, by man shall his blood be shed, for God made man in his image" (Gen 9:6). This covenant with Noah and his sons creates civil government as a way to protect the sanctity of human life. It shows, says Cairns, that even fallen humanity is "said to be of dignity" (126).

We must now go one step further and say that this primal dignity, reaffirmed by God after the Fall, could not be fully human, not even fully "like God" without another voice of reaffirmation, the one made by humanity itself. We are not speaking here, however, of autonomy in the sense of aseity (e.g., as in Kant, Sartre, or Madalyn Murray O'Hair, our most visible atheist; it is an autonomy, if that is the word, growing out of an *imago-dei* based pre-autonomy. Dignity is God-given, humanly affirmed.

Objections must be dealt with. Brunner surmises of "the first human pair" that their pre-Fall innocence "was not merely that of children or of primitive man; rather it was that of fully mature human beings in union with God" (85). But if this situation had prevailed, this pair need not have fallen; there was nothing they needed. The innocence of "childhood" is just what they had to surpass to be God's managers of human experience. Maturity involves the loss of innocence.

Cairns claims, in similar vein, that one in "rebellion against God cannot be like him," that human dignity "gives man no rights over against God" (194, 247). I would argue that for finitude to be like God, it must assert itself, or its freedom, against its source, freedom being a part of the likeness that we are entitled to and the ability to create *ex nihilo* being a part of the likeness that we are forever barred from. Unless humans are created as robots or puppets, creative freedom also implies "rights," a word I do not especially defend, to self-actualization, even "over against God."

A better surmise for the *imago dei* in the American world of reference is implicit in Erik Erikson's description of the transition from childhood through adolescence. This process is complete, he says, only when we have subordinated (not left behind) our "childhood identifications" to a new identity, "achieved in absorbing sociability and in competitive apprenticeship with and among . . . age mates" (155). To make this transition, we must break away—for a time, not permanently—from our pasts, our roots, our *source*.

Erikson thinks of this not as break, not as dropping-out, not as permanent estrangement, but rather as a "psychosocial moratorium," during which the fledgling adults, now on their own, may find themselves, find a place to invest their awesome new energies (genital, physical, intellectual), find their niche. It is finally a quest for fidelity, "the search for something and somebody to be true to," based not on pre-adult easy acceptance of unquestioned role, but upon "the genuineness of convictions and the reliability of commitments" (235). From this estimate we theologians may take two clues. First, the Fall, in its full scope, is "curved." If we depart to actualize our dignity (or identity) we also hope to return. Perhaps the completion of this process takes us beyond the boundaries of community based on *imago dei*, and into the realm of such religious addenda as the evangelical concept of reconciliation. Second, Erikson speaks of freedom as a means to identity (or dignity); his talk of "free role experimentation" in the hiatus or moratorium is clearly an example. Thus we are encouraged to think of human dignity or personhood or identity, not freedom per se, as the quality that is reaffirmed in the break.

As I have already said, we pay a high price for this actualization of the *humanum*, and theology, in its age-old doctrine of depravity, has already said so. In Erikson's terms, there is no guarantee that the moratorium will be temporary or curved, or that things will work out at all. "The moratorium may be a time for horse stealing and vision-quests, a time for *Wanderschaft* or work 'out West' or 'down under,' a time for 'lost youth' or academic life, a time for self-sacrifice or for pranks—and today, often a time for patienthood or delinquency" (157).

One can be crushed in the process. One can "fall away" and never come back. If America is the place where the modern idea of dignity has been given a unique chance—its advocates run from Jefferson through Lincoln to King—it is also the place where the moratorium can most spectacularly fail. In America, the land where the illusion of innocence vies with the refusal of moral obligation as the worst sin, freedom can damn. Jonathan Edwards, in his *Thoughts on the Revival*, spoke of America as the place where the Reformation, born in Europe, would be completed. We might add that America could also be the place where the Reformation doctrine of total depravity comes to its most horrifying exemplification. Examples are plentiful—in the American penchant for racism, jingoism, and violence. The latter is easiest to document with figures. In 1980 in Sweden there were about two murders per 100,000 people; in the United States in the same year there were about ten murders per 100,000 people—more than half of them done with handguns (*U.S. News and World Report*, May 31, 1982, p. 38; *Houston Post*, September 27, 1981). Most of us are not murderers. But American individualism—which we might think of as freedom really fallen, heedless of the *telos* to fold it back into community—takes such a toll on our humanity that we need have no further doubts that with dignity goes depravity.

We may glimpse the community-damaging aspects of depravity by referring to the story of the Fall itself.

1. We try to get by through deception and blaming the others. When God queried the man about eating the fruit, the man answered: "The woman whom thou gavest to be with me, she gave me the fruit" (Gen 3:12). It was not only the woman's fault, but behind that, God's fault! The woman gets in the act, too: "The serpent beguiled me" (Gen 3:13).

Once an entrancing sector of Houston, Texas, almost old-world-like, the Montrose area used to offer European restaurants, gift shops, book stores, and old townhouses. Now it is a hotbed of crime, prostitution, and drug dealing—a study of community in disarray. What is worse, "The police blame the street people. The street regulars blame visitors. Gays blame straights. Straights blame gays. . . . Residents blame topless bars and gay bars. The bar owners blame drug dealers" (*Houston Chronicle*, October 25, 1981).

There is still a community in Montrose, but it is troubled, and its troubles are compounded by the all-too-human refrain that runs from Adam to Camus's Meurseult in *The Stranger*: "Ce n'est pas de ma faute."

2. The male–female relationship is plagued by conflict. The woman seems doubly penalized, not only by threatened pain in childbirth (a threat happily meliorated by medical management) but also by the imposition of male chauvinism. "Your desires shall be for your husband and he shall rule over you" (Gen 3:16). In a broader sense we may say that suffering, both physical and psychic, tinges all human relationships—from starving babies in the Sahel to battered wives and lonely old

people in America, and much of it is political chauvinism, for the strong are constantly tempted to impose power upon the weak.

3. The mandate to "have dominion," while not withdrawn, now comes only by blood and toil, sweat and tears. Luther actually interprets Gen 3:17–19 as a loss of dominion consequent upon the Fall: "What we achieve in life, is brought about, not by the dominion which Adam had but through industry and skill" (1960:67). One wonders at first if this is any real loss. Then one reflects that industry also means the crushing boredom of the assembly line, and skill may be stretched into manipulation and cunning. Certainly the uneven distribution of arable soil tells us that, for much of the world at least, "cursed is the ground because of you." It is no accident, moreover, that the weak seem to have inherited most of the "thorns and thistles," for the transition from innocence to experience brings injustice along with the sense of justice.

4. The "dust to dust" sentence indicates to some theologians—Luther is one—that mortality is a penalty of the Fall. But if Adam was created he was finite from the beginning. What our guilty act of self-actualization introduces is the "denial of death" (Ernest Becker), death-phobia (Philippe Aries).

5. Is the root of the matter our estrangement from God, as much mainstream theology—especially that fueled by existentialism—maintains? The form this question must take for us is: does the break with God, before the curve of the moratorium is completed, estop community, wreck the *polis*? Put this way, the answer is clearly no. Even with a strained relation to God, humankind is capable of political community. But it is community troubled by blaming the others, partner-abuse, the unjust use of power, fear of death, and perhaps at its limit the longing for restoration. That is why sin condemns us to ethics—and to politics, if Aristotle was right in yoking the two—another aspect of the Fall to which we now turn./6/

The Curse and the Promise of Ethics

> Behold, man has become as one of Us, so that he knows good and evil. (Gen 3:22)

These are very nearly God's last words in the story of the Fall before he puts the man and the woman out of the garden. What do the words mean? Taken literally and "straight," Adam is pictured as having so nearly succeeded in his bid, his rebellion, that God himself seems to grant the point (if a bit grudgingly).

Luther says (sounding to American ears like a paleo-orthodox if not a neo-orthodox theologian) that these words are not to be taken at face value. God spits them out in "sarcasm and very bitter derision" (1960: 222). He does not elaborate. Luther is more interested, for his part, in pursuing the meaning of the word "Us" here than in the new responsibility (and "curse") of knowing good and evil. So he fills his lines as a proselytizing preacher, putting down the Jewish error of thinking that "Us" means something other than the Trinity (1960:223).

But even Luther sees more here than a divine taunt to a bootless pretender. The sarcasm encourages Adam to self-examination, to realizing that even if a human being is created in the image of God, he is more like the devil than like God. Adam is in the middle. He is indeed like God in a way—God concedes it. But in being so—knowing good and evil, cursed with the responsibility for moral choice—he is very much less than God.

Building upon Luther's insight, what does American ethics make of this story? Ethics, unlike simple piety, cannot ever be theonomous. It is always in league with the world, whatever our hopes for the future. It is always a reminder of a lost, unattained pinnacle, for it must fall back, despite its godlikeness, to the grubby business of dealing with the sores and wounds that are the price we pay for actualizing our humanity.

But ethics is not, in that case, just a curse, even as a product of the Fall. It is a way of keeping things in repair until the moratorium curves back and ends. It is a symbol of what was lost and what might be hoped for. On the average, it is a sign that we are perhaps over our heads in our pretensions to know good and evil. At its best, it is a prophetic force for both proximate and future community.

When medical ethicists, among others, wonder about whether the physician ought to "play God," we can see the ambiguous character of this possibility. No person can possibly do so; every responsible person (not just the physician) must.

If ethics is an introjection into the human condition after the Fall, we next have to consider a disturbing thought: ethics must depend in large part upon the secular. With a direct, unbroken connection to divinity, the man and the woman have no decisions to make. After the transition from innocence to experience, they have taken on a new responsibility of godlikeness, making ethical judgments. But now they make these judgments as free agents—acting, to be sure, when they act righteously, as God's agents, but still acting as free agents.

"Religious ethics," we can say, lacks substance unless it draws maxims from its time and place, from reflection on ethical choice made by the man who is now, in part at least, on his own. Thus for Augustine, Platonism furnishes a "secular" base for Christian ethics; for Aquinas, Aristotle's ethics looms even larger. All ethics, as we have said, is inextricably mixed up with the world. For Americans thinking in the image of God surely must attend to the American tradition of justice—mixed up with the world, too, like its predecessors, but offering a program for management of experience that betters fallen humanity without ethics, Hobbes's war of all against all.

This is not, after all is said, really so heterodox, even for the neo-orthodox. Does Barth, for example, argue differently? "The Christian community," he says, "has no exclusive theory of its own to advocate in face of the various forms and realities of political life." This is a way of saying, it seems to me, that ethics is inherently creational—and maybe also fallen. There is no such thing, Barth goes on to say (1960:160–61), "as *the* Christian doctrine of the just State." For political ethics bears the indelible stamp of its provenance in "human inventions." In the political sphere, Barth decides (1960:184), "Christians can bring in their Christianity only anonymously."

Even when he thinks he is discussing specifically "religious ethics," Barth relies in fact on secular moral conceptions, indeed, on the Swiss penal code! In his discussion of abortion under the general rubric of God's command to protect life, for example, his conclusions, if one reads the fine print, seem not to be much at variance with those expected of any law-abiding Swiss citizen (1961:415–22).

One wonders, in fact, if there can be a specifically "Christian" ethics at all. But we must attend to another matter. What I have been saying about the secular origins of ethics brings up the question Am I not arguing, in another fashion, for the now-familiar "civil religion"? Am I not saying either that we must define ethics from the base of "religion in general" (one approach to civil religion), or else saying that this definition must come from some kind of sacralization of national values?/7/ And what might this do to biblical imagery?

Civil religion, understood in either of these ways, appears to me to be more concerned with the constitution of a new "canon" than with recognizing the curse (and promise) of ethics as a function of the image of God. This tendency is especially noticeable in the more egregious form of civil religion, in which the American founding documents—the Declaration of Independence, the Bill of Rights, the Civil War amendments, and so on—are proposed as an "American Bible," perhaps on the analogy of the *Book of Mormon* and Mary Baker Eddy's *Science and Health with Key to the Scriptures* (see Bellah: 33, 36 in Richey and Jones: 21–44).

But the disruption of ethics in the *imago dei* does not alter the canon; rather it makes plain that the canon, ever and always, must be interpreted by fallen humans doing their best to hold community together in their own time and place. Thus ethics intrudes as interpreter of the canon, but never as a replacement for it.

The American experience decisively reconfirms that scripture is never self-evident nor self-communicating. Every religious community depends on its own interpreting functionaries to make scripture available. Luther thought he was ousting for good an interposed set of interpreting functionaries when he insisted that the laity read scripture for themselves. He was right in insisting on the believer's right to participation. He was wrong in thinking that he had removed interposed interpreters. He substituted one way of understanding the gospel for another. To be an authentic Christian now is indeed to read scripture for oneself—but according to Luther's catechisms and the later Lutheran confessions. The same may be said of Calvinists, Anglicans, American Puritans, even the Bible-specific American Campbellites: each proposed some body of interpretation, congruent with time and place and the contingent intrusion of ethics, to be used by the faithful in appropriating the meaning of scripture.

American ethics—or hermeneutics, really—carries this process a step further. It grants that scripture is interpreted not only by religious functionaries but also by the (secular) moral tradition. That is a large step. But America affords a novel new form of the problem: not only the shift to new ground, but the shift to *pluralistic* new ground. Here various interpretations of religious symbols vie in open competition. More important, religious symbols are no longer the only ones for which ultimacy is claimed. Science, politics, and the irreligion of atheism all make claims to offer the answers. The canon remains the canon. But when the churches are reduced to enclaves within a larger political community, who or what now has the authority to interpret the canon insofar as it has meaning for this larger trans-religious community?

Here is the true function of the American tradition of justice (Sellers, 1979) and of its supporting documents./8/ They represent that creative, historical intrusion of ethics. They are the new tradition coinherent with gospel, the new catechism, the new communal judgment, our Aristotle.

It is true that scripture continues to function classically within the several religious communities. Here it may very well decisively shape personal identity "in the context of the common life of Christian community" (Kelsey: 91). But this tells us, in the new pluralist context, that scripture can function as scripture only when it is also under the complementary or dialectical authority of the American community, not just the churches, for identity-shaping goes on here too, and in an ethical context that at its limit approaches the religious quality of the *imago dei*.

For the American use of scripture, then, ethics and the tradition of justice become part of biblical hermeneutics. If an example needs to be given that this intrusive interpretation of scripture is in fact taking place, we need only consider recent movements by a committee affiliated with the National Council of Churches to call "for a new rendering of the Revised Standard Version of the Bible to eliminate 'sexist' language in references to God, Christ and humanity." Such changes would be made as the substitution of "human beings" for "men," Jesus as "Child of God" rather than "Son of Man," and even outright additions, such as appending "and Eve" in places which now speak only of "Adam" (*Houston Post*, June 13, 1980).

Ethics, as an epiphenomenon of the Fall, is a "curse." It introduces the values of time and place into what some still think of as the "eternal verities." It asks human beings who are going to die to play God. If it is not exactly the work of the devil, as Luther thought, it is still tied to the perversities of fallen existence. And yet ethics can also be prophetic. In the American tradition of justice, ethics speaks for dignity and fairness, for consent of the governed. The Reformation distinction between grace and nature, between love and justice, is revised. Justice becomes a kind of "beauty" for Jonathan Edwards, if an "inferior" kind. In our own day justice pulls ahead of love, in some senses, as the chief medium of political community (see Edwards, 1960: chap. III).

At its limit, when the *imago dei* is shining through, American ethics becomes what Sidney Mead calls "the religion of the Republic." It is "essentially prophetic. . . . its ideals and aspirations stand in constant judgment over the passing shenanigans of the people, reminding them of the standards by which their current practices and those of their nation are ever being judged and found wanting" (Mead: 65). At its limit such an ethics, or religion, shows a yearning for the rebellion to become a moratorium. It shows that "man's being is essentially of the nature of a response to God" (Cairns: 189)./9/

Three-Dimensional Community

We began by considering two competing religious versions of community, a "narrow" and a "wide." We went on to find fault with both— with the "narrow" for its loss of larger ethical concern; with the "wider" for its loss of religious substance in a slide toward secularity. I have argued for a new religious vision of community that is somewhere between the two, based on the biblical story of the *imago dei* and its inseparable sequel, the story of the Fall. To go with the "horizontal" transcendence that we have outlined after reflecting upon the biblical story of the *imago dei*, we must now ask: What is to be said, in this same American context, for the "vertical" transcendence that is spoken for in our "born-again" religious communities?

The first step is to place in perspective the actual significance of these evangelical communities in the American context. This entire camp, from the irenic conservatives to the warlike fundamentalists, speaks as if New Testament religion were the primary stuff of reality in America. But the last Americans to live in anything like "Christendom"—a state of culture essentially or ontologically Christocentric—were the Puritans, and Christendom did not last long for them—no longer, at the outside, than from about 1630 to 1679 (the year of the Reforming Synod), when "declension," for which we may read "secularization," after earlier adumbrations, was owned to.

Since then, every quarter of a fragmented Christianity has been confronted with a reality that not all have faced up to. This reality, growing over the generations, is that religion (especially of the "born-again" variety) is no longer the substance of culture. It is rather one *option* (or one option fragmented), one of a number of "subuniverses" (William James), one of a number of "finite provinces of meaning" (Schutz). Even if the message is of the sovereignty of Almighty God, the medium qualifies the message, and the medium is one camp speaking (in several voices) in a cacophony of camps in a new world of reference, a world of non-Christendom. Even in eras when one of the religious camps gains ascendancy—say, liberal Christianity in the late 1800s or fundamentalism in the early 1900s or the "Moral Majority" in the Reaganesque early 1980s—these front-runners are enjoying nothing more than temporary heteronomous hegemony. Their sway is not that of Anselm's pervasive Christian culture, not that of authentic "religious affections" or of "the nature of true virtue," for they are at the top of polls without having overtoppled either the worst or the best in the pluralist American experience.

To be sure, evangelical Christians have made efforts to reckon with twentieth-century reality. Karl Barth, toward the end of his career, thought he had come to terms with modernity by speaking of the new situation as embracing two realities: the "civil community" and the "religious community." But he posited (perhaps rightly for Europe, certainly wrongly for pluralistic America) the "Christian community" as the kernel, the center, with the "civil community" a larger and less central surrounding sector. Barth has at least here relinquished the earlier vision of a pervasive substance of Christendom. But the spirit of Christendom, in his schema, lives on: The Christian, if not the all, is at least at the center. The American experience cannot go even that far in the direction of Christendom. For the American tradition of justice, the Christian vision is "side by side" with various competing visions, not at all at the center.

Schutz, who builds on the pluralism of William James, speaks convincingly of the "multiple worlds" we all live in. The dominant reality for most of us is not the world of religion—unless we are losers in the other arenas—but rather the world of "working in daily life," which is the "archetype of our experience of reality." For what it is worth (and to the dismay of devotees of scientism) this dominant reality is not the world of science. It is not the world of the child, though that world has bequeathed us all something to remember. All of these subordinate worlds—art, play, science, religion—are subordinate to the outer world of work and everyday life, which we all live in "by means of our bodies, which are themselves things in the outer world." This world is filled with objects of its own—freeways, shops, specification manuals—which guide and delimit what we do and think. We are always bumping into these constraints, and what they influence us to do is far more important than either Clark Maxwell's electromagnetic equations or John Wesley's rules for holy living. It is only in this realm, supervening the various provinces of finite meaning, that we can have political community (see Schutz, 1967:342).

"Whether God exist, or whether no God exist," says William James, "we form at any rate an ethical republic here below" (223–24). In Walker Percy's novel, *The Second Coming*, Will Barrett understands the place of religion in this new world of reference. Most of the people he knew seemed to be more or less normal, more or less happy. What made them so? "They played golf, kept busy, drank, talked, laughed, went to church, appeared to enjoy themselves, and in general were both success-ful and generous" (4–5). "Went to church." Sandwiched between golf and drinking, success and generosity. The conclusion is inevitable. Religion is an option. That is all, but also: that is something.

What can be done with this option? Langdon Gilkey is troubled by an analogous question, set not, as we have considered it, in the context of American pluralism, but rather more universally, given "the present *close* encounter" of world religions—Christianity and all the others in a new global side-by-sideness. Gilkey confesses bafflement: These other religions are ardently believed by other human beings deserving our respect; these competing claims to allegiance stand, given the inter-dependent contemporary world, in some kind of equality. We have to recognize, for example, "the truth and grace, the spiritual power of another faith," such as Buddhism (128–30).

The "watershed" in theological reflection that Gilkey speaks of is also present at home. It is not only a matter of the encounter among world religions. Domestically we must ask whether evangelical Christianity is really prepared to accept pluralism. Under American principles of jus-tice, is a pretender to hegemony—born-again Christianity—morally jus-tified in demeaning "the truth and grace, the spiritual power" of other faiths?

It is against this background—the call to honor the religious integrity of others in the *polis* and even to make common cause with them through reinterpreted *imago dei*—that we must ask our question: What is the distinctive role of "vertical" Christianity now to be?

Kierkegaard insists that the ethical and the religious—roughly, what I have been calling the horizontal and the vertical—are always in conflict, and that the religious is higher in respect of the divinity to whom it turns, and that in fact it transcends, leaves behind, the ethical. Buber, on the other hand, suggests that the ethical and the religious interpenetrate. The religious and the ethical do indeed at times come into conflict. But in a pluralistic world of reference, where both are in danger of becoming what Jonathan Edwards called "private systems"—closed to being— neither can always be the "higher." It may well be, at times, that the religious is to be found wanting, lacking in ethical substance. We may from time to time have to call for a teleological suspension of the religious by the ethical, for God is as surely imaged in our ethical tradition as in our religious communities, especially when these yield to the temptation for small-minded closure. Strictly speaking, what is at stake is not the "ethical" versus the "religious," but two versions of the "religious"—the horizontal and the vertical. Given the shape of the twentieth century, most of our lives are lived in the horizontal. "By and large," says Salomon Bochner, thinking more of art and science than religion, "the nineteenth century was predominantly horizontalist." Cezanne's cubism was "three-dimensional," thus reflecting the vertical. Picasso's *Guernica*, though "tumultuously agitated and action-packed," is spatially totally flat (4).

Guernica shows the power of the horizontal for prophetic ethics. Its message fairly leaps out of the flatland: "a lone, snarling bull, a wounded horse, a mother with child crying in agony, groping arms, mutilation and a sun reduced to a glimmering lightbulb" (Brand). Picasso said he was protesting the horror of the Spanish Civil War, of militarism, of "racism and the death of art."

Long before Picasso, America was a cradle of horizontal spirituality. Even in a Jonathan Edwards we can see its unfolding. His *Religious Affections*, the work of a Puritan retrencher, still represents a significant turn not away from the vertical but to the horizontal as the locus of the vertical. For here the Reformed doctrine of election is in effect "lowered" from the reaches of the vertically transcendent, somewhere in the serene mind of God, to the realm of the human psyche. We are now to look for the holy in the depths of the human heart, once it has, in grace, taken on a new taste or relish for the excellency of God.

To say that the authentic signs of God's favor are to be found in the realm of the affections is a firm statement that God makes himself known or felt (Edwards's "relished" is better) on the human plane. Yet what goes on here is of God, it is his "most glorious work" (Edwards, 1961:131). The horizontal may have a life of its own, we can go on to say, even an ethics of power and passion (in Tom Paine or *Guernica* or Erik Erikson) that at its limit approaches the religious. The horizontal is thus never without God, even when he is unnamed. But to live in the horizontal only is to miss a dimension. That is the real message of evangelical faith, which seeks three-dimensional existence.

But the message is also *for* evangelical faith: our "vertical" religious communities are radically dependent on the *polis*, for the "horizontal" in its full life as *imago dei* is needed for three-dimensional community./10/

NOTES

/1/ Recent studies of the relevance of biblical themes to ethical matters tend to stress the variety of the biblical materials, their diversity and richness as the basis of ethical reflection; see, e.g., Sleeper; Birch and Rasmussen: 70, 75). Given this variety, we must also recognize that for any ethics concerned with the creation of community, the variety is underlain by a fundamental tension, two competing models. I see them as the tension between *imago dei*, an ethics of creation, and the "born-again," an ethics of evangelical faith. The history of theology is witness to the endless permutations of this basic twoness: two cities, nature and grace, two realms, etc.

/2/ Although I prefer, for the purposes of this essay, the more unpretentious term "story," what I mean by this term corresponds more or less to what I meant by "myth" in *Warming Fires* (1975:77–88)—the "cash value" being measured by its capacity to change identity, enlarge it when we are thinking of the problem of community. I use "story" here rather than "myth" to underline the fact that, although I am writing of biblical themes, I do so not as a biblical scholar but as a theological ethicist. I have attempted to attend to the story in that act of theological imagination that is "logically prior" to any professional expertise in biblical exegesis (Kelsey: 199). This imaginative response to a hermeneutically decisive biblical "story," I might add, is powerfully influenced by one's time and place.

I should also explain at this point why I have based my creational ethics on the *imago dei* rather than on the favorite symbol of the Social Gospel, the "Kingdom of God," which Walter Rauschenbusch opposed to churches in the same way that I am opposing the "image of God" to the "born-again." Here I agree with Karl Barth. Neither church nor political community can, as yet, identify itself with the kingdom of God. In our terms, neither the "born-again" church leaders nor the human beings acting under the color of the *imago dei* in political community can claim to represent the kingdom of God. The "real Kingdom of God," as Barth says, will follow both of these preliminary representations (1960:168).

/3/ There is, indeed, a nonhistorical, cyclical aspect of our lives that is still valuable, even acceptable as part of the *imago dei*. This is the reassurance afforded by noncumulative repetition, which offers stability, an anchor against the strange, the new, the unexpected, all of which are part of the historicity. We celebrate Thanksgiving, for example, in very much the same way every year: turkey and dressing, the televised football game. But there is also a historical aspect blended in: we grow older together, doing "the same old thing." To take an example from the personal realm alone, to have one poached egg on toast every morning is evidence of the inexorable cyclical character of life; to have deviled eggs at the park on Saturday afternoon with one's spouse, growing "older together" (Schutz) is part of our historicity.

/4/   What I call here the horizontal corresponds to what Marc Spindler, in a provocative critique of classical theology, which was more interested in time than space, calls "une théologie de l'espace." Spindler attempts to rescue "space" as a theological medium: "L'espace, profondément, est . . . ce qui me permet de coexister avec d'autres hommes, c'est la chance d'un dialogue possible avec Dieu" (61).

/5/   After the Fall, this process of management and confrontation takes on a "meanness" not foreseen in the state of innocence. We must now manage by manipulation, distrust, suspicion (see the following subsection). Regarding the question of whether God must be recognized in acts of creation management, Feldman, in his discussion of Jewish ethics, cites Maimonides: the person who observes the basic laws of the covenant with Noah and his sons is "righteous" if he sees they are commanded of God; the person who observes them because of his own reason is "wise" instead of "righteous" (56).

/6/   Space does not permit the elaboration of three further considerations: (1) Personal sin, perhaps an overworked topic in any case, has not been addressed in this estimate. Perhaps personal refusal of larger community, however, should count more importantly in the internal counsels of the evangelical churches than now appears to be the case. (2) Christian orthodoxy is quite right in insisting on the reality of original sin, but perhaps not for the reasons it advances. Original sin is not the transferred guilt of an earlier Other; it is our own eager latching onto the refusal of fellowship commanded to us by our predecessors. One needs only to reflect on the history of racism, for example, to see that this is so. We modify, decry, prettify the more crass racism of our fathers; but in their spirit, if more in the direction of sophistication, we endorse their setting of one group over against another. (3) Depravity, unwittingly perhaps, shows us what must be protected in the humanum as a matter of human dignity. A convict in a prison of the overcrowded Texas penal system, testifying before a federal judge, told how he was forced to sleep on a mattress rigged over urinals: "I wake up when someone uses it, and he's staring at me." Cruel and unusual punishment is forbidden by our Bill of Rights. Thus the profane—its degradation and its sense of injustice, even against the lowliest among us—teaches us to value dignity.

/7/   For a fuller account of the typology of civil religion, see Richey and Jones, chaps. 1, 2, 7, 12.

/8/   By this phrase I do not suggest that there is only one *conception* of justice in America. There are obviously many, of which three may be mentioned: (1) The "order" or "harmony" theory that has antecedents in Plato and Calvin. Justice means accepting one's place in a hierarchy or whole. While there is a valid place for this view, it also provided the rationale for slavery and economic oppression. (2) The "contract" theory, running from Hobbes and Locke to John Rawls. "Consent of the governed" or the establishment of a system of justice based on remarkably rational deciders (in Rawls's "original position") is the ostensible basis of this theory. But like the "order" theory, justice here seems determined by an elite, the non-envious rational ones among us. (3) The "sense of injustice" theory, which begins not with the necessity of hierarchy or with rational speculation but with the declaration (in King's phrase) that "I'm somebody!" This cry, uttered in the field (rather than in the philosopher-king's library or in the Rawlsian conclave of thinkers) seeks to overcome injustice rather than to elaborate a theory of justice. In my *Soundings* essay I have explicated at greater length why I consider the third of these the most representative of the American moral tradition.

/9/   Whether God need be named, even at the limit of ethics, is debatable. Cairns (181): "We may even, as existential philosophers following Jaspers, study man in his relation to the transcendent, without filling in the form of that concept with the content of Christian belief about God." Stackhouse (73): "In working toward an urban theology, the symbol 'God' does not necessarily focus on the question of a theistic being. . . . 'God,' as a symbol, focuses . . . [on] *worthy* power, capable of making urban constructs work for human good."

/10/   Within the Christian enclaves, there is a further task imposed by the gospel, which I have not been able to comment on here. This task surely includes bolstering of the faint-hearted, the lonely, the losers in this businesslike world; educating persons about their traditions; and (perhaps most importantly) challenging them to the broader ethical imperative of community that is laid on all of us in pluralistic America, but perhaps laid most compellingly on those who profess to see the renewal of humanity in Christ, who comes as reconciler rather than divider.

Regarding the capacity of the "vertical" enclaves to accept the ethics of the horizontal, there may be a glimmer of hope in the otherwise quite misguided program of "creationism." In the days of Bryan and Scopes, fundamentalists argued that the biblical creation story was the truth, evolution theory a lie; a reductionist remnant of the illusion of Christendom. Today the creationists, though wrong in claiming that their schema is science rather than faith, at least are willing to see evolution theory as existing side by side with their own—implicitly recognizing their own views as another finite province of meaning within a larger pluralistic social context.

WORKS CONSULTED

Barth, Karl
1958   *Church Dogmatics* III/1. Edinburgh: T. & T. Clark.
1960   *Community, State and Church.* New York: Doubleday.
1961   *Church Dogmatics* III/4. Edinburgh: T. & T. Clark.

Birch, Bruce C., and Larry L. Rasmussen
1976   *Bible and Ethics in the Christian Life.* Minneapolis: Augsburg.

Bochner, Salomon
1981   "Three Dimensionality in Science and Art." *Sallyport* 38 (September): 4–5.

Bonhoeffer, Dietrich
1959   *Creation and Fall.* London: SCM.

Brand, David
1981   "'Guernica' Returns to Spain and Controversy." *Wall Street Journal* 70 (October 27): 22.

Brunner, Emil
1939   *Man in Revolt.* London: Lutterworth.

Brunner, Emil, and Karl Barth
 1946   *Natural Theology*. London: Geoffrey Bles.

Cairns, David
 1953   *The Image of God in Man*. New York: Philosophical Library.

Cameron, J. M.
 1981   "Can We Live the Good Life?" *New York Review* (November 5):
               44–48.

Cheever, John
 1963   *The Wapshot Scandal*. New York: Harper & Row.

Edwards, Jonathan
 1959   *Select Works II (Sermons)*. London: Banner of Truth Trust.
 1960   *The Nature of True Virtue*. Ann Arbor: University of Michigan.
 1961   *Select Works III (Religious Affections)*. London: Banner of
               Truth Trust.
 1974   *Works*. London: Banner of Truth Trust.

Erikson, Erik H.
 1968   *Identity: Youth and Crisis*. New York: W. W. Norton.

Feldman, David M.
 1978   *Marital Relations, Birth Control and Abortion in Jewish Law*.
               New York: Schocken Books.

Fletcher, Joseph
 1966   *Situation Ethics*. Philadelphia: Westminster.

Fox, Marvin, ed.
 1975   *Modern Jewish Ethics*. Columbus: Ohio State University.

Gilkey, Langdon
 1981   "The New Watershed in Theology." *Soundings* 64 (Summer):
               118–31.

Gunn, Giles, ed.
 1981   *New World Metaphysics*. New York: Oxford.

Haroutunian, Joseph
 1970   *Piety Versus Moralism*. New York: Harper & Row.

Houlden, J. H.
 1977   *Ethics and the New Testament*. New York: Oxford.

Hyatt, J. Philip
               The Heritage of Biblical Faith. Saint Louis: Bethany.

James, William
 1963   *Pragmatism and Other Essays*. New York: Washington Square.

Jervell, Jacob
 1960   *Imago Dei*. Göttingen: Vandenhoeck & Ruprecht.

Jung, L. Shannon
 1980   *Identity and Community*. Atlanta: John Knox.

Kaufman, Gordon D.
 1968   *Systematic Theology*. New York: Charles Scribner's Sons.

Kelley, Dean
　　1972　　　　*Why Conservative Churches Are Growing.* New York: Harper
　　　　　　　& Row.

Kelsey, David H.
　　1975　　　　*The Uses of Scripture in Recent Theology.* Philadelphia: For-
　　　　　　　tress.

Lasch, Chistopher
　　1979　　　　*The Culture of Narcissism.* New York: Warner.

Luther, Martin
　　1958, 1960　　*Lectures on Genesis, 1, 2.* Saint Louis: Concordia.

McDermott, John J.
　　1965　　　　"The American Angle of Vision." *Cross Currents* (Winter): 69–
　　　　　　　93; (Fall): 433–60.

Mead, Sidney E.
　　1975　　　　*The Nation With the Soul of a Church.* New York: Harper &
　　　　　　　Row.

Muckenhirn, Sister M. Charles Borromeo
　　1963　　　　*The Image of God in Creation.* Englewood Cliffs, NJ: Prentice-
　　　　　　　Hall.

Percy, Walker
　　1980　　　　*The Second Coming.* New York: Pocket Books.

Porteous, N. W.
　　1962　　　　"Image of God." *Interpreter's Dictionary of the Bible.* Nash-
　　　　　　　ville: Abingdon.

Richey, Russell E., and Donald G. Jones
　　1974　　　　*American Civil Religion.* New York: Harper & Row.

Schutz, Alfred
　　1967　　　　*Collected Papers, I.* The Hague: Nijhoff.

Sellers, James
　　1975　　　　*Warming Fires.* New York: Seabury.
　　1979　　　　"Human Rights and the American Tradition of Justice." *Sound-
　　　　　　　ings* 62 (Fall): 226–55.

Sleeper, Freeman
　　1968　　　　"Ethics as a Context for Biblical Literature." *Interpretation* 22
　　　　　　　(October): 443–60.

Spindler, Marc
　　1968　　　　*Pour une Théologie de l'Espace.* Neuchâtel: Delachaux et
　　　　　　　Niestlé.

Stackhouse, Max L.
　　1972　　　　*Ethics and the Urban Ethos: An Essay in Social Theory and
　　　　　　　Theological Reconstruction.* Boston: Beacon.

Thoreau, H. D.
　　1966　　　　*Walden and Civil Disobedience.* New York: W. W. Norton.

Tocqueville, Alexis de
　　1961　　　　*Democracy in America, 1, 2.* New York: Schocken Books.

Index